THE SOPHISTIC MOVEMENT

The sophistic movement

G. B. KERFERD

*Hulme Professor of Greek
in the University of Manchester*

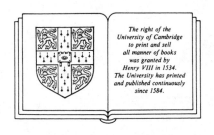

The right of the
University of Cambridge
to print and sell
all manner of books
was granted by
Henry VIII in 1534.
The University has printed
and published continuously
since 1584.

CAMBRIDGE UNIVERSITY PRESS

CAMBRIDGE

NEW YORK   PORT CHESTER
MELBOURNE   SYDNEY

Published by the Press Syndicate of the University of Cambridge
The Pitt Building, Trumpington Street, Cambridge CB2 1RP
40 West 20th Street, New York, NY 10011, USA
10 Stamford Road, Oakleigh, Melbourne 3166, Australia

First published 1981
Reprinted 1984, 1989

Printed in Great Britain by
Redwood Burn Limited, Trowbridge, Wiltshire

British Library Cataloguing in Publication Data
Kerferd, George Briscoe
the sophistic movement.
1. Sophists (Greek philosophy)
I. Title
183'.1   B288   80–41934

ISBN 0 521 23936 2 hard covers
ISBN 0 521 28357 4 paperback

Contents

Preface

The present study of the sophistic movement is the fruit of many years of study and reflection, of teaching and of argument, and was completed in all essentials in 1978. What I have attempted is in no sense a comprehensive treatment of individual sophists and their doctrines – this would require much more space and much more technical detail. I have simply tried to provide an overall re-interpretation and re-assessment of the nature of the movement as a whole, in the belief that this is now a matter of some urgency. My thanks are due to many over the years, but most recently to the readers and staff of the Cambridge University Press, and above all to Professor G. S. Kirk without whose help publication might well not have taken place, at least in its present form. Naturally I alone am responsible for the particular views expressed, and no-one but myself is to be taken to task if any of these views are judged to be unacceptable.

Details of the books and articles to which reference is most frequently made will be found in the select bibliography. The standard collection of surviving texts relating to the sophistic movement is that of Diels, re-edited by Kranz (abbreviated DK) for which see bibliography p. 177. Texts concerning individual authors are divided into two sections lettered A and B, of which the first contains *testimonia* or statements in later writers concerning the life, writings and doctrines of the sophist or thinker in question, and the second collects passages which in the opinion of the editors constitute actual quotations from their writings. So for example the fourth fragment attributed to Protagoras is referred to as DK 80B4. References to particular ancient writers whose works do survive are abbreviated in standard form and it is hoped that these abbreviations will not cause any difficulties.

University of Manchester　　　　　　　　　　G. B. KERFERD
October 1980

vii

1

Introduction

Not one barrier but two stand in the way of anyone who seeks to arrive at a proper understanding of the sophistic movement at Athens in the fifth century B.C. No writings survive from any of the sophists and we have to depend on inconsiderable fragments and often obscure or unreliable summaries of their doctrines. What is worse, for much of our information we are dependent upon Plato's profoundly hostile treatment of them, presented with all the power of his literary genius and driven home with a philosophical impact that is little short of overwhelming. The combined effect has been fairly disastrous. It has led to a kind of received view according to which it is doubtful whether the sophists as a whole contributed anything of importance to the history of thought. Their major significance, it has often been said, was simply that they provoked their own condemnation first by Socrates and then by Plato. In all the essentials of this quarrel it was Plato who was judged to be right and the sophists who were in the wrong. Even the revulsion from Plato felt by those to whom Plato has tended to appear as a reactionary authoritarian has done little for the sophists. Condemned to a kind of half-life between Presocratics on the one hand and Plato and Aristotle on the other, they seem to wander for ever like lost souls.

This result is paradoxical. The period from 450 to 400 B.C. was in many ways the greatest age of Athens. It was a period of profound social and political changes, in which intellectual and artistic activity was intense. Established patterns of life and experience were dissolving in favour of new patterns. Beliefs and values of previous generations were under attack. The sophistic movement gave expression to all of this. We whose fortune it is to live at the present time, it might be supposed, are particularly well placed to understand what was likely to happen in such a situation, and to proceed to investigate and, so far as may be, establish by scholarship what actually did happen.

The modernity of the range of problems formulated and discussed by the sophists in their teaching is indeed startling, and the following list should speak for itself. First, philosophic problems in the theory of knowledge and of perception – the degree to which sense-perceptions are to be regarded as infallible and incorrigible, and the problems that result if such is the case. The nature of truth and above all the relation between what appears and what is real or true. The relation between language, thought and reality. Then, the sociology of knowledge, which cries out for investigation because so much of what we suppose that we know appears to be socially, indeed ethnically, conditioned. This opened the way for the first time to the possibility of a genuinely historical approach to the understanding of human culture, above all through the concept of what has been called 'Anti-primitivism', namely the rejection of the view that things were much better in the distant past in favour of a belief in progress and the idea of an unfolding development in the history of human beings. The problem of achieving any knowledge at all about the gods, and the possibility that the gods exist only in our minds, or even that they are human inventions needed to serve social needs. The theoretical and practical problems of living in societies, above all democracies with the implied doctrine that at least in some respects all men are or ought to be equal. What is justice? What should be the attitude of the individual to values imposed by others, above all in an organised society requiring obedience to the laws and to the state. The problem of punishment. The nature and purpose of education and the role of the teachers in society. The shattering implications of the doctrine that virtue can be taught, which is only a way of expressing in language no longer fashionable what we mean if we say that people in their proper position in society can be changed by education. This in turn raises in an acute form the question what is to be taught, and by whom and to whom it is to be taught. The effect of all this on the younger generation in relation to the older. Throughout all, two dominant themes – the need to accept relativism in values and elsewhere without reducing all to subjectivism, and the belief that there is no area of human life or of the world as a whole which should be immune from understanding achieved throughout reasoned argument.

A long list, and one may be pardoned for feeling that it represents something like the very process of transition from an earlier, traditional picture of the world to a world that is intellectually our world, with our problems. Yet the attempt to interpret the sophists along these lines has as yet hardly got under way. What follows in the present book is very much a first beginning. Before proceeding to actual interpretations along these lines, it will however be helpful, I judge, to deal at some slight length with two preliminary topics – the history of past attempts at assessing the sophistic movement, essential for an understanding of why its significance has been so underrated up to now, and the social and historical situation which produced the activities of the sophists.

2

Towards a history of interpretations of the sophistic movement

Plato's hostility to the sophists is obvious and has always been recognised. But exactly what he says about them has not always been described with precision. In two places in his dialogues he provides what may be seen as set-piece treatments. In the *Gorgias* 462b3–465e6 he distinguishes between on the one hand a range of genuinely scientific activities which he here calls *technai*, whose aims or objectives are the highest degree of excellence in each of their proper spheres, and on the other hand various empirical activities. These are not scientific since they are not based on rational principles and are unable to provide explanations, they aim at pleasing rather than excellence, and do so by pandering to people's desires and expectations. They are deceptive imitations of the genuine *technai*. In the general area of concern for the human soul Plato includes the declaration of norms of behaviour,[1] and this he regards as a genuine *technē*. Corresponding to it however is a counterfeit activity, the empirical pursuit known as sophistic.

In the dialogue the *Sophist* the analysis is more elaborate and the hostility no less marked. No fewer than seven different definitions of the sophist, with one possible exception all derogatory, are discussed in turn. There has been discussion as to whether Plato regarded them all as satisfactory descriptions or not, but it is clear, I think, that he did regard each of them as expressing at least particular aspects of the sophistic movement. They define the sophist (1) as the hired hunter of rich young men, (2) as a man who sells 'virtue', and, since he is selling goods not his own, as a man who can be described as merchandising in learning, or (3) who sells it retail in small quantities, or (4) as a man who sells goods that he has fabricated in person for his customers. On another view, (5) the sophist is one who carries on controversies of the kind called Eristic (an important term discussed further in Chapter 6 below), in order to make money from the discussion of right and wrong. (6) A special aspect or kind of sophistry is then identified as a

---

[1] *Nomothetikē*, usually translated 'law-giving', but here much wider in its meaning.

kind of verbal examination called Elenchus which educates by purging the soul from the vain conceit of wisdom. Just what Plato is trying to convey here has been a matter of controversy, but he does seem to regard this essentially negative function as one of the less undesirable results of sophistic activity when he labels it as 'the sophistic which is of noble family', presumably in order to distinguish it from other aspects of the activities of the sophists. Finally at the end of the dialogue, after a long digression, we come to (7) where the sophist is seen as the false counterfeiter of philosophy, ignorantly framing contradictions that are based on appearances and opinions rather than reality.

It will be necessary to return later to what Plato has to say about Eristic, Elenchus and the Art of framing contradictions. But it is clear that his characterisations in the *Sophist*, which can be matched by similar statements in other dialogues,[2] constitute an outright condemnation. When we find Aristotle telling the same story – the sophistic art, he says, consists in apparent wisdom which is not in fact wisdom, and the sophist is one who makes money from 'apparent and not real wisdom' (*Sophistici Elenchi* 165a22–23, and *Metaphysics* Γ. 1004b25 ff.) – it is not surprising that this remained the standard view for the next two thousand years. If anything the reputation of the sophists became still worse – they provided what seemed ready-made material for moralising and christianising interpretations of history. They came to be seen as 'ostentatious imposters, flattering and duping the rich youth for their own personal gain, undermining the morality of Athens public and private, and encouraging their pupils to unscrupulous prosecution of ambition and cupidity. They are even affirmed to have succeeded in corrupting the general morality, so that Athens had become miserably degenerated and vicious in the latter years of the Peloponnesian war, as compared with what she was in the time of Miltiades and Aristeides.'[3]

The question of the alleged degeneration of the Athenians raises larger issues and it may suffice to mention the reply of the historian Grote who declared that the Athenian character was not really corrupted between 480 B.C. and 405 B.C. But the question of the nature

---

[2] Well-meant attempts by some nineteenth-century scholars to show that in the earlier dialogues Plato took a more favourable view of some sophists have not been generally accepted.

[3] Grote, *History of Greece*, new edn, London 1883, Vol. VIII p. 156. This of course is not Grote's own view.

of the sophists' teachings is very much the subject of this present book and will be considered fully later on. At this point it may be of interest to repeat a further characterisation of the standard view of the sophists obtaining before the reconsiderations of the nineteenth century, which has become a classic description:

> The old view of the Sophists was that they were a set of charlatans who appeared in Greece in the fifth century, and earned ample livelihood by imposing on public credulity: professing to teach virtue, they really taught the art of fallacious discourse, and meanwhile propagated immoral practical doctrines. They gravitated to Athens as the Prytaneum [here = central place of assembly] of Greece, they were there met and overthrown by Socrates, who exposed the hollowness of their rhetoric, turned their quibbles inside out, and triumphantly defended sound ethical principles against their plausible pernicious sophistries. That they thus, after a brief success, fell into well-merited contempt, so that their name became a byword for succeeding generations.[4]

Thus formulated, the charges really amounted to two: that the sophists were not serious thinkers and had no role in the history of philosophy, and secondly that their teachings were profoundly immoral. Both these contentions had to face a certain degree of reconsideration with the growth of new approaches to history in the first half of the nineteenth century. While the two charges are interrelated it will be convenient to treat them to some extent separately.

First the question of the place of the sophistic movement within the history of philosophy. The history of the study of Greek philosophy has been profoundly influenced in modern times down to and including the present by the treatment adopted by Hegel in his *Lectures on the History of Philosophy*.[5] Hegel did indeed restore the sophists to an integral position in the history of Greek philosophy, but in such a way that his successors were able for a hundred more years to continue with only a partial modification of the previous profoundly hostile view of the sophistic movement.

Hegel saw the history of philosophy as the progressive unfolding of the Universal Mind or Spirit. The movement of its thinking follows the pattern that is universal for all thought: it begins by laying down a positive thesis which is then negated by its antithesis. Further thought produces a synthesis of thesis and antithesis and the process

---

[4] Henry Sidgwick, 'The Sophists', *Journal of Philology* 4 (1872) 289.
[5] These were first published in German at Berlin in 1833–36, when they had been collated after his death in 1831 from lecture notes taken by his students over the previous twenty years. An English translation was published at London in 1892.

continues with the synthesis forming the thesis of a fresh cycle in each case until all that was implicit in the original starting point has been made explicit. This movement of thought Hegel called Dialectic, and it proceeds by negations because each step, thesis, antithesis and synthesis, negates the step that comes before it. It is able to do this just because each step in itself is partly true and partly false.

The application of this scheme to the history of Greek philosophy gives three periods, Hegel supposed. The first extends from Thales to Aristotle, the second constitutes the Hellenistic period or 'Greek philosophy in the Roman world' (Stoicism, Epicureanism and Scepticism), and the third consists of Neoplatonism. Within the first period Hegel saw a further three-fold or triadic division, namely (1) from Thales to Anaxagoras, (2) the sophists, Socrates and the followers of Socrates, and (3) Plato and Aristotle. The first of these subdivisions is described by Hegel as that in which thought is found initially in sensuous determinations. In non-Hegelian language we might say that these determinations are viewed as merely objective, as stating scientific facts about the world which we are perceiving and studying. So Thales and the other Ionians grasped Universal Thought in the form of natural determinations of it, as water and air, out of which they supposed our physical universe was made. The second subdivision contained those who through sceptical criticism came to negate this view and to substitute for it as its antithesis the principle of subjectivity, according to which it is supposed that it is the thinking and perceiving subject himself who determines his own thoughts and perceptions. The conflict of thesis and antithesis in due course predictably gave rise to synthesis, in this case the systems of Plato and Aristotle which form for Hegel the third subdivision of the first period.

For our purposes the important feature of all this is that Hegel reinserted the sophists into the history of philosophy and did so by treating them as subjectivists. For Hegel their subjectivism was a necessary stage in the self-determination of Thought which is what the history of philosophy was. It was a necessary stage despite its negative character because negation was an integral part of the movement of Universal Thought. But throughout the nineteenth century and for the first third of the present century the tradition of idealist philosophy continued to dominate the minds of students of Greek philosophy. As a result the characterisation of the sophists as subjectivists was widely accepted. But so far from re-establishing their reputation as philosophers the effect was the opposite. It seemed to confirm the hostile judgments of

7

Plato and Aristotle. Truth and reality were objective, not subjective. All those who denied this were opposed to truth and reality, and as such were not merely not philosophers, they were enemies of philosophy; and such were the sophists. Paradoxically the traditional view of the sophists would seem thus to have been confirmed. Nowhere was this more strongly felt than in the sphere of morals. Here to many it seemed that to claim that right and wrong were subjectively determinable was fundamentally to deny the validity of moral values altogether.

The next stage in the story is reached with the famous sixty-seventh chapter of George Grote's *History of Greece*.[6] Grote was a Radical and a free-thinker and he entered the circle of the utilitarians Jeremy Bentham and James Mill. For a period he was a member of the House of Commons, and from its beginnings he was associated with the movement to set up the then new London University in Gower Street, later to become University College, London. As a reformer and utilitarian he was himself much concerned with attacking the dead hand of tradition. It was no accident that he set himself to revalue the sophists. He saw them as the champions of intellectual progress and rejected crucial features of the traditional assessment of their work. In particular he argued first of all that they were not a sect or school but a profession, and that there was no community of doctrine. So, if one doctrine put forward by an individual sophist was objectionable, this was no ground for condemning the movement as a whole. Secondly as regards the alleged teaching of immoral doctrines, not even Plato brought this as a charge against the principal sophists, Protagoras, Prodicus, Hippias and Gorgias. Grote refused to believe that either Thrasymachus or Callicles could ever publicly have taught the antisocial theories of justice attributed to them by Plato in the *Republic* and the *Gorgias*. Even if they did, it would be wrong to infer from this anything as to the other sophists. Basically Grote regarded the sophists as teachers who simply represented the standard opinions of their age.

A vigorous controversy followed Grote's defence. His main point eventually received very general acceptance – it was simply not a matter of historical fact that they had poisoned and demoralised, by corrupt teaching, the Athenian moral character. But he had done little to rehabilitate the sophists intellectually. Indeed by denying that the

[6] First edition, London 1846–56.

persons styled sophists possessed doctrines, principles or methods both common to them all and distinguishing them from others he made it as difficult to defend them as a class as he had intended to make it difficult to attack them.

A different path was followed in the influential history of Greek philosophy by Eduard Zeller.[7] While critical of many features of Hegel's approach, Zeller nonetheless adopted his basic pattern. He accepted the idea of a kind of internally generated development of Greek philosophy – this was reflected in the title of his work *Die Philosophie der Griechen in ihrer geschichtlichen Entwicklung*. He included the sophists, and, unlike Grote and many who followed him, he claimed that they all had so much in common despite individual differences that we were justified in treating them as all representing the same educational discipline. He argued persuasively against attempts to divide or distribute the sophists in any fundamental way into early and later kinds, or into different schools, and proceeded to attempt to characterise the movement as a whole. He did so very much in the way Hegel had done it. First the negative side. Their calling things into question destroys all scientific endeavour at the root, their Eristic has as its final result only the bewilderment of the interlocutor, their rhetoric is concerned with appearance and serves the cause of wrong as well as truth, their views of scientific knowledge are that it is worth little, their moral principles are dangerous. But on the positive side, the philosophic validity of the principle of subjectivity was now asserted, and for the first time. The previous period had confined itself in its consideration of practical behaviour to the existing moral and religious tradition and in its science to the contemplation of nature. Now people become conscious that this is not sufficient. Man loses his respect for the actual and the given as such, he will accept nothing as true which he has not himself approved, he will act only on the basis of his own judgment. But for Zeller this also is inadequate. Instead of completing physics by a system of ethics, physics are now entirely set aside; instead of seeking a new scientific method, the possibility of knowledge is denied. Likewise with morals. Instead of searching for the internal grounds of obligation in the nature of moral activities and relations men are satisfied with a negative result, the invalidity of existing laws.

---

[7] First published in German at Tübingen in three volumes, 1844–52, but expanded in successive editions, by Zeller himself until the fifth, and subsequently by W. Nestle in a sixth edition (Leipzig 1920).

The result for Zeller was something superficial and onesided, unscientific and dangerous in its results. But this onesidedness was not to be avoided and it had its place in the history of philosophy. As the Germans would scarcely have had Kant without the Period of the Enlightenment, so the Greeks would scarcely have had a Socrates and a Socratic philosophy without the sophists. Such was the assessment provided by Zeller in 1892.[8] The sixth edition published in 1920 contained an extra appraisal by Wilhelm Nestle,[9] which continued the same viewpoint as Zeller, but showed a retreat on one point. The sophists are now differentiated *from* philosophers (without qualification) and not simply from earlier philosophers. They differed in the objects with which they were concerned (men, not natural science, and above all men in society); in their methods, which were empirical and based on experience, rather than deductive and based on assumed first principles or first beginnings for the physical world; and their aim was different. They were concerned with subjective knowledge for practical purposes, to secure mastery over men and over life, whereas the philosopher is concerned with knowledge pursued for its own sake. But while Nestle contrasted the sophists with philosophers he stressed their ultimate connection so strongly[10] that in effect he treated them as a kind of philosopher. What he was really doing was what his predecessors had done, namely restricting the term philosopher to a certain kind (the approved kind) of philosopher. It has become common[11] to classify the defenders of the sophists into two groups, the one, which labelled the sophists 'positivists of the Enlightenment', stemming from Grote, and the other the Hegelian. Nestle, together with Zeller, belongs to the second group.

To attempt to distribute writers in the present century between the two groups is dangerous, since almost all in one way or another would probably now wish to combine elements from both groups. But predominant sympathies can still be recognised. The positivist approach concentrates the greater attention on what the sophists were and did, rather than on what they thought. Here belong the views that they were inspired above all by the educational ideal of rhetoric, that they were the encyclopaedists or illuminators of Greece, that they

[8] See *Philosophie der Griechen*, Leipzig I.2, 5th edn, 1147–64 = I.2, 6th edn, 1423–39.

[9] *ibid.* I.2, 6th edn, 1291–6.

[10] See his later treatment in his book *Vom Mythos zum Logos*, Stuttgart 1940, 2nd edn 1942, 250–2.

[11] See e.g. K. Joël, *Geschichte der antiken Philosophie*, Tübingen 1921, 674.

were above all teachers of the ideal of political virtue (or more simply how to succeed in politics) or of the ideal of virtue or success in life in all its aspects, or that they were humanists in that they put man and his values in the central place in the interpretation of the universe. All of these views tend to be associated with the contention that we cannot hope to find any really specific common intellectual or philosophical doctrines shared in by the movement as a whole.

On the other hand many have continued to place the sophists firmly within the history of philosophy and have sought to characterise the movement as a whole in terms of its doctrines, thus following at least in a general way the tradition begun by Hegel. Here I would place the most recent full treatment of the sophists in English, that by W. K. C. Guthrie,[12] who contrasts the empiricism and scepticism of the sophists with the idealism of Plato on the one hand and the interest in natural phenomena which was typical of most of the Presocratics before them. His own sympathies are however, I think it would be fair to say, with what I would call generally the idealist tradition, and not with their opponents.

Very different is the controversial approach developed in Italy by Mario Untersteiner during the last thirty years. In his work *I sofisti*[13] he presents a distinctive view. He writes that 'the sophists agree in an anti-idealistic concreteness which does not tread the ways of scepticism, but rather those of a realism and a phenomenalism which do not confine reality within a single dogmatic scheme, but allow it to rage in all its contradictions, in all its tragic intensity'. For Untersteiner, if I understand him correctly, the starting point is always the experiences encountered by the individual including those coming to him from society and from other individuals. These are almost always as a matter of course in conflict and mutual contradiction. Through the power of his mind man can achieve mastery over the manifold of his experience, and so in effect generate or regenerate its contents for himself. Much of this is readily intelligible only within the general framework of thought of the expressionist philosopher Benedetto Croce.

It should be clear even from the above very incomplete survey how much the sophists have suffered from being set in conflict with the idealist tradition. Sometimes the effects have been curious and

[12] *History of Greek Philosophy*, Vol. III, Cambridge 1969, 3–9.
[13] 1st edition, Turin 1949, English translation *The Sophists*, Oxford 1954, 2nd edition in Italian, 2 vols., 1967.

extreme. Writing before the publication of Hegel's lectures, Heinrich Ritter of Berlin, in his *Geschichte der Philosophie*,[14] regarded the materialist doctrines of Democritus and the Atomists, while admittedly differing in character from those of the sophists, as nonetheless equally anti-philosophical in that they would deprive us of all access to the truth. Even more remarkable in some ways was the conception found in the book by Th. Funck-Brentano, *Les sophistes grecs et les sophistes contemporains*, Paris 1879. Here the second part of the book is devoted to 'Les sophistes contemporains anglais', and these are primarily John Stuart Mill and Herbert Spencer. With them should be classed the scholastic predecessors of Bacon and Descartes at the Renaissance, who followed after the great doctors of the Church. In each case it comes to be supposed that contrary opinions are equally legitimate, truth becomes a deceptive decoy, attempts to attain it folly. The result is intellectual and moral disorganisation. Protagoras, Polus and Thrasymachus fulfil the same role as Adam Smith, Diderot, Helvétius and Rousseau, who were to be followed by the positivists Comte, Mill and Herbert Spencer.

Certain conclusions may, I think, legitimately be drawn. The historical approach in itself is clearly essential. We do need to understand the sophistic movement both in relation to the earlier history of Greek thought and in relation to Plato and Aristotle. But it is dangerous to move too quickly. In particular the attempt to arrive at answers in advance of detailed study is unsatisfactory. When coupled with a prior schematisation of the supposed direction of development in human thought the result can be disastrous. The danger was not so much the imposition of a fixed scheme derived from Hegel – this was in fact soon criticised and then largely abandoned – but something deeper. This was the feeling that the right and desirable direction for the evolution of human thought was towards an increasing understanding of the importance of *Geist* or Spirit in contrast with the inadequacies of materialism and interpretations based on sense perceptions and no more. This when coupled with the belief that all the past history of thought must have consisted of attempts however misguided to arrive at the one true philosophy however interpreted is a sure recipe for historical distortion. It follows that what is wanted is not a re-evaluation of the sophists that is still *within* this framework, e.g. by those for whom a contrary direction of thought is more com-

---

[14] Vol. I, Hamburg 1829, 552.

mendable. Such would see the sophists as anticipating anti-idealist positions, positivism, liberalism, materialisms whether dialectical or otherwise. This also is basically to *accept* the Hegelian framework, whereas what is wanted is an approach that is more cautious, that aims to avoid premature schematisations of the history of thought. This will involve starting from the actual evidence about the sophists, about the Presocratics and about Plato, without presuppositions, but with an alertness always as to the possibility of unifying interpretations nonetheless, which in due course may constitute elements in overall patterns.

A few examples must suffice by way of illustration. A favourite pattern was to see the importance attached to *Nous* or Mind in the thought of Anaxagoras as enormously significant, and indeed as a formative influence on the sophistic movement. Anaxagoras himself had given it only a limited role, as Plato complained in the *Phaedo* 97b–98c, perhaps confining it to getting the process of world formation started. Nonetheless this represented an important beginning in that it enabled the sophists to generalise the importance of the (individual) mind over the whole area of philosophy. But there is very little sense or substance in this view. There is no evidence that the sophists were influenced by Anaxagoras' view of *nous*, and chronology makes even the possibility of such an influence uncertain for the earliest sophists, including Protagoras. Moreover, Anaxagoras' *nous* was material not spiritual – it is described as the thinnest and purest of all things, – fr. 12 DK,[15] but it is still clearly material. Secondly, it is often said that the sophists represented a turning away from physical speculation towards something new – the introduction of the human mind as the determining factor in the shaping of our thought. There is, however, quite good evidence that the sophists *retained* a lively interest in physical speculation. More importantly, however, the characterisation of their predecessors as exclusively concerned with the objectively observed physical world is simply false. From a very early stage they were fundamentally concerned with what we would call the philosophy of mind. Both Heraclitus and Parmenides began movements in which the way things seem to people and the reasons why they so seemed were right in the centre of their speculations and this continued through the pluralists as well. There was in these matters much more continuity and much less of a dramatic contrast

---

[15] DK 59B12. For the abbreviation DK used here and elsewhere see under Diels–Kranz in the bibliography, p. 177 below, and Preface, p. vii.

between the sophists and their predecessors than has commonly been supposed.[16] Exactly the same applies, it will be argued, between the sophistic movement itself and the thought of Plato. What is now wanted is a series of detailed studies of the actual evidence relating to individual sophists, which will take this evidence seriously and will not be inhibited at its very starting point by the conviction that any attribution of significant doctrines to a particular sophist is unlikely to be correct because 'the sophists were not the kind of people to entertain serious doctrines'. Of course the evidence is often deficient, inadequate and difficult to interpret. But the same is true of the Presocratics, and in their case detailed scholarly investigations and reconstructions can hardly be said to have been deterred to any serious extent. May the same kind of approach now be applied to the sophists.

---

[16] See e.g. Erik Wolf, *Rechtsphilosophie und Rechtsdichtung im Zeitalter der Sophistik* (Griechisches Rechtsdenken Bd. II), Frankfurt 1952, 9–16.

3

The sophists as a social phenomenon

Individual sophists came from all over the Greek world and many though not all of them continued to travel extensively as part of their professional activity. Nonetheless they all came to Athens and it is clear that Athens for some sixty years in the second half of the fifth century B.C. was the real centre of the sophistic movement. So much so indeed that it would seem probable that without Athens the movement would hardly have come into existence at all. What was there then about Athens in this period which was responsible for this happening?

The answer should probably be given under two headings.[1] First, social and political conditions which created a need for the sophists, and, secondly, the direct influence of a single individual, namely Pericles. Greece as a whole in the fifth century B.C. would appear to have surpassed all previous periods in the products of agriculture, industry and trade. But the transformation at Athens amounted to an economic revolution which has been described as a passing from the economics of a city state to the economics of empire. The great and extensive public building programme which restored the temples destroyed by the Persians on a new scale never matched before, was paralleled, if we can believe Thucydides (II.38), by elegance, comfort and luxurious consumption in private. While it would be quite wrong to attempt to infer from this last statement that poverty had been eliminated, it *is* likely that the claim reflects a general belief that private affluence was very much greater than in earlier generations at Athens, or indeed in other Greek cities.

In one sense the development of democratic institutions at Athens had been a gradual one from the time of Solon onwards. In another it

---

[1] In what follows I can proceed only by generalisations which will inevitably be subject to qualification. For fuller discussions of the controversial question of the economic development of ancient Greece see M. M. Austin and P. Vidal-Naquet, *Economic and Social History of Ancient Greece*, London 1977, and C. G. Starr, *The Economic and Social Growth of Early Greece*, New York 1977.

would be true to say that right down to the beginning of the Peloponnesian War it remained largely the same leading class and the same leading families which governed the increasingly democratic state. But there were changes. The constitutional reforms which began at Athens in 462/461 B.C. brought into being what some regarded as a full or unmixed democracy (so Plutarch, *Cim.* 15.2). In fact it is clear from the carefully phrased statement of Thucydides (II.37.1) that Periclean democracy rested on two fundamental principles: 'It is called a democracy because the conduct of affairs is entrusted not to a few but to many, but while there is equality for all in civil affairs established by law, we allow full play to individual worth in public affairs.'[2]

These two principles are (1) that power should be with the people as a whole and not with a small section of the citizen body, and (2) that high offices carrying the right to advise and act for the people should be entrusted to those best fitted and most able to carry out these functions. In practical terms the first principle was expressed in the power of the assembly and of the mass juries and the gradual extension of the system of selection by lot to the majority of civic magistracies. The introduction of payment made it possible for poorer citizens to offer themselves for possible selection, and its importance is evidenced by the fury which it inspired in the conservative opposition.

On the other hand no attempt was made to extend the principle of selection by lot to the strategiate or generalship. This was no doubt common sense from a military point of view. The author of the Pseudo-Xenophontine treatise *On the Constitution of Athens* (I.2–3) contrasts the offices to which everyone is admitted with 'those magistracies which when well conducted bring safety to the whole people, but when badly conducted bring danger; in these magistracies the people do not ask to have any share – they do not think they should share in the generalship by drawing lots, nor in the office of cavalry commander. For the people are aware that it is more advantageous for themselves not to hold these offices, but to leave them to the ablest men.' The importance of this second principle was not confined to military matters since it was as *strategos* or general that Pericles secured for himself virtually uninterrupted power, such that Thucydides could say that under him what was in name a democracy was in fact in process of becoming rule by one man.

---

[2] following the interpretation given by Gomme, 'Thucydides Notes', *CQ* 42 (1948) 10–11 and *Historical Commentary on Thucydides* Vol II, Oxford 1956, 107–10.

Both of the above two aspects of Periclean democracy were no doubt significant in the development of a demand for the services of the sophists. But we shall probably be right if we place the main emphasis on the second. What the sophists were able to offer was in no sense a contribution to the education of the masses. They offered an expensive product invaluable to those seeking a career in politics and public life generally, namely a kind of selective secondary education, intended to follow on after the basic instruction received at school in language and literature (*Grammatikē* and *Mousikē*), arithmetic (*Logistikē*) and athletics (*Gymnastikē*) – see e.g. Plato, *Prot.* 318e1, Xenophon, *Constitution of the Spartans*, II.1. As the earlier school education was normally completed at the point at which a boy passed from being a child (*Pais*) to becoming a youth or young man (*Meirakion*) (see Plato, *Laches* 179a5–7, Xenophon, *Const. of the Spartans* III.1), and since becoming a *Meirakion* was equated with the age of puberty, traditionally assigned to the fourteenth year (Aristotle, *HA* VII.581a12ff.) we can say, if we wish, in modern terms that the sophists provided a selective education at the age of fourteen-plus.

This education, though it varied in content, seems always to have been to a considerable extent career-orientated. By the beginning of the Peloponnesian War, if we can believe Plato in the dialogue *Protagoras*, it was already sufficiently well established to have a further function – that of training further teachers who were in turn to become professional sophists (*Prot.* 312a–b). But as its main purpose remained to prepare men for a career in politics, it should cause no surprise that an essential part of the education offered was training in the art of persuasive speaking. On this it has been well said by J. B. Bury: 'The institutions of a Greek democratic city presupposed in the average citizen the faculty of speaking in public, and for anyone who was ambitious for a political career it was indispensable. If a man was hauled into a law-court by his enemies and did not know how to speak, he was like an unarmed civilian attacked by soldiers. The power of expressing ideas clearly and in such a way as to persuade an audience was an art to be learned and taught. But it was not enough to gain command of a vocabulary; it was necessary to learn how to argue, and to exercise one's self in the discussion of political and ethical questions. There was a demand for higher education.'[3]

The sophists, then, were supplying a social and political need. But in

---

[3] *History of Greece*, London [4]1975, 241.

addition they owed much to individual patronage, and above all to the patronage of one man, Pericles. This is something that has perhaps not always been recognised as fully as it should in accounts of the sophistic movement. Lack of evidence makes it difficult for us to form any clear and reliable judgment about the personality of Pericles. But his intellectualism is not to be doubted. His closest associates and, it would seem, his only personal friends, were artists, intellectuals and philosophers. One of the sophists, the Athenian Damon, a friend of Socrates and the constant associate of Prodicus, was spoken of as his 'trainer and teacher in politics', and Isocrates said of Damon that he was considered to be the wisest man of his day. He was subsequently of sufficient political importance to be expelled from Athens for ten years by the process of ostracism.

Of even greater importance was Anaxagoras. According to Plutarch this was the man whom Pericles admired even to excess. From him he acquired his gravity of thought and appearance, and in addition his scientific rationalism and rejection of superstition. This was illustrated by the story that Pericles was able to explain the eclipse of the sun in 431 B.C. and to calm those who were frightened, by explaining the movements of the sun and moon, and illustrating what he said by holding his cloak up, apparently so as to cover his own face. More important, however, than this story, is the evidence that he attempted to base all his actions upon reasoned judgment and rational calculation (*Gnomē*) in preference to feelings (*Orgē*), hope or chance.[4]

In addition to Anaxagoras there were other intellectuals who were closely associated with Pericles (cf. [Plato] *Alcib.* I 118c). Protagoras was certainly one. He praised Pericles for his philosophical attitude after the death of his two illegitimate sons in the plague in 429 B.C. (DK 80B9) Much earlier he had been chosen, clearly by Pericles, to write the laws for the new city of Thurii, an important foundation in southern Italy in the year 444/443 B.C., the lay-out of whose streets was entrusted to the political theorist and town-planner Hippodamus of Miletus who was also responsible for arranging the street-pattern of the port of Athens at the Piraeus on a grid-plan. We are further told that Protagoras once spent a whole day talking with Pericles about the question, who or what was to be rightly blamed for an accidental

---

[4] see Thuc. I. 140 with V. Ehrenberg, *Sophocles and Pericles*, London 1954, 94–5, P. Huart, *Le vocabulaire de l'analyse psychologique dans l'oeuvre de Thucydide*, Paris 1968, *Gnomē chez Thucydide et ses contemporains*, Paris 1973.

death in the celebration of an athletic festival – the weapon (a javelin) or the man who threw it, or the organisers of the games.

A further tradition preserved by Plutarch (*Per.* 4.3), but probably known also to Plato (DK 29A4), tells us that Pericles heard lectures by Zeno the Eleatic. Others in his circle were Herodotus the historian, Phidias the sculptor and Sophocles the tragedian.

The probable influence of sophistic thought on Pericles has indeed not gone unnoticed. But *his* importance in promoting the sophistic movement was clearly no less important. It was not an accident that sophists came to Athens from all over the Greek world. This was due in part to Athens itself, first of all because it offered excellent opportunities for a sophist to make a great deal of money, and, secondly, at a higher level, in that in many ways it was in process of becoming a real intellectual and artistic centre for the whole of Greece. But individual patronage was also important. Plato's dialogue the *Protagoras* opens with a brilliant scenario at the house of Callias in Athens. The dramatic scene is placed just before the beginning of the Peloponnesian war. Staying in the house of Callias are Hippias and Prodicus and they have just recently been joined by Protagoras who has arrived from abroad two days ago, and there are present many of their followers and disciples assembled to hear their discourses. This Callias belonged to one of the richest families in Athens and according to Plato in the *Apology* (20a4–5) he spent more money on sophists than was spent by all others put together. It cannot be without significance that his mother had previously been Pericles' first wife before marrying Callias' father Hipponicus.[5] Moreover, Callias was not the only private patron of sophists – we learn from Plato that Gorgias stayed and was prepared to lecture at the house of Callicles (*Gorg.* 447b7–8), and later speculations suggested that Protagoras gave a reading of his work *On Gods* either at the house of Euripides or at the house of a certain Megaclides (Diogenes Laertius IX. 54).

But important though this private patronage clearly was, it can hardly have been of the same importance as that of Pericles. We do not know that he ever had sophists to stay in his house, but we are told of discourses held in his home with sophists, apparently on numerous occasions (Plut. *Per.* 36.2). But his great personal interest in them we have seen already. In view of his position, the importance of this interest may reasonably be assumed to have been considerable. The pro-

---

[5] see J. K. Davies, *Athenian Propertied Families*, Oxford 1971, 262 ff.

fession of a sophist at Athens was not without danger. Here the starting point must be the words which Plato puts into the mouth of Protagoras:

When a man who is a foreigner makes his way into great cities and there persuades the best of the young men to abandon their associations with others whether kinsmen or strangers, whether older or younger than themselves and to associate with himself under the idea that they will become better through their association with him, a man so proceeding needs to be on his guard. For great are the jealousies that arise together with other resentments and attacks made upon him. Now I declare that the sophistic art is of great antiquity, but those who practised it in ancient times, fearing the odium it involved, constructed a shield and veil for themselves, some of them poetry, as in the case of Homer, Hesiod and Simonides; some religious rites and prophecies, as did Orpheus, Musaeus and their followers, some I have observed also athletics, as with Iccus of Tarentum and another still living, Herodicus of Selymbria, originally of Megara, as much a sophist as any; and music was the disguise adopted by your own Agathocles, a great sophist, and Pythocleides of Ceos and many others. All of these, as I say, from fear of ill-will used these arts as screens (*Prot.* 316c5–e5).

Protagoras goes on to say that he himself has not taken this road. He admits that he is a sophist and that he educates men. He considers this a better precaution than outright denial. But he has thought out 'other precautions as well' (317b6–7) the nature of which are not specified, so that as a result he suffers no harm from his admission that he is a sophist.

At one point Plato actually puts into Socrates' mouth the claim that Athens allows greater freedom of speech than at any other place in Greece (*Gorg.* 461e2) and this remained one of the features upon which Athenians prided themselves down into the fourth century (cf. Demosthenes IX. 3). The 'Note of Freedom' has almost regularly been claimed as one of the glories of the Greek genius, exhibited nowhere more than at Athens in the fifth century B.C. Yet, as E. R. Dodds has written, 'the evidence we have is more than enough to prove that the Great Age of Greek Enlightenment was also, like our own time, an Age of Persecution – banishment of scholars, blinkering of thought, and even (if we can believe the tradition about Protagoras) burning of books. This distressed and puzzled nineteenth-century professors, who had not our advantage of familarity with this kind of behaviour. It puzzled them the more because it happened at Athens, the "school of Hellas", the headquarters of philosophy, and, so far as our information goes, nowhere else. Hence a tendency to cast doubt on the evidence wherever possible; and where this was not possible, to explain that the real motive behind the prosecutions was political.'[6]

There is no need to doubt that in attacking philosophers at Athens those concerned were attacking Pericles. This is simply evidence of the close involvement and patronage of Pericles in relation to the sophistic movement. But the evidence is strong indeed that there were a whole series of prosecutions brought against philsophers and others at Athens in the second half of the fifth century B.C., usually on the charge of *Asebeia* or Impiety.[7] It is preserved not by one source but in many. The victims included most of the leaders of progressive thought at Athens, Anaxagoras, Diagoras, Socrates, Aspasia, Protagoras, and Euripides, though in his case it looks as if the prosecution was unsuccessful. Protagoras was said to have been exiled from Athens and his books burnt (DK 80A1 and 3); there seems no doubt that Anaxagoras was exiled though the date is uncertain. Phidias, after condemnation for embezzlement either died in prison or went into exile. Damon as we have seen was ostracised. It is hard to believe that all of this was simply invented, despite uncertainty about some of the details.

Plutarch (*Per.* 31–32) gathers a number of these charges together and places them about the beginning of the Peloponnesian war, where he associates them with a decree of Diopeithes providing for public prosecution (by the process of *eisangelia*) of those who did not believe in things divine or who gave lessons in astronomy. Attempts to date the decree after the beginning of the war are clearly motivated by a desire to associate it with war hysteria and even emotions evoked by the plague,[8] should be dismissed. It is even possible that some of the actual prosecutions were earlier than 432 B.C. Finally, reference should be made to an intriguing statement in Aristotle's *Rhetoric* 1397 b24 according to which the rejection of a probable statement is accepted as a good argument for the rejection of another less probable statement. So if other technical experts are not to be despised, neither should philosophers. If generals are not despised because they frequently are subject to death, neither are sophists. Here the reading of the text *thanatountai* is secure and should not be altered. But it does

---

[6] *The Greeks and the Irrational*, Berkeley 1951, 189–90.
[7] for a survey of the evidence see E. Derenne, *Les procès d'impiété intentés aux philosophes au Vème et au IVème siécles*, Liège 1930, reprinted New York 1976. The trials are discussed also by K. J. Dover, 'The freedom of the intellectual in Greek Society', *Talanta* 7 (1975) 24–54 in a way, however, which seems to me excessively sceptical.
[8] so Adcock, *Cambridge Ancient History*, Cambridge, V 478.

not mean actually put to death, only subject to the threat of death.[9] What Aristotle is saying is that the sophistic profession was a dangerous one, though less so than that of a general.

In view of the above evidence we need not doubt the genuineness of the tradition that some felt that a sophist might be well advised to conceal the fact that he was a sophist. We find this not merely in the passage cited earlier from Plato's *Protagoras* but also applied to Damon in Plutarch's *life of Pericles,* treated as a joke by Socrates in the case of himself in *Theaetetus* 149a7, and as a serious argument in *Apology* 33c4–34b5, and applied to others in addition to Protagoras in *Meno* 91e3–92a6. If sophists could on occasion feel insecure at Athens, it must surely follow that they would have looked to Pericles for support. We are told that Pericles intervened directly to help Anaxagoras and Aspasia. We need not doubt that his influence was available to help others as well, and it is likely that Pericles' support was the undisclosed source of security upon which Protagoras relied (*Prot.* 317b6–7).

In view of all that has now been said we can conclude that it was not merely the general situation at Athens but also the direct encouragement of Pericles that brought so many of the sophists to Athens. Their coming was not simply something from without, but rather a development internal to the history of Athens. They were a part of the movement that was producing the new Athens of Pericles, and it was as such that they were both welcomed and attacked. They attracted the enthusiasm and the odium which regularly accrues to those who are deeply involved in processes of fundamental social change. The change that was taking place was both social and political on the one hand and intellectual on the other. But these two aspects were not separate, they were aspects of a single complex process of change.

This chapter has been concerned with an attempt to understand the sophistic movement as a social phenomenon within the context of fifth-century Athenian society. I believe that no apology is needed for the stress laid upon the special features obtaining at Athens and in particular for the importance assigned to the personal influence of Pericles, while conceding that on both these points I am perhaps going rather further than some other scholars have done. Nonetheless it would be a mistake to give the impression that the sophistic

[9] cf. Xenophon *An.* II.6.4 as against Solmsen's review of Dodds' *Greeks and the Irrational*, *AJP* 75 (1954) 192 n. 1.

movement was something confined to Athens. Individual sophists came from many parts of the Greek world, they travelled extensively, visiting cities everywhere (Plato, *Ap.* 19e5), or at least the larger cities (Plato, *Prot.* 316c6), from which cities, it would seem, they were liable to be expelled, just as was the case at Athens (Plato, *Meno* 92b3). Some sophists however were not foreigners, but citizens of the cities in which they taught (Plato, *Meno* 91c2, 92b3, *Soph.* 223d5). When a sophist travelled he was likely to be accompanied by pupils who like him came as foreigners to the cities which he was visiting (Plato, *Prot.* 315a7). Gorgias taught pupils in Argos, where he attracted much hostility from the Argives (see DK Vol. II 425.26), and at another period of his life he seems to have settled in Thessaly (DK 82A19). Hippias travelled very widely, especially in the Dorian world, and so to Sparta and Sicily, and Protagoras also lived for a time in Sicily.

4

The meaning of the term sophist

The name sophist is clearly related to the Greek words *sophos* and *sophia*, commonly translated 'wise' and 'wisdom'. According to the received account, built both into our lexica and our histories of philosophy, these terms went through a kind of evolution in their meanings, from (1) skill in a particular craft, especially handicraft, through (2) prudence or wisdom in general matters, especially practical and political wisdom, to (3) scientific, theoretic or philosophic wisdom. I have tried to argue elsewhere[1] that this sequence is artificial and unhistorical, being essentially based on Aristotle and his attempt to schematise the history of thought before his own time within a framework illustrating his own view about the nature of philosophy, above all that it proceeds from the particular to the universal. From the beginning *sophia* was in fact associated with the poet, the seer and the sage, all of whom were seen as revealing visions of knowledge not granted otherwise to mortals. The knowledge so gained was not a matter of technique as such, whether poetic or otherwise, but knowledge about the gods, man and society, to which the 'wise man' claimed privileged access.

From the fifth century B.C. onwards the term '*sophistēs*' is applied to many of these early 'wise men' – to poets, including Homer and Hesiod, to musicians and rhapsodes, to diviners and seers, to the Seven Wise Men and other early wise men, to Presocratic philosophers, and to figures such as Prometheus with a suggestion of mysterious powers. There is nothing derogatory in these applications, rather the reverse. It is to this honourable tradition that Protagoras wishes to attach himself in the passage already quoted from Plato's dialogue the *Protagoras* (316c5–e5).[2]

---

[1] *Images of Man in Ancient and Medieval Thought, Studia Gerardo Verbeke ab amicis et collegis dicata*, Louvain 1976, Ch. I: The Image of the Wise Man in Greece in the period before Plato, and also earlier in 'The first Greek sophists', *Class. Rev.* 64 (1950) 8–10.

[2] above, p. 20.

Nonetheless, Protagoras both claimed to be and was a professional. In fact the professionalism of the sophists in the second half of the fifth century B.C. distinguishes them quite markedly from all their supposed predecessors. The first element in their professionalism is the fact that they received fees for their teaching. According to Plato this was an innovation compared with those who came before them (*Hipp. Mai.* 282 c6) and it is clear that to many it was the mere fact that they took fees, not the size of the fees, which was objectionable. Why should this be? There was certainly no disapproval for the sale of goods for money at Athens (cf. Plato, *Gorgias* 520d). Poets, artists and doctors all received fees. Pindar writing soon after the end of the Persian invasion of 480 B.C. (*Isthm.* II) says that the days are now past when poets wrote songs without receiving money payments – money makes the man! In fact we are told he received 10,000 drachmas as a present for his poem in praise of Athens (Isocrates XV.166), and Simonides also received payment for his odes (Ar. *Rhet.* 1405b23ff.). For payments of a talent and more to the physician Democedes we have the evidence of Herodotus III.131.

Why then? The standard answer has been that it was not the fact that they charged fees as such which gave offence, it was the fact that they sold instruction in wisdom and virtue. These were not the kind of things that should be sold for money; friendship and gratitude should be sufficient reward (cf. Xen. *Mem.* I.2, 7–8). But it is doubtful if this really would have been sufficient to separate the professional sophists from poets, for example, and when we look more closely at the repeated objections recorded in Plato and Xenophon we find that almost regularly the objection has an extra feature not much stressed in modern literature. What is wrong is that the sophists sell wisdom *to all comers* without discrimination – by charging fees they have deprived themselves of the right to pick and choose among their pupils. So it is said to involve lecturing before 'all kinds of people' (*Hipp. Mai.* 282d1), an expression as contemptuous in Greek as it is in English, and taking money from any one who chooses to come along (Xenophon, *Mem.* I.2.6,I.5.6,I.6.5,I.6.13). One of the consequences, it was said, was to deprive the sophist of his freedom and to make him the slave of all and sundry who came to him with money. But it is doubtful whether it would have been solicitude for the independence of the sophist which was the real basis for this objection. Indeed it was not even certainly true that this was the case with sophistic teaching. Clearly in the *Protagoras* the young Hippocrates is not at all sure that he is going to be able to persuade Protagoras to take him on as a pupil and is anxious that Socrates should speak to the great man on his behalf (310d6–e3).

It is consequently likely that the real reason for the objection was not concern to protect the sophists from having to associate with all kinds of people, it was objections to all kinds of people being able to secure, simply by paying for it, what the sophists had to offer. What they had to offer, in the words attributed to Protagoras, included teaching a man about matters of state, so that he might become a real power in the affairs of the city both as a speaker and as a man of action, in other words become an effective and successful politician (*Prot.* 319a1–2). It was surely this that was the source of the powerful attraction exercised by the sophists at Athens, and also the hatred for them that led to the attacks by the writers of comedy, the prosecutions and eventually to the death of Socrates himself as the fifth century B.C. passed into the fourth.

A subsidiary, but difficult, question is the size of the fees received by the sophists for their services. Here the general statements that have come down to us conflict, and the particular statements are hard to interpret. Thus we are told that Gorgias and Prodicus both made remarkable sums of money, as did Hippias and Protagoras (Plato, *Hipp. Mai.* 282b8–283b3), and the wealthy Callias was said to have paid 'much money' to these same three sophists (Xen. *Symp.* I.5). Protagoras was said to have earned more money than Phidias together with any ten other sculptors (Plato, *Meno* 91d). As against this Isocrates could write (XV.155–156):

Overall none of those known as sophists will be found to have accumulated much money, but some lived in poor, other in moderate circumstances. The man who in our recollection secured most was Gorgias. Now he spent his time in Thessaly when the Thessalians were the most prosperous people in Greece; he lived a long life and devoted himself to the making of money; he had no fixed domicile in any city and paid nothing for public needs nor any tax; he was not married and he had no children . . . yet all the same he left at his death only a thousand staters [say 20,000 drachmas].

None of this really amounts to very much. First of all we have no means of knowing whether the statements are literally true or not. Secondly we should by now be familiar enough with the way arguments of this kind tend to be conducted at the present day over the remuneration of professional men, say doctors, lawyers or university professors – the discussion tends to be influenced by both the feelings and the interests of the parties concerned.

So we might expect more help when we turn to some actual figures. But here also there are marked divergences, and the figures can be placed under three separate headings. (1) Pythodorus, son of Isolochus, and Callias, son of Calliades, paid 100 minas (10,000 drachmas) each to Zeno, according to the statement in the dialogue which is probably Pseudo-Platonic, the *First Alcibiades (Alc.* I.119a1–6). According to later sources Gorgias charged each pupil 100 minas (DK 82A2 & 4), and this was the charge also made by Protagoras according to Diogenes Laertius (DK 80A1). (2) On the other hand Socrates in the *Apology* of Plato (20b9) says that Callias paid Euenus of Paros 5 minas for the education of his two sons, Isocrates charged 10 minas (Plutarch, *Mor.* 837d), and Prodicus normally charged half a mina for a single lecture (DK 84A11). At first sight the second group represents a much lower scale than the first and this has caused doubts as to whether the higher figures may not be grossly exaggerated.[3] We do not get much help either from a third set of figures (3) which tell us that Hippias claimed that he once went to Sicily at a time when Protagoras was also there, and, despite his competition, Hippias made more than 150 minas in a short space of time, including 20 minas in one small village, and that in general his earnings constituted more than those earned by any two other sophists.

Two major difficulties stand in the way of any very reliable inferences from these figures. First it is clear that there was an enormous difference between fees. Socrates, in the passage already cited (DK 84A11), after telling us that the normal charge for one of Prodicus' lectures was half a mina, goes on to say that he could not afford this, so instead went only to the one drachma lecture, i.e. at one fiftieth of the cost. And Isocrates (XIII.3–4 & 9), after saying that some ask for three or four minas, adds that others tried to collect the greatest number of students by making very small charges. Secondly we are given no information as to the relation between the charge, the number of students and the length of the course which could be as long as three or four years (Isocrates XV.87). So while we may be suspicious that the 100 mina fee is too high, it is, I think, not possible to be certain that it is simply false.

Whatever be the truth about the range of fees charged, it is of in-

---

[3] so G. Vlastos 'Plato's testimony concerning Zeno of Elea', *Journ. Hellenic Studies* 95 (1975) at 159–60.

terest to ask what was the social significance of any particular fee. One mina has been calculated as containing approximately 425 grams of silver, at the price of silver current in 1978 (i.e. before the period of price instability), equivalent at a mint-par rate of exchange to some £38 or US $74. But more informative is the comparison of one mina containing 100 drachmas, with the computed average daily wage of an artisan of one drachma, or some 3 to 4 minas a year, based on records of payments for temple constructions at the end of the fifth century B.C. This would suggest that a payment of four or more minas for a course spread over a year might not have been regarded as particularly demanding for those who could afford to pay, and, exceptionally, higher fees may not have been impossible of achievement by a sophist at the height of his powers and career. If Prodicus could really secure half a mina for one lecture from each student attending, then the total income if 20 students attended the lecture would be 10 minas, and a course of 10 lectures might even produce 100 minas. This inference would be invalidated if the half mina was not for one lecture but for a whole course, and many translators of the passage do suppose just that. But in favour of the view that it was for a single lecture is the use of the singular noun *epideixis*, normally used, as we shall see, for a single display lecture, and in any case if it was a whole course then a drachma for a whole course would surely be a derisory sum for Prodicus to have demanded. It is perhaps worth noticing that in the Pseudo-Platonic *Axiochus* 366c1–3 (DK 84B9) charges of a half drachma, two drachmas and four drachmas are mentioned for what seems to have been a single performance.

When the fees, whatever they might be on the particular occasion, had been either paid or promised, what actually happened when a student began his attendance upon a sophist? It will be convenient to distinguish three aspects, (1) matters of organisation, (2) teaching methods and (3) curricula, though naturally these were all interrelated.

One quite distinct type of performance was the *epideixis* or public display lecture. Hippias gave such performances regularly at the Panhellenic games at Olympia in the sacred precinct where he offered to speak on any one of a prepared list of subjects, and to answer any questions (*Hipp. Min.* 363c7–d4) and it appears that this may have been a regular feature there (Lysias, XXXIII.2). Gorgias offered to speak on any subject whatsoever in the theatre at Athens (DK 82A1a) and he spoke also at Olympia and at the Pythian games at Delphi (DK

82B7–9). On occasion both Hippias and Gorgias adopted the purple robes of the rhapsode, as though to emphasise their continuation of the functions of poets in earlier days (DK 82A9). Other *epideixeis* were given in public places and buildings in various parts of Athens – in the Lyceum by Prodicus (DK 84B8), in 'the school of Pheidostratus' by Hippias (DK 86A9), perhaps in a Gymnasium by Gorgias (Plato, *Gorg.* 447 a1–b3). Still other epideictic performances were given in private houses e.g. that of Callias in the case of Prodicus (DK 84B9).

An *epideixis* was normally a single lecture. According to Diogenes Laertius IX.52 (DK 80A1) Protagoras had been the first to introduce 'contests in arguments' (*logōn agōnas*) and this provided one of the starting points for the elaborate theory propounded by Gilbert Ryle which deserves a mention here.[4] According to Ryle these constituted what he called 'eristic moots' or public debates between competing speakers, and he believed that the earlier dialogues of Plato were dramatisations, indeed possibly virtually minutes, of what had taken place at actual eristic moots, and that they themselves were first published by being recited in public, with Plato taking the part of Socrates. So far as concerns Plato, there is simply no evidence of any kind to support this theory, and all probability is strongly against it.

That there were sometimes public debates and confrontations between sophists of the kind supposed is not impossible, and is just possibly supported by one piece of evidence, Hippocrates, *De Natura Hominis* 1 where we are told that when the same men are contradicting one another (*antilegontes*) in front of the same listeners, the one is never victorious three times in succession in his argument, but now one prevails, now another, and now the one with the most glib tongue in the face of the crowd. But it is not certain that this refers to any actual debates, since the same debate would hardly be repeated three times over in public. The reference may be simply to the unpredictable and inconclusive effect of opposed arguments when presented to successive audiences. The nature of these 'opposed arguments' is discussed further below. All that is meant by the phrase *agōn logōn* is the kind of conflict between arguments found in all cases of Antilogic, written or otherwise, in public or in private (see DK Vol. II 292.8, Plato, *Prot.* 335a4), as was correctly understood by Guthrie.[5] If formal public debates did take place from time to time, it does not seem that they were a major part of sophistic activity. What is

[4] G. Ryle, *Plato's Progress*, Cambridge 1966.
[5] *History of Greek Philosophy*, III, 43–4.

likely to have been more frequent were the kind of debates described in Plato's *Protagoras* and still others which were essentially class exercises and which were internal to the teaching situation. Something more will be said about these shortly, under the heading 'teaching methods'.

The main instruction by sophists, however, was given quite certainly neither in public lectures nor in public debates, but in smaller classes or seminars such as are depicted in the house of Callias when the young Hippocrates comes to seek instruction from Protagoras. Here Hippias was seated on a chair in a portico, discoursing to a group of listeners, apparently on nature and astronomical matters and replying to questions. Prodicus is in a converted store-room, talking in a loud, booming voice, while Protagoras is walking up and down in the front portico followed by a whole crowd of Athenians and foreigners, dancing attendance upon him. Many of these had left their own cities to follow Protagoras on his travels – if board was supplied by Protagoras in such cases it might explain why some of his charges were so high. Certainly there does seem to be some emphasis placed on the close association of teacher with pupil, in a kind of living together as part of the process of education. The result will of course have been that students gained not only from their close contact with the mind and personality of the sophist, but also from the intellectual stimulus of associating with each other in a group of young men all concerned with the same studies. No doubt this is part of the source of the intense excitement which we can sense in the young Hippocrates at the prospect of joining the group of students associated with Protagoras, an excitement so intense that he cannot wait until the normal times, but comes to Socrates' house while Socrates is still in bed, all aflutter with his emotions.

This leads naturally on to (2) the question of teaching methods. First there was the prepared lecture on a set theme. Some of these were essentially rhetorical exercises on a mythical topic, such as the surviving *Helena* and *Palamedes* of Gorgias. More directly related to the training of future speakers in the law courts or the assembly were rhetorical exercises of the type that have come down to us in the collection of the Tetralogies of Antiphon – each of these consists of a set of four speeches, giving speech of the accuser, reply of the defendant, then a second speech on each side. They are as it were specimen skeletons for speeches, and the second Tetralogy deals with the theme already mentioned – the question of blame when a boy is accidentally hit by a javelin while a spectator in a gymnasium. It is clear that sample speeches of this kind were provided for students to study and imitate.

Cicero in the *Brutus* (46–47) provides us with further valuable information which he has taken from a lost work of Aristotle, probably his collection of early rhetorical handbooks known as the *Technōn Synagogē*. According to this: 'Protagoras prepared written discussions of important matters, now called commonplaces [*loci communes*]. Gorgias did the same, composing eulogies and invectives against particular things, because he regarded it as especially the function of the orator to be able to increase merit by praising and to diminish it again by invective. Antiphon of Rhamnus had similar compositions written out.' It can hardly be in doubt that it is commonplaces of this kind which the pupils of Gorgias were required to learn by heart (DK 82B14), rather than whole speeches as is sometimes asserted, and one must assume that they would then be deployed in practical exercises under the master's supervision.

What Cicero refers to in Latin as the *locus* is in Greek the *topos* or 'place', and in its most general sense it was probably originally the position or standpoint from which you assail your opponent or defend your own thesis. Others would confine it however to meaning simply the place where the orator finds a needed argument. Aristotle in his treatise the *Topics* gave a kind of primer of dialectic showing how one could defend a thesis by taking as starting points appropriate premises that were already generally acceptable. Topics are for him lines of argument, such as arguments from contraries, arguments from definitions and arguments from mistake. His approach is formal, and his topics are not the same as the *loci communes* to which Cicero refers. But the conclusion of the *Sophistici Elenchi* shows that he was well aware of the existence of these also, and his *Rhetoric* II. 23 gives examples, such as the quotation from Euripides, *Thyestes*, 'If men are in the habit of gaining credit for false statements, you must also believe the contrary, that men often disbelieve what is true.'

Many of these commonplaces were antithetical in character, and it would seem that written collections were made. Protagoras wrote a *Technē Eristikōn* or Art of Eristica, which was either the same as or similar but distinct from the two books known as *Antilogiai* or *Antilogikoi*, and there are good reasons for supposing that either or both of these contained 'commonplace' materials, in antithetical form as the name *Antilogiai* implies, ready for use either by students or in real life. How many such collections of passages there may have been we do not know. But there were certainly others, and Plato refers also to the practice of Euenus of Paros (DK 80A26) who invented Insinuation, Indirect Praises, and, as some say Indirect Censures, composing them in verse as an aid to memory, presumably as examples for pupils, rather than so that he could remember them himself.

A further method of teaching that was widely used was by question and answer. This was frequently associated with another theme, the ability to speak briefly. Thus both are said to be the mark of the man who knows the truth about things, in the treatise known as the *Dissoi Logoi* 8.1 and 8.13 (DK 90). In a number of Plato's dialogues Socrates is presented as objecting to long speeches and calling for brief answers to questions. In the *Protagoras* he is quite emphatic that Protagoras is equally skilled and at home in each of these two methods of teaching (329b1–5, 334e4–335a3), the second method being only in the power of a few. Exactly the same claim is made for himself elsewhere by Gorgias (*Gorg.* 449c1–8), and possibly for Polus (461d6–462b3). We are told in the *Phaedrus* (267a6–b9) that both Tisias, the Sicilian rhetorician who had taught Gorgias, and Gorgias himself

realised that probabilities deserve more respect than things that are true, and further made small things seem large and large things seem small by the power of language, and new things seem old fashioned and vice versa, and discovered both conciseness in arguments and very long treatments about all things. And when Prodicus heard this mentioned he laughed and said he and he alone had discovered what speeches are required by the art – neither long nor short ones but ones that are moderate . . . But are we forgetting Hippias? I think the man from Elis also would join his vote to that of Prodicus.

The evidence of this passage is important in a number of ways. It shows that Plato knew that there were two recognised methods of instruction in the sophistic period. But more than this, it shows that there was debate about their respective merits among named sophists. The references to the power to change the way things appear by interchanging their importance ties all in clearly with the *technique* of sophistic argument. As will be seen below in due course, this is the technique of making the weaker argument into the stronger. As we saw from other evidence before quoting the passage from the *Phaedrus* the method of speaking briefly was quite clearly related by Socrates to the method of question and answer (see *Prot.* 329b3–5, 334d4–7, 335a6, b1–2) – indeed, one might ask, how should it have been otherwise, above all with a sophist, who would be least likely of all men to wish to speak briefly, and then be silent in argument. Consequently it is not plausible to suggest[6] that the brevity in speech of Protagoras and Gorgias was simply a laconic style, 'putting a thing in the fewest possible words', and not a technique of investigation. At the very least, if not a technique of investigation, it was certainly a technique of argument and of teaching.

This is an issue where a great deal has seemed to many to be at stake. For the technique in question is the basis of what we know as the Socratic tradition in education, and in fact Diogenes Laertius records the tradition that Protagoras was the first to develop the Socratic method of argument. The attempt, as it was seen, to rob Socrates of the credit for this achievement, perhaps inevitably aroused strong partisanship. This emerges very clearly in the discussion by Henry Sidgwick[7] who considered it 'quite incredible' if Protagoras had really invented methodical disputation by short questions and answers that he could ever have been represented as Plato represents him in the dialogue which bears his name. He was disposed to think that the art of disputation which is ascribed to the sophists later on in some of Plato's dialogues such as the *Euthydemus* and the *Sophist* originated entirely with Socrates, and that he is altogether responsible for the form at least of this 'second' species of Sophistic.

This view has often been quoted with approval, either with or without qualification.[8] The most careful recent discussion of this question known to me is by Norman Gulley.[9] He is aware, I would say, that the view of Sidgwick simply cannot stand, and that the sophists did develop a method of argument by question and answer. This, I would say, is the only possible view based on the evidence that we have. But Gulley feels constrained to hedge the conclusion as much as possible by arguing as follows. The sophists' procedure was probably a fairly late development, influenced in its formulation by Socrates' question and answer method of examination. It is probable that any element of questioning in the method of Protagoras was an almost incidental element, and had a dramatic rather than a philosophical significance. So, he concludes, we might be best advised to

---

[6] as E. R. Dodds, commentary on *Gorg.* 449 c 2 in his *Plato, Gorgias*, Oxford 1959 p. 195.

[7] in *Journal of Philology* 4 (1872) 298–300.

[8] see e.g. R. Robinson, *Plato's Earlier Dialectic*, Oxford 2nd edn. 1953, p. 88.

[9] *The Philosophy of Socrates*, London, 1968 28–37.

follow Plato and call the Socratic method 'dialectic' in contrast to the 'eristic' of the sophists.

Now the contrast between the terms 'dialectic' and 'eristic' will be discussed below. For the remainder of the contentions just mentioned there is simply no evidence and no inherent likelihood that would suggest that the method of Protagoras and other sophists was later than that of Socrates. But we do have reason to associate Protagoras' method with his doctrine of Two Logoi each opposed to the other. Indeed Plato in the *Sophist* in a passage to be discussed further shortly (232b) picks out one feature as distinctive of all sophists as such, namely that they were *Antilogikoi* who opposed one Logos to another. This means that what I have been calling the method of Protagoras has a base in Protagoras' own theorising, and this surely does suggest that his method is likely to have been his own rather than simply derived from Socrates. So the following schematisation[10] of the 'method of Protagoras' has considerable plausibility, though in its details it perhaps does run a little beyond the evidence: (1) a formal expository style whether lecture or text-book, (2) the verbal exchange of a small informal discussion group, and (3) the antithetical formulation of public positions and the setting of party lines. What we can say with certainty is that we have every reason to attribute to Protagoras the use of a kind of tutorial method to supplement set expositions, and that there is no reason to suppose that this originated with Socrates.

So, to sum up, I would say that in one sense the problem is not nearly as important as it had been made to seem. The Socratic method, to the extent that it may have originated with Socrates, nonetheless originated from within the sophistic movement, if only because Socrates himself was a part of that movement. Once it is granted that sophists other than Socrates did use the question and answer method, and this surely we must grant, then the degree of Socrates' originality and the degree to which he was influenced by other sophists is both an unanswerable question, and also one of subordinate importance from almost every point of view other than that of Socratic partisanship.

I turn now (3) to the curricula taught by the sophists, and the range of studies which they prosecuted. From time to time in the past, attempts have been made to argue that the sophists were wholly or predominantly concerned with a single area of study and teaching,

---

[10] cf. E. Havelock, *The Liberal Temper in Greek Politics*, London 1957, 216 and F. A. G. Beck, *Greek Education*, London 1964, 166.

which concern was then taken as the distinguishing mark of a sophist as such – the educational ideal of rhetoric, the opposition of nature and convention, political success, the ideal of education in general, the rejection of physical science, a turning away from religion, the humanistic view of man as at the centre of the universe, man as a tragic figure of destiny. All these in turn or in combination have been suggested by different modern scholars at different times. The actual references that we have to sophistic teachings suggest that these covered an extremely wide range, and in any case the question is complicated in part by the need to decide in advance just which figures are to be included and which are to be excluded from the title of sophist. Then there is the difficulty that the writings of the sophists have not survived. It is clear that they were in fact numerous and it is sometimes said that in general they disappeared from circulation within a few decades of their production. After all, it has been suggested, they were mostly not scholars and their most serious educational work was meant for living men, not future readers. So Jaeger in his influential work *Paideia* Vol. I Eng. trans. 1939, p. 302, which was cited with approval by Untersteiner.

About this it must be said, as about so many of the general statements regularly repeated about the sophists, that it is only partly true. This the mention of some facts is sufficient to demonstrate. For Protagoras the manuscripts of Diogenes Laertius give a list of 'surviving works' comprising 12 titles, and Diogenes' actual list may have been longer. It is natural to suppose that this comes from a library catalogue, perhaps at Alexandria. Another of his works seems to have got itself somehow listed in the so-called Lamprias catalogue of Plutarch. Porphyry in the third century A.D. came by chance on a copy of another work and claims to have summarised its arguments (DK 80B2), and we have a piece of literary criticism of Homer by Protagoras in a piece of papyrus from Oxyrrhynchus not before the first century A.D. (DK 80A30). On the other hand it is probable that the so-called new fragment of Protagoras, published in 1968 from a biblical commentary by Didymus the Blind, comes merely from a sceptic doxographical work of some kind and not directly from Protagoras' writings, and this is likely also to be the case with the valuable new information about Prodicus from another of Didymus' commentaries.[11] But for Antiphon what is in fact our main information comes

---

[11] for Protagoras, M. Groenewald, 'Ein neues Protagoras-Fragment', *Zeitschr. f. Pap. u. Ep.* 2 (1968) 1–2, with J. Mejer, 'The alleged new fragment of Protagoras', *Hermes* 100 (1972) 175–8, for Prodicus see below p. 89 n. 4.

from two separate pieces in the series of *Oxyrrhynchus Papyri*, which means that his major work was known and copied in Egypt. If Antiphon the sophist is identifiable with Antiphon from Rhamnus we have of course in addition the surviving collection of speeches known as the Tetralogies together with two other speeches. The identification was regarded as uncertain by Hermogenes in the late second century A.D. because the style or, perhaps better, the literary form of the sophist's writings was so distinct. This would imply that he had read one or more of them, and the *De Concordia* was in fact quoted from quite extensively by John Stobaeus about the middle of the fifth century A.D. For Gorgias we have the two surviving *Encomia* and two summaries of his *On Nature* of which that by Sextus Empiricus belongs to the late second century A.D. Iamblichus, about 300 A.D. was able to quote extensively from the treatise known as a result to us as the *Anonymus Iamblichi* (DK 89). A Memphis book catalogue of the third century A.D. preserved in a St. Petersburg papyrus contained the title of a work by Hippias (DK 86B19), and a treatise by Prodicus, *On the Nature of Man,* appears to have been known to Galen in the second century A.D. (DK 84B4).

From this it would appear that a not inconsiderable number of writings did survive for quite some time. Where the sophists have been less fortunate than others among the Presocratics has been in the virtual absence of doxographic accounts. For this their rejection as thinkers by Aristotle was probably the major reason. This meant they were virtually excluded from the series of surveys commissioned in Aristotle's school, which were a major source of subsequent information. They probably were included in his survey of rhetorical writings and this is at least one reason why the subsequent tradition has so heavily stressed this aspect of their work. Their general omission from the doxographic tradition, coupled with the Platonist and Aristotelian view that their thought and teaching was bogus, meant that they were indeed virtually ignored by Hellenistic scholarship, and even such of their works as did survive were not read. In the imperial period it was only members of what is known as the Second Sophistic movement starting with the second century A.D. who were prepared to take them at all seriously. This was a movement, however, that really was concerned with language and rhetoric rather than philosophy. In the third century A.D., Flavius Philostratus, a member of the intellectual circle of the Syrian Empress, Julia Domna, wrote his *Lives of the Sophists* in which he included Gorgias, Protagoras, Prodicus, Polus, Thrasymachus, Antiphon and Critias. But he appears actually to have seen only works by the last two on the list, and his almost exclusively rhetorical interests meant that he said nothing about doctrines even when information about these was available to him, e.g. for the Man-measure doctrine of Protagoras.

The curriculum of sophistic education did not begin from nothing – it followed on after completion of the primary stage. According to Aeschines the orator it was Solon early in the sixth century B.C. who first made the learning of reading and writing compulsory at Athens (Aeschines, *In Tim*. 9–12), and by the middle of the fifth century and probably earlier there was a well-established system of primary schools. Attendance was the general pattern for free-born boys, though there is no evidence that school-attendance was compulsory. The widening of education throughout Athenian society that this involved was not popular with those who looked back to an age of greater aristocratic privilege in such matters. Pindar (*O1*.II.86–88) opposed those whose wisdom comes by nature (and so family and birth) to those who have had to learn. While it is not certain exactly to whom he was referring, it may fairly be taken as a move in what it is convenient to call the Nature–Nurture controversy, which was important in the sophistic period; cf. also his Nemean ode, III.41. If *aretē* or excellence can be taught then social mobility is immediately possible, and it is clear that Protagoras was concerned with just this Nature–Nurture controversy when he wrote that 'teaching requires both Nature and Practice' (DK 80B3; cf. B10).

In the primary school the standard system of education consisted of three parts, each with its own specialist teacher. The *paidotribēs* was responsible for physical education and sporting activities, the *citharistēs* for music. Thirdly the *grammatistēs* taught reading, writing, arithmetic, and his pupils were required to read and memorise writings of the great poets, Homer, Hesiod and others, chosen because of the moral wisdom which they contained (cf. Plato, *Prot.* 325d7–326a4).

This was the kind of education already possessed by a student who handed himself over to a sophist for further instruction. There was no such thing as a standard sophistic curriculum of studies, as has been repeatedly pointed out by modern scholars. But there is one piece of evidence which suggests that there may not have been quite so much diversity as has commonly been supposed. For when Protagoras has been asked by Socrates what it is that the young Hippocrates will learn from him, his reply is given by Plato as follows (*Prot.* 318d7–319-a2):

'When Hippocrates has come to me he will not be treated as he would have been, if he had come to any other sophist. For the others cause damage to those who are young, and when they have got away from those studies that are specialised, they take hold of them once again against their wills and pitch them back into specialised studies, teaching them mathematical calculations and astronomy, geometry, music and literature' – and as he said this he looked at Hippias – 'but if he comes to me he will learn about nothing else, but only what he has come to learn about. And the subject-matter is good policy, in private affairs, how to manage his own household in the best possible way, and in public affairs how to speak and act most powerfully in the affairs of the city.'

It is often assumed that Protagoras is simply poking fun at a method of instruction that was peculiar to Hippias. This could be right, but it is not what Protagoras says. His words are quite clear – what he is rejecting is the approach of *all* other sophists, *all* of whom, he implies, teach specialised studies (318d8 and 9). It is true that references elsewhere do suggest that the programme announced by Protagoras was not only his, but in some sense represented what was taught by other sophists as well as himself (cf. *Meno* 91a1–b8, *Gorg.* 520e2–6, *Rep.* 600c7–d2, Xen. *Mem.* I.2.15). But equally there is evidence that the kind of knowledge taught by Hippias was to be learned from other sophists as well. Thus Protagoras made a detailed and apparently technical attack on geometricians (DK 80B7). A question that we know was of great interest throughout the period was the problem of the squaring of the circle, which concerned Anaxagoras (DK 59A38), and Antiphon claimed to have discovered how to do it by a method of exhaustion. We are fortunate to have a detailed account of what he proposed preserved by Simplicius (DK 87B13). The method is of course based on a mistake, and Aristotle could reasonably claim that it was not based on sound geometrical principles. Nonetheless it *was* an attempt to solve a problem in geometry. Hippias himself was credited with the discovery of a curve, the *quadratrix*, used in attempts to square the circle, and also for the trisection of an angle. It is natural to suppose that when in the *Meno* Socrates proceeds by means of a diagram, no doubt drawn in sand, to elicit answers from the slave boy, he is following a well established method of illustrating geometrical problems by actual drawings. That there were geometrical discussions in sophistic circles is surely established by Socrates' casual remark in that dialogue (85b4) that the line drawn across an oblong from corner to corner is called a diagonal by the sophists. As this is only the second time the word *diametros* for 'diagonal' is found in Greek (the first being in Aristophanes, *Frogs* 801) it is probable that the word was a relatively new and unfamiliar technical term – indeed it is not impossible that the word was actually invented by one of the sophists. In the case of astronomy we have very strong evidence from Aristophanes' *Clouds*. There Prodicus is described as a kind of 'upper air sophist' (*meteorosophistes*) and Socrates is shown on stage swinging in some kind of basket to enable him to see more clearly the objects in the heavens which he is engaged in contemplating.

It is said from time to time that the sophists were simply not interested in physical speculations. If we exclude thinkers such as Empedocles, Anaxagoras and Democritus from the ranks of the sophists, then it is true that no major theoretic contributions came from the rest. But it is equally clear that they did regularly talk about physical questions. An interest in physical questions both in discussions and in their writings is in fact attested by Cicero (DK 84B3) for Prodicus, Thrasymachus and Protagoras. Xenophon seeks to defend Socrates and does so by claiming that Socrates did not even talk about the topic discussed by so many of the sophists, namely the nature of the universe, how the cosmos arose, and the necessary laws governing the heavenly bodies, arguing that those who thought about such matters were out of their minds (*Mem.* I.1.11). Here Xenophon is no doubt appealing to the evidence of the *Phaedo* to defend Socrates against the view that he was interested in physical science which stems from the *Clouds*. But he does claim that Socrates was more or less unique in his avoidance of such topics. Protagoras is credited by Sextus Empiricus with a doctrine of physical effluences similar to that of Empedocles and the atomists (DK 80A14) and he was satirised for his interest in physical questions by Eupolis the comic poet (DK 80A11). Gorgias likewise was interested in Empedocles' theory of pores and effluences (DK 31A92 and 82B5). He appears to have said that the sun was a red-hot mass (DK 82B31) and he was represented on the tomb of Isocrates as gazing at an astronomical sphere (DK 82A17). Prodicus is said to have discussed the four elements identifying them with gods and also with the sun and the moon as the source of the vital force in all things, thus qualifying for a place next to Empedocles and Heraclitus (Epiphanius, *Adv. Haeres.* III.2.9.21 = Diels,

Doxographi Graeci p. 591), and there is probably a reference to his theories in Aristophanes *Birds* 685 ff. He was in addition credited by Galen with a particular view about the nature of phlegm (DK 84B4).

Relevant here is the passage mentioned earlier in Plato's *Sophist* (232b11–e2), where, after suggesting that the sophist is characterised by his being an *antilogikos*, the Eleatic Stranger asks what is the range of topics with which such persons are concerned, and himself replies with a list: things divine that are mostly unseen, visible objects on earth and in the sky, the coming into existence and the being of all things, laws and all matters of politics, each and every art (*technē*), and he insists that these were not merely discussed in writings by Protagoras, but by many others as well.

This provides us with a wide-ranging list of topics, including one unexpected heading, things divine. But it is here that Protagoras' book *On the Gods* should be placed, where the opening words give us an application of the two-opposed arguments doctrine – 'concerning the gods I cannot come to know either as to how they are or how they are not or what they are in appearance', and also the work *On things in Hades*. Prodicus (DK 84B5) discussed the origin of men's belief in gods in psychological and naturalistic terms, and Critias (DK 88B25) held that gods were invented deliberately by governments to secure the good behaviour of their subjects.

Finally literature. Here we have Protagoras reported as saying (*Prot.* 338e6–339a3) that it is his opinion that the greatest part of a man's education is to be skilled in the matter of verses, that is, to be able to understand in the utterances of the poets what has been rightly and what wrongly composed, and to know how to distinguish them and to account for them when questioned. And he goes on to introduce an elaborate discussion of a poem by Simonides, which in turn provokes further analyses by Socrates and Prodicus, and the offer of an exposition by Hippias, which is hurriedly refused on behalf of the assemblage by Alcibiades with the request that he do it some other time. That Hippias' rejected exposition might have been lengthy is suggested by the references to his *epideixis* on Homer and other poets in the *Hippias Minor* 363a1–c3. The whole discussion in the *Protagoras* takes up something like a sixth of the complete dialogue, and we know independently from a papyrus fragment that Protagoras did indulge in literary criticism of Homer (DK 80A30). Somewhat later Isocrates (XII.18) tells how once in the Lyceum three or four plain and ordinary sophists were sitting together discussing poets, especially

Hesiod and Homer, and it is clear that the practice followed by Protagoras continued long afterwards.

The evidence so far cited would indicate that the contrast between Protagoras and Hippias may not have been as great as is suggested by the statement which Plato puts into Protagoras' mouth. This statement is indeed likely to be substantially correct in what it actually says. But there is a difference between the two approaches which is historically of considerable importance. Protagoras in his criticism of Hippias and others like him is raising the question of relevance, by suggesting that he, Protagoras, will teach what the student really wants to be taught as a preparation for the life he is intending to lead. Associated with this is a further issue also. Heraclitus had attacked Hesiod, Pythagoras, Xenophanes and Hecataeus on the grounds that Polymathy or learning in many subjects did not produce understanding (DK 22B40), no doubt because it had not led men to an understanding of what he regarded as his own special insight into the nature of the universe. From then on the value of Polymathy was a matter of debate, and we find Democritus saying (DK 68B65) that what is needed is not Polymathy in the sense of learning many things but rather an understanding of many things. This is the issue between Protagoras and Hippias, not that of the range of things which we need to understand. It is probable that Protagoras' position is summed up in the statement attributed to him (DK 80B11): Education does not sprout in the soul, unless one goes to a greater depth. It is likely that this means that it is not enough to stay at the level of phenomena which are the materials of polymathy, but that we must proceed to what is now called study in depth, in an attempt to understand underlying principles common to all the subjects that are to be studied.

5

The individual sophists

We know the names of upwards of twenty-six sophists in the period from about 460 to 380 B.C. when their importance and activity was at its height. In the fourth century they were effectively replaced by more systematic, organised schools, often with more or less permanent buildings of their own, as was the case with the Academy of Plato, the Lyceum of Aristotle and quite a number of others. Of the sophists known to us by name perhaps eight or nine were outstandingly famous, and to these should be added the authors of two surviving anonymous works, the *Dissoi Logoi* and the so-called *Anonymus Iamblichi*. It will be convenient to say something about each of these separately. The evidence is in general to be found conveniently presented in the collection of Testimonia and Fragments by Diels–Kranz cited as DK.[1]

(1) *Protagoras*

By far the most famous was Protagoras, and Plato suggests that he was the first to adopt the name of sophist and to charge fees for the instruction he offered (*Prot.* 349a2–4). Born in Abdera not later than 490 B.C. he probably died soon after 421 B.C. He may have been educated as a boy under Persian religious teachers in Thrace. He is represented in Plato's dialogue the *Protagoras* as having recently arrived in Athens from abroad (309d3), and reference is made to the occasion when he was last previously in Athens a few years before (310e5). This misled Athenaeus into supposing that he had made only two visits to Athens at the time envisaged in Plato's dialogue (DK 80A11) and this has led to some rather profitless speculations by

---

[1] Diels, H. & Kranz W., *Die Fragmente der Vorsokratiker*, 6th and later editions, 3 vols Berlin 1951–52. There is an edition by M. Untersteiner with Italian translation and commentary in four fascicules, entitled *Sofisti, Testimonianze e Frammenti*, Florence 1949–62, which is quite distinct from his interpretative volume *I Sofisti*, Turin 1949, 2nd edn in 2 vols Milan 1967.

modern scholars. It would be very difficult to believe that Protagoras had actually only been to Athens once before his present visit towards the end of the thirties – his close association with Pericles and his selection by him to frame the constitution for the new colony at Thurii must mean that he was already well known at Athens by 444 B.C. It is probable that his first arrival there was as early as about 460 B.C., since we are told by Plato [DK 80A8] that he had been a sophist for forty years at the time of his death. In fact there is no reason at all to believe that there had been only one previous visit by him to Athens, since all that the passage in the *Protagoras* says is 'when he visited Athens previously i.e. before', not 'when he visited Athens the first time'.[2]

According to the preserved tradition it appears that Protagoras died by drowning on a sea voyage after leaving Athens because he had been tried and convicted of impiety and his books burnt in the agora after they had been called in from those who possessed them by herald's proclamation. The essentials of the story are found already in Timon of Phlius and in Philochorus in the third century B.C. and I believe that there is no reason not to accept them. In the *Meno* (91e3–92a2), it is true, Socrates says that right down to the day at which he is speaking (dramatic date of the dialogue, perhaps 402 B.C.) Protagoras has not ceased in any way to be of high reputation. It has been argued that these words prove that Protagoras never suffered any serious public disgrace, and that consequently the story of his trial cannot be true. But it is hard to feel that this objection is conclusive. It has been pointed out[3] that Plato would have said the same about Socrates, who was in fact put to death as well as tried for impiety.

The list of Protagoras' 'surviving books' preserved by Diogenes Laertius reads as follows: *Art of Eristics, On Wrestling, On Sciences* (or possibly *On Mathematics*), *On Government, On Ambition, On Virtues, On the Original State of Things, On those in Hades, On incorrect Human Actions, Imperative, Trial over a Fee, Antilogies* in two books. Not included as such in this list were also his works *On the Gods,* and *Truth.* In most cases we have no positive indication of the actual scope or contents of these works.

In the years 1851–54 some eleven statues in a half-circle of wall

---

[2] *to proteron*, and not *to prōton*. Correctly translated by W. K. C. Guthrie, *Plato Protagoras and Meno*, London, Penguin 1956: 'Last time he came to Athens I was still a child.'

[3] Guthrie, *History of Greek Philosophy*, III, 263.

facing the end of the so-called Sphinx alley leading to the Serapeum at Memphis in Egypt were uncovered in excavations conducted by Mariette. They were left *in situ* and were covered again by drifting sand. They were rediscovered in 1938 but work was suspended during the Second World War. They were eventually uncovered once again in 1950 and then published in full.[4] On the eastern half of the semi-circle we have Plato, Heraclitus, Thales and Protagoras identified by the inscription of their names on the statues. Despite the use of omicron for omega in the spelling of Protagoras' name, the identification seems secure and has not been queried. The date is uncertain, except that the statues certainly belong to the Ptolemaic period. What is remarkable is that Protagoras should be included in a series of philosophers facing a set of poets on the opposite side, a clear testimony, it would seem, to the importance with which he was invested in the Hellenistic period.

(2) *Gorgias*

Gorgias came from Leontini in Sicily and was said to have lived to a very great age. Pausanias (DK 82A7) tells us that Gorgias won even more respect at Athens than the famous Tisias and that when Jason had become tyrant in Thessaly he put Gorgias before Polycrates though Polycrates' school was by then in high repute at Athens. On the basis of this it has been inferred that he lived at the court of Jason of Pherae after the latter became tyrant not before about 380 B.C. But the inference is quite unjustified since the story merely relates a comparison between Gorgias' brand of rhetoric with that of his pupil Polycrates. All we can say with any probability is that his birth was perhaps about 485 B.C. and that he lived into the fourth century B.C.

There is a clear tradition that he was a disciple of the Sicilian philosopher Empedocles, and he made a famous visit to Athens in 427 B.C. as leader of an embassy from Leontini, to persuade the Athenians to make an alliance with his native city against Syracuse. He addressed the Assembly and was said to have been much admired for his rhetorical skill. It may have been his first visit to Athens. But we are not actually told this in any source, and consequently the inference is quite uncertain. He certainly travelled extensively, without settling in any particular city, and he is recorded as having spoken at Olympia, at

---

[4] J. Ph. Lauer and Ch. Picard, *Les statues ptolémaiques du Sarapieion de Memphis* Paris 1955. See also K. Schefold, 'Die Dichter und Weisen in Serapieion', *Mus. Helv.* 14 (1957) 33–8.

Delphi, in Thessaly, in Boeotia, and in Argos where he was so disliked that his pupils were subjected to a penalty of some sort, and he both gave epideictic speeches and also taught pupils at Athens (cf. Plato, *Hipp. Mai.* 282b4–c1) for which he received considerable sums of money.

In all this Gorgias was clearly functioning as a sophist and was clearly known as such. Modern suggestions that he should not be classed as a sophist rest on an arbitrary narrowing of the concept of a sophist and even then are not supported by ancient evidence.[5]

His treatise *On Nature* was said to have been written in the 84th Olympiad i.e. 444–441 B.C. (DK 82A10). Summaries or parts or references survive from speeches entitled *Funeral Oration, Olympian Oration, Pythian Oration, Encomium to the Eleans, Encomium to Helen, Apology of Palamedes*. It is probable that he also wrote a technical treatise on rhetoric, whether its title was simply *Art* or possibly *On the Right Moment in Time (Peri Kairou)*. Finally there is no reason to doubt the attribution to him of the *Onomastikon* mentioned by Pollux in the preface to his own Lexicon as there used by him (IX.1 p. 148 Bethe), but not included, I believe, in any of the standard books on the sophists before 1961.[6] The title was also apparently that of a separate work by Democritus (DK 68A33, XI.4).

(3) *Prodicus*

Prodicus came from the island of Ceos in the Cyclades which had also been the birthplace of the poet Simonides. He was probably born before 460 B.C. and was still alive at the time of the death of Socrates in 399 B.C. He went on many embassies for Ceos to Athens, and on one occasion spoke before the Council. Like Gorgias he gave epideictic speeches and also private teaching for which he earned a great deal of money, and he visited many cities, not Athens alone. According to Philostratus, Xenophon was for a time a prisoner in Boeotia, but obtained his release on bail in order to listen to a discourse by Prodicus. Certainly Xenophon was very impressed with one *epideixis* by Prodicus, on the Choice of Heracles, which he summarised in the

---

[5] For such an attempt see E. R. Dodds, *Plato Gorgias* Oxford 1959, 6 ff. For the contrary view, Guthrie, *History of Greek Philosophy*, Cambridge III. 36 n. 4 and E. L. Harrison, 'Was Gorgias a Sophist?' *Phoenix* 18 (1964) 183–92.

[6] For the reference see V. Goldschmidt, *Essai sur le Cratyle*, Paris 1940, 7 n. 3 with Untersteiner, *Sofisti, Test. e Framm.* II² (1961) 209.

mouth of Socrates in his *Memorabilia* II.1.21–34. It came from a work entitled *Hours (Horae)* which included encomia on other persons or characters as well as Heracles according to Plato (DK 84B1). He also wrote a treatise *On the Nature of Man*.

Prodicus was above all famous for his work on language, and Plato's satire on him in the *Protagoras* has suggested to some that he may have left specific writings *On the correctness of names*. The philosophic importance of this side of his work is very great, but we have no actual references to anything other than lecture courses. But it was on the basis of these lectures and their contents that Socrates regarded himself as a pupil of Prodicus (Plato, *Prot.* 341a4, *Meno* 96d7) and says that he has sent many pupils, not suited to associate with himself as they are not philosophically pregnant, to be attached profitably to Prodicus and other wise and inspired men (*Theaetet.* 151b2–6). That his linguistic theories had a definite quasi-metaphysical base is suggested by the new papyrus fragment discussed below.

There was a tradition in later sources (DK 84A1) that Prodicus died at Athens by drinking the hemlock apparently after condemnation for 'corrupting the young'. This is usually and probably rightly dismissed as involving a confusion between Prodicus and Socrates – if it had been true we would surely hear much more about it in earlier sources. But there was a story, preserved in the Pseudo-Platonic *Eryxias* (398e11–399b1) that Prodicus was expelled from a gymnasium for speaking unsuitably in front of young men, so it is not impossible that he did have to face the kind of opposition which Protagoras spoke of as the common lot of all sophists.

(4) *Hippias*

Hippias of Elis is mentioned in the *Protagoras* in similar terms to Prodicus and it is reasonable to suppose that he may have been about the same age. He was apparently alive in 399 B.C. and probably died early in the fourth century – certainly there is not the least likelihood that he lived until the middle of that century, as has been suggested. Like other sophists he travelled extensively and made much money.

He claimed to be at home in all the learning of his day and Socrates not unnaturally refers to him as a polymath (DK 86A14). In this he was no doubt aided by exceptional powers of memory, apparently developed by special techniques, which he also taught to others, but which enabled him to remember fifty names after a single hearing. It is interesting to read, though it is unlikely to have been true, that his art of memory was aided by drinking certain potions.

In addition to epideictic displays, it appears that he was known to have been ready to teach astronomy, mathematics and geometry, genealogy, mythology and history, painting and sculpture, the functions of letters, syllables, rhythms and musical scales. Moreover he wrote epic verses, tragedies and dithyrambs, as well as many writings of all kinds in prose. All this would be remarkable enough. But there is good evidence that his knowledge was not merely superficial, and not based merely on a glib facility to talk without preparation about any subject whatsoever. Rather we must conclude that it was based on scholarship that was both wide and deep.

The evidence for this is of two kinds. First there are indications that Hippias developed some kind of general philosophical position of his own. Though it is difficult to reconstruct, it seems to have been based on a doctrine of classes of things dependent on a being that is continuous or carried right through physical bodies without interruption, in a manner, we are told, like the slices of beef cut the whole length of the back given in Homer to a very important guest as a special privilege at a feast (see *Hippias Maior* 301d5–302b4, unfortunately not in DK). More important however, because it can hardly be challenged, is the evidence of an exceptional scholarly interest in the study of subjects as such, including their history. Hippias seems himself virtually to have inaugurated this kind of study. In this he anticipated the kind of systematic surveys commissioned by Aristotle in the Lyceum. What is so remarkable in the case of Hippias is that he was able to accomplish so much without the help of established libraries and an organised school of research students.

He produced a list of Olympic victors, based on local records at Olympia, which probably enabled Thucydides to give precise dates, whereas Herodotus had not been able to do so.[7] A quotation from the list, either direct or indirect, may be found in what survives in a papyrus from Oxyrhynchus dating from the third century A.D. (no. 222). Certainly it formed part of the evidence for the later full list of which we know from Eusebius. Hellanicus produced a similar list for the priestesses of Hera in Argos and Aristotle (frs. 615–617) produced another comparable list for Delphic victors. Here may be mentioned a

---

[7] see F. Jacoby, *Fragmente der griechischen Historiker*, Leiden 2nd edn 1957, I p. 477, and the full discussion in III b Text 221–228, III b Noten 143–154.

further work, a list, if that is what it was, of names of peoples compiled by Hippias under the title *Ethnōn Onamasiai* (DK 86B2).

The whole of this work was fundamental for the establishment of a basic chronology for Greek history. Nor was this all by any means. In mathematics he was credited with the discovery of the curve known as the quadratrix used for the trisection of an angle and in attempts to square the circle. The way in which this is referred to by later writers makes it reasonably certain that he left an account of his discovery in writing, see Proclus' *Commentary on the First Book of Euclid's Elements* (p. 356, a passage not in DK). In this same commentary Proclus gives (pp. 65–8) a sketch of the history of geometry, apparently based directly or indirectly on a copy of the history by Eudemus of Rhodes, the disciple of Aristotle, no longer available to us. Proclus makes it clear that at least some of Eudemus' information for the period before Plato was derived from Hippias. As the particular point cited is a small one otherwise unknown it looks as if Hippias in his enquiry (Proclus says *historēsen*) went into considerable detail.

Finally it looks as if a further work, known simply as the *Synagoge* or *Collection*, was a work of much more importance than was commonly supposed not so very long ago. Clement of Alexandria in order to argue that Greeks were incorrigible plagiarists quotes what may have been part of Hippias' own introduction to the work (DK 86B6):

Some of these things may perhaps have been said by Orpheus, some briefly here and there by Musaeus, some by Hesiod, some by Homer, some by others among the poets, some in prose-writings whether by Greeks or by barbarians. But I will put together the most important and inter-related passages from all these sources, and will thus make this present piece both new and varied in kind.

This suggests that the *Synagoge* was a collection of various passages, stories and pieces of information concerned with the history of religion and similar matters. There the matter rested until 1944 when Bruno Snell in a remarkable article pointed out that the above passage established that Hippias was the earliest systematic doxographer or collector of the opinions of earlier writers of whom we have any knowledge. He then went on to demonstrate, with as near an approach to certainty, I would say, as is possible in questions of this kind, that Hippias was the source that had connected the doctrine of

48

Thales that all things were made out of water and that the earth rests on water with the cosmogonical statements in Homer, Hesiod and elsewhere that Oceanus and Tethys were the source of all things. Certainly Plato was familiar with a schematisation of the thought of the Presocratics according to which one line of thinkers, extending from Homer, Hesiod and Orpheus through Epicharmus, Heraclitus and Empedocles held that all things are the offspring of flow and motion, and the other line from still earlier thinkers through Xenophanes, Parmenides and Melissus held that everything is one and is stationary within itself (*Crat.* 402a4–c3, *Theaetet.* 152d2–e10, 180c7–e4, *Soph.* 242d4–6). While this further step cannot be proved, it begins to look not impossible that this schematisation also came from Hippias. Certainly it is clear that Hippias stands at the very beginning of the writing of the history of philosophy.[8]

(5) *Antiphon*

There was no great amount of interest shown in Antiphon as a thinker until 1915. Then the position was changed dramatically by the publication of two sizeable papyrus fragments from his work *On Truth*, followed by a further fragment in 1922. These made it clear that he was an acute and original thinker. But the immediate effect was to compound a previously known difficult question by adding to it a second.

The first question was whether Antiphon the Sophist was to be identified or not with the Antiphon of Rhamnus who is known to us from Thucydides as a member of the oligarchy known as the Four Hundred who held power in Athens for some four months in 411 B.C. and on whose overthrow Antiphon was executed together with Archeptolemus. This Antiphon was an orator and was the author of the extant collection of oratorical exercises known as the *Tetralogies* to which are joined three forensic speeches. No one seems to have separated the two Antiphons until the grammarian Didymus of Alexandria, nicknamed Chalcenterus, in the first century B.C. argued that they must have been two because of the difference in literary form or

---

[8] for the above see Bruno Snell, 'Die Nachrichten über die Lehren des Thales', *Philologus* 96 (1944) 119–28, reprinted in his *Gesammelte Schriften*, Göttingen 1966 and in C. J. Classen, *Sophistik* (Wege der Forschung) Darmstadt 1976. See also Classen 'Bemerkungen zu zwei griechischen Philosophie-Historikern', in *Philologus* 109 (1965) 175–81.

genre between *On Truth, On Concord* and the *Politicus* on the one hand, and the remaining writings. As a result modern scholars have been divided into two groups, those who believe in one Antiphon and those who believe in two. The weakness of the so-called stylistic argument has, I think, been adequately exposed by J. S. Morrison,[9] and I will content myself with quoting his conclusion: 'the distinction, of which there is no trace before Didymus, is quite arbitrary and appears to have been already rejected (*sc.* by Hermogenes) while the works on which it was based still survived. The reasons for maintaining it now are quite insubstantial.'

But that is not the end of the matter. In the fragments known before the papyrus discoveries, especially those quoted from *On Concord* e.g. fr. 61: 'There is nothing worse for men than lack of rule. With this in mind men of old accustomed children to being ruled and to do what they are told so that when they became men they should not become confused in a great change', we seemed to have an Antiphon who spoke as a right-wing conservative. Yet in the papyrus fragments we appear to see a thinker who rejects laws in favour of nature and who is preaching a thorough-going left-wing egalitarianism. This led to the view that the Antiphon with these views could not possibly be the same as the extreme oligarch who was particularly strong in his opposition to democracy.

The question so posed is of considerable interest and importance. But it arises not simply as a difference between the two supposed Antiphons, but within the one Antiphon who has been traditionally accepted as Antiphon the Sophist. And it will be suggested later on that the matter may not involve quite such a sharp contradiction as has been supposed, and that in any case it arises primarily from the attempt to set up two rather artificial stereotyped categories each mutually exclusive, those of the left-wing thinker and of the right-wing thinker. In any case it will be convenient to treat the issue as one *internal* to the interpretation of Antiphon the Sophist, since even if there were two Antiphons it will be the first that is of primary importance for the history of political thought.

Finally it should be said that one or two, they both lived at the same time – born perhaps about 470 and dying in 411, in the one case certainly, in the other not long afterwards, since the sophist was regarded as contemporary with Socrates and Protagoras. In addition to *On*

[9] see his summary in R. K. Sprague, *The Older Sophists*, Columbia S.C. 1972, 109–11.

Truth in two books and *On Concord* there were ascribed to him a *Politicus*, and a work *On the Interpretation of Dreams*. A number of fragments show that he was interested in the problem of squaring the circle by the method of exhaustion (DK 87B13) and also in physical and astronomical problems (B9, 26, 27, 28, 32). Antiphon of Rhamnus was credited with manuals of rhetoric, perhaps in three books, with an *Invective against Alcibiades*, with composing tragedies, and an intriguing *Art of avoiding distress (Technē Alupias)*. Paralleling the treatment given by physicians to those who are ill, he was said to have set up a kind of citizens' advice bureau or modern-style Samaritan service in a room near the market place at Corinth, claiming to be able to treat those who were in distress by asking questions and finding out the causes and so by his words encouraging those in trouble. We do not know what words were used. But in the Hippocratic Corpus anxiety is recognised as a pathological state (*De Morbis* 2.72). Euripides in a fragment (964N²) makes a character say that he has learnt from a wise man to contemplate disasters such as unseasonable deaths in advance so that they will not come unexpectedly when they do come. The same is cited as a Pythagorean precept much later on by Iamblichus (DK 58D6) and it may well have formed part of the psychological therapy offered by Antiphon. That he was interested in psychological problems is suggested by his work on the interpretation of dreams. Against the view that dreams have direct perceptual origin as held by the atomists, or a direct and natural predictive value, he followed the path later labelled that of *divinatio artificiosa* (DK 87B79). On this view dreams were signs which required interpretation not literal application, and indeed often could mean the opposite of what they appeared to say.[10] This rationalisation of dreams was no doubt part of the movement against superstition which we have seen was associated with the circle of Pericles.

(6) *Thrasymachus*

Thrasymachus of Chalcedon in Bithynia is made famous for us by one thing only, his encounter with Socrates, in the first book of Plato's *Republic*. He was well known as an orator and teacher of rhetoric in Athens in 427 B.C. and made a speech *On behalf of the people of Larisa* which must be later than 413 B.C., but otherwise nothing is

[10] for the whole subject see E. R. Dodds. *The Greeks and the Irrational*, Berkeley 1951, 117–21 with references.

known of the course of his life. He is credited with a number of rhetorical treatises and exercises, and we know from the *Republic* that he travelled extensively and received fees.

(7) *Callicles*

Whereas we do know something of Thrasymachus from sources other than Plato, nothing is known about Callicles apart from the vivid portrait of him in Plato's *Gorgias*. As a result his existence as a real person was doubted by Grote and some other scholars, although the majority have been prepared to accept him as a historical figure. According to Plato he came from the deme of Acharnae in Attica and it is at his house that his friend Gorgias was staying at the opening of Plato's dialogue (447b2–8). Socrates describes him (520a1–b2) as preferring rhetoric to teaching virtue to the young, and elsewhere in a famous passage (484c4–486d1) as scornful of philosophy when adopted as an adult pursuit. But he supports his preference for the successful life of action by arguments which are in a general way comparable with those of Thrasymachus, and which as a result make him beyond argument a very important figure in the history of the sophistic movement.

(8) *Critias*

Critias was a cousin of Plato's mother, and a bitter opponent of democracy at Athens. After the end of the Peloponnesian War in 404 B.C. he was elected one of the commission of Thirty, familiarly known as the Thirty tyrants. He was personally responsible for the death of Theramenes, and he was himself killed in the civil war in 403 B.C. He was not paid for teaching nor did he teach, but stood rather on the fringe of those classed as philosophers according to an anonymous scholiast (DK 88A3). But he wrote, and he was portrayed as present at the gathering of sophists in the house of Callias which sets the scene for Plato's dialogue the *Protagoras*. He was in a sense a pupil of Socrates and other sophists rather than himself a sophist. But he was included by Philostratus in his *Lives of the Sophists* and perhaps for this reason was included by Diels in his *Fragmente der Vorsokratiker* when others with better claims were excluded, and since then he has always been discussed as part of the sophistic movement, and it is perhaps too late for this easily to be altered.

His writings were considerable, both in prose and in verse. The latter included political elegies, and hexameters on literary and political themes. But his interest for the history of the sophistic movement is really confined to the contents of three tragedies and a satyr play, *Tennes, Rhadamanthys, Pirithous* and *Sisyphus,* and primarily the last of these. All were generally attributed to Euripides in antiquity, but an anonymous *Life of Euripides* says that the first three are spurious (DK 88B10) and Athenaeus speaks of the *Pirithous* 'whether it be by Critias or Euripides'. The fragment from the *Sisyphus* (DK 88B25) is attributed to Critias by Sextus Empiricus and to Euripides by Aetius. Wilamowitz-Moellendorff gave the weight of his great authority to the view that none was by Euripides, but it is beginning to appear that he was probably wrong.[11] The *Sisyphus* fragment gives a naturalistic account of the origins of religion which is of considerable interest and certainly sophistic in inspiration. But if it not by Critias there is not very much left of Critias' claims to be ranked among the sophists.

(9) *Euthydemus and Dionysodorus*

If Critias should perhaps be excluded from standard lists of sophists, there are two other persons who should certainly be included.[12] These are the two brothers Euthydemus and Dionysodorus, natives of Chios, who joined the colony of Thurii, but then went into exile, spending their time as sophists on the mainland of Greece. In Plato's dialogue the *Euthydemus* they are presented as having recently come to Athens as professional teachers of wisdom and virtue. Socrates met them walking with a large number of their students – he had known them on previous occasions before this – and so the scene is set for the dialogue that follows. The dramatic date is not determinable but may have been about 420 B.C. or later since Socrates is already an old man. That both Euthydemus and Dionysodorus were real persons is established by references to them by Xenophon and Aristotle, and we know from the *Cratylus,* 386d3–7 that Euthydemus differed from Protagoras on the application of the Man–measure doctrine. The evidence

[11] for the view that the *Pirithous* was by Euripides see Kuiper, 'De Pirithoo Fabula Euripidea', *Mnemosyne* 35 (1907) 354–85, and D. L. Page, *Greek Literary Papyri* I, London 1942, 120–2; for the ascription of the *Sisyphus* to him Dihle, 'Das Satyrspiel "Sisyphos"', *Hermes* 105 (1977) 28–42.

[12] so, rightly, by R. K. Sprague, *The Older Sophists*, Columbia S.C. 1972, 294–301, where the relevant evidence is given in translation.

of Aristotle would suggest that he had before him a writing of Euthydemus containing sophistic arguments not in Plato's dialogue.

(10) *The Dissoi Logoi*

The *Dissoi Logoi* is an anonymous text found at the end of manuscripts of Sextus Empiricus. Written in a kind of Doric dialect, it opens
with the words 'twofold arguments are spoken in Greece by those who
philosophise, concerning the good and the bad', and the modern title
is simply taken from the opening two words. It was composed after
the end of the Peloponnesian War, but the inference that it must have
been written soon after its ending is based merely on a misunderstanding of what is said in I.8 where the words 'most recent events first'
simply mean that he is starting with the Peloponnesian War and then
going back in time to earlier wars. The nature of the work is curious
and some have thought it may represent either a lecturer's speaking
notes, or possibly notes made by a listener. Its basic structure clearly
consists in setting up opposing arguments about the identity or non-
identity of apparently opposite moral and philosophic terms such as
good and bad, true and false. As this is an application of the method of
Protagoras it has led to the suggestion that it is based on the *Antilogiai*
of that sophist. But, as the method of Protagoras, it will be argued
in this present book, was in effect the method of the whole of the
sophistic movement, this conclusion does not follow. Nor is it safe to
assign it to any one particular source of inspiration.

(11) *The Anonymus Iamblichi*

The *Protrepticus* of Iamblichus is known to contain much material
taken often word for word from earlier writers. It contains considerable portions of the lost *Protrepticus* of Aristotle, and in 1889 Frie-
drich Blass demonstrated that some ten pages of printed Greek text in
Iamblichus were taken virtually straight out of an otherwise
unknown piece of writing of the fifth or fourth century B.C. That it
involves discussion of a sophistic theme is now accepted without
question, since it defends the cause of *nomos* or conventional law and
morality against those who would overthrow *nomos* in favour of
nature. But all proposals to assign it to a particular known author or
even to his school have been unsuccessful through lack of any kind of
hard evidence.

An attempt to identify a further sophistic 'piece' in defence of *nomos* has however been less successful than the hypothesis of Blass. In 1924 Pohlenz claimed that three separated sections in the *Speech against Aristogiton* found in the manuscripts of Demosthenes (*Or.* XXV), namely paragraphs 15–35, 85–91 and 93–96, constituted what he called an anonymous treatise *Peri Nomōn* or *On Laws*. His claim was widely accepted and the text was added to the material available for the study of the sophists. That there was any such *separate* treatise was however successfully challenged by Gigante in 1956[13] and it now appears that the *Peri Nomōn* itself is no more than an invention by Pohlenz. But Gigante never denied that the speech, which is probably itself too late to have been written by Demosthenes, did contain considerable 'Socratic' and 'Platonic' material, and as such it can certainly be used as source material for the *nomos-physis* debate. Indeed it may point the way to a conclusion of considerable value, namely that there were wide ranging debates and arguments on most of the issues raised by the sophists, and that these continued long after the end of the fifth century B.C.

(12) *Socrates as a member of the sophistic movement*

The very idea of including Socrates as part of the sophistic movement is at best a paradox and to many absurd. Plato seeks to present Socrates as the arch-enemy of the sophists and all that they stood for. Down the centuries the gulf between Socrates and the sophists, it would seem, has become even wider and more unbridgeable, as Socrates has become a symbol and a rallying-cry. He has often been regarded as exceeded in moral grandeur only by the founder of Christianity, and as embodying in his own life and personality whatever is highest and most valuable in the intellectual traditions of western civilisation.

Yet Socrates was a human being living in a particular period in time. He can only be understood if he is seen in his own contemporary world. This is how Plato portrays him, living in that world, and participating eagerly in fifth century controversies, with opponents such as Protagoras, Gorgias, Prodicus and Hippias. Moreover we can say with some certainty that Plato was not satisfied that the arguments of these opponents had been adequately met, and that he saw it as his

[13] in his *Nomos Basileus*, Naples 1956, 268–92.

own task to develop a new and fuller vision of reality in order to arrive at the kind of answers that were required.

But does any of this, or for that matter anything else, justify us in thinking of Socrates as a sophist? I want to suggest that in part at least our answer to this question should be yes. First there should be no real doubt that he was so regarded by his contemporaries, including Aristophanes when he made fun at his expense in the *Clouds* in 423 B.C. But there is a problem in citing Aristophanes, since in the *Clouds* Socrates is portrayed as head of a school where the students are resident boarders, and Socrates is teaching for payment. There are other fundamental differences, apart from these two points, between the Aristophanic portrait and the way Socrates is depicted by Plato and Xenophon. Thus in Aristophanes for example Socrates is depicted as engaged in physical speculations, and in the *Apology* of Plato he denies any such interest. It is not plausible simply to say that Aristophanes was right and Plato and Xenophon were wrong, and it is not much more plausible to say that both accounts are right, but are true only of different stages in Socrates' life. We must conclude that at least to some extent Aristophanes is distorting the picture by attributing to Socrates characteristics belonging to the sophists in general but which did not belong to Socrates.[14] To some extent, yes, but to what extent?

The 'autobiographical' section of the *Phaedo* (96a6–99d2) is clear evidence for an early interest in science by Socrates, and when facing death he was said to have spent his last hour discussing the geological structure of the earth (*Phaedo* 108d2–113c8). He was associated with the physical philosopher Archelaus already by Ion of Chios (DK 60A3) in the fifth century, who said that Socrates travelled with him to Samos. The formal accusation of impiety brought successfully against Socrates in 399 B.C. claimed that he was guilty of not accepting the gods whom the city accepted, of introducing other strange divinities, and of corrupting the young. Plato in the *Apology* (19b2–c1, 23d5–7) argues that behind the formal charges lay popular prejudices, according to which Socrates *was* concerned with physical speculations, did not believe in the gods, made the worse argument better and taught these things to others. While these charges are denied by Socrates in his defence, it is there also freely admitted that young men of the richer

---

[14] see *Aristophanes Clouds* ed. K. J. Dover, Oxford 1968, introduction xxxii–lvii reprinted with slight changes in G. Vlastos, *The Philosophy of Socrates* New York 1971, 50–77.

classes came to him of their own accord, without any payment, and then went to apply what they learnt from him in arguments with others.

It is thus clear that Socrates *was* quite widely regarded as part of the sophistic movement. Through his well-known friendship with Aspasia it is likely that he was in fairly close contact with the circle of Pericles, and his intellectual and educational impact on the aspiring young men at Athens was such that *in function* he was correctly so regarded. The fact that he took no payment does not alter his function in any way.

But were there *no* differences between him and the rest of the sophists? The answer requires an attempt to discover what was the method and what was the content of Socrates' teaching, and this is difficult, especially so in the case of content. Some suggestions will be made below as to how this content bore on problems raised by other sophists, taking as a starting point the statement of Aristotle (*Met.* 1078b27–31) that there are two things that we are justified in ascribing to Socrates, *epactic logoi*, which probably refers to the process of generalising from examples which have the power to lead one on beyond themselves, and general definitions. This fits in very well with the picture found regularly in Plato's dialogues in which Socrates is shown as endeavouring to discover What is x, i.e. what is the correct logos of x, where x is something appearing in the world around us, above all a virtue or a moral or aesthetic quality. Unlike the Platonists, Aristotle tells us, Socrates did not separate either universals or definitions from the things to which they applied. But it fits in also very well with the picture of others among the sophists who also were concerned with the search for the stronger logos or the correct logos in relation to the conflicting claims of apparently opposed logoi. It is from this point of view that I propose that Socrates should be treated as having a part to play *within* the sophistic movement.

(13) *The Hippocratic Corpus*

A full account of the sophistic movement in the fifth century B.C. would require a consideration of the sophistic elements in the collection of medical writings attributed to Hippocrates. This is a large area of study in which much still remains to be done, and only a very little will be said here.[15] Many of the treatises in the Corpus show little or no

[15] For a recent view see the remarks by G. E. R. Lloyd, *Magic, Reason and Experience*, Cambridge 1979, pp. 86–98.

signs of specific sophistic influences. But this is certainly not the case with two treatises *On the Art* and *On Breaths* which seem not to have been written by professional physicians but to be more in the nature of *epideixeis* or exhibitions of sophistical argumentation. Thus *On the Art*, in the process of defending the art of medicine against those who attack it, begins with a reference to those who have made an art of vilifying the arts in order to make a display (*epideixis*) of their own learning, which reminds readers of the *Protagoras* of the attack by Protagoras on the practice of Hippias, and proceeds to defend the art of medicine as possessing an independent existence, by appealing to sophistic doctrines about the relation between names and classes of things. Earlier attempts to assign the authorship to either Protagoras or Hippias are not persuasive, but its place within the sophistic movement is difficult to deny.

The work *On Breaths* argues that air, which is so powerful in nature generally, is also, in the shape of breaths, the most active agent during all diseases, while all other things are secondary and subordinate causes. In a different position is the treatise *On Ancient Medicine* which holds that the arts are human inventions developed over a long period of time, and proceeds (in Chapter 20) to attack certain physicians and sophists, who claim that in order to understand medicine it is necessary to know what a man is. In reply it is argued that such questions as the nature of man belong to speculations about physical philosophy and are no part of medicine and no help to it. What is needed is the detailed study of individual diseases and individual case-histories.

6

Dialectic, antilogic and eristic

Aristotle in his lost dialogue the *Sophistes* declared that the founder of dialectic was Zeno the Eleatic (fr. 65 Rose = DK 29A10). Inevitably this statement has provoked much discussion in view of the prominence of the concept of dialectic first in Plato, then in Aristotle, and also because of the important and indeed emotive role of the term in the subsequent history of philosophy down to the present day. Elsewhere Aristotle himself seems to attribute the origins of dialectic, in part to Socrates, in other cases to Plato, and in other cases again to himself. These attributions are not inconsistent in view of the rather wide range of meanings attaching to the word already in antiquity.[1]

Some older suggestions entertained by modern scholars attempted to reduce the original meaning of the term dialectic to that of dialogue and the writing of dialogues, and these suggestions may be disposed of first. 1. According to Diogenes Laertius (III.48 = DK 29A14) some said that Zeno was the first to write dialogues. But this conflicts with all other evidence including quotations that survive from Zeno's written work, and if it had been true we would surely have heard a great deal more on the subject than this one reference. 2. A modern guess has been that the reference may originally have been not to dialogues written by Zeno, but to dialogues written by others in which he appeared as a speaker. We actually have a passage of dialogue of this kind given by Simplicius (DK 29A29) expounding the paradox of the millet-seed in conversation with Protagoras. But it is not very likely that this is the source of the story that Zeno was the first to *write* dialogues. 3. One of the later meanings of the verb *dialegesthai* from which *dialectic* was derived was 'to discuss by the method of question and answer', and a passage in Aristotle, *Sophistici Elenchi*, 10, 170b19 = DK 29A14 seems to say that this method was used by

---

[1] See discussion by P. Wilpert, 'Aristoteles und die Dialektik', *Kant-Studien* 48 (1956–57), 247–57 and J. D. G. Evans, *Aristotle's Concept of Dialectic*, Cambridge 1977, 17–30.

Zeno. Many recent editors however would remove the name Zeno from the text at this point, and even if it is kept it is still possible to suppose that Aristotle is fabricating a hypothetical example using the case of Zeno rather than referring to his supposed actual practice whether in real life or in his writings. 4. A rather weaker form of this same interpretation was suggested by Wilamowitz when he maintained (*Platon* II² 28) that the evidence of Plato's dialogue the *Parmenides* suggested that at least in parts Zeno's writing had been in the form of catechism by question and answer. It has indeed been pointed out that this is of course entirely possible within a continuous discourse and need not imply anything like dialogue form.

All these interpretations are suggestive and may be regarded in a general way as pointing the right direction. But none of them is entirely convincing. Whenever Aristotle uses the word dialectic, whether with reference to Zeno, to Socrates, to Plato or to himself, he seems always to be referring to methods of argument. What Aristotle does, almost regularly and as a matter of habit, is to take a current philosophical term or expression already in use, and then to refine it in such a way as to demonstrate that his own analyses and ideas were somehow already imperfectly present in earlier ideas already in currency. In order to explain the attribution of the origin of dialectic to Zeno we need to find some aspect or aspects of philosophic *method* which Aristotle supposed he could detect as already present in Zeno before its later development in Socrates, Plato and his own thinking. We reach firm ground immediately we turn to a further piece of evidence, that of Plato in the *Phaedrus* 261d6–8 = DK 29A13: 'Are we not aware of how the Eleatic Palamedes speaks with art, with the result that the same things appear to his hearers both like and unlike, both one and many, both resting and moving.' That the Eleatic Palamedes was Plato's way of referring to Zeno was recognised in antiquity and may be taken as securely established. There is every reason also to suppose that when he wrote these words Plato was well aware of the contents of Zeno's book. On this basis Gregory Vlastos has recently argued most persuasively that Zeno supposed that the contradictions 'like – unlike', 'one – many', and 'resting – in motion' all followed from a single initial hypothesis, 'if things are many'.² But this is not essential for my purposes. What is important is that, however he arrived at such pairs of contraries, Zeno *is* being credited with using

---

² See the section in his article 'Plato's testimony concerning Zeno of Elea', *Journ. Hellenic Studies* 95 (1975) 150–5.

an art which sets up contradictory predicates for the same subjects – so the same things are alike *and* are unlike.

If we look at the whole passage in the *Phaedrus* from 261c4–e5 it becomes clear that Plato is there equating the art of the Eleatic Palamedes with an art which he calls *antilogikē* (hereafter glossed as 'antilogic') which consists in causing the same thing to be seen by the same people now as possessing one predicate and now as possessing the opposite or contradictory predicate, so e.g. just and unjust, an art 'which is not confined to law courts and to public speeches, but which applies as a single art (if it is an art) to whatever things men speak about'.

The art of antilogic as we shall see is attributed by Plato to the sophists above all others. The consequences drawn by scholars from the attribution of antilogic to Zeno are of considerable interest. Cornford[3] contrasted modern writers, who regard Zeno's arguments as subtle and profound and valid against the position he was attacking, with Plato who seems to have regarded him as a mere sophist, practising a rhetorical art of deception. In an influential article on Zeno published in 1942[4] Herman Fränkel argued that this (Platonic) picture of Zeno as 'playfully, lustily and defiantly' deceiving and mystifying his readers was not in fact wholly without substance. The combination of the comments by Cornford and Fränkel provoked Gregory Vlastos, who argued strongly that this view of Zeno was not correct, because 1. Zeno was never elsewhere classed as a sophist either by Plato or anyone else, 2. Plato did not portray him as such in the *Parmenides*, 126a–128e, where he is depicted as a committed supporter of Parmenides, and by implication as observing the same respect for truth as that which inspires his master's poem, and 3. while Plato has a low opinion of antilogic as a style of philosophical debate, he does not suppose that its practice establishes that its practitioner is therefore a sophist. It is not in itself dishonest or directed to deceive.

A good deal of the difficulty here is conceptual and terminological. What I may call the Cornford view involves the following: 1. Sophists were not honest thinkers, 2. Plato credits Zeno with antilogic, 3. Antilogic is a rhetorical art of deception, ignorant of truth and going

[3] *Plato and Parmenides*, London 1939, pp. 67–8.
[4] 'Zeno of Elea's Attacks on Plurality', *American Journ. Philology* 63 (1942) 1–25, 193–206 = *Wege und Formen frühgriechischen Denkens* Munich, 2nd edn 1960, 198–236 = R. E. Allen and D. J. Furley, *Studies in Presocratic Philosophy* Vol. II, London 1975, 102–42.

in chase of mere belief. 4. Therefore Plato treats Zeno as a sophist. Vlastos accepts 1. and 2. but denies 3. and consequently denies the inference which is 4. Now 1. represents the traditional view of the sophist. The historical correctness of this view is something which I am concerned to challenge in this present study of the sophistic movement. But it *is* the traditional view, and *does* represent what Plato wants to say about the sophists. It follows that the difference between Cornford and Vlastos here turns upon 3., namely the true nature of antilogic.

A solution to this question, namely what is the true nature of antilogic, is a matter of some importance and indeed of urgency. It is in many ways the key to the problem of understanding the true nature of the sophistic movement. What is needed is a distinction, which will be as precise as possible, between three terms, dialectic, eristic and antilogic, and these three terms will need to be brought into relation with another concept, that of the Socratic Elenchus. Plato uses both eristic and antilogic fairly frequently – precise figures can now in fact be given on the basis of L. Brandwood, *A Word Index to Plato* (Leeds, 1976), which for the first time gives us complete and reliable information on such matters. There is a long tradition in Platonic studies of treating the two words as simply interchangeable.[5] But this is certainly a mistake. What needs to be said is this: Plato frequently uses the two terms to *refer* to the same procedure, and he likewise on occasion uses the derived adjectives *eristikos* and *antilogikos* to refer to the same people. But, equally, on occasion, he will apply one term only without the other. Sometimes the missing second term is simply omitted, but in other cases the context suggests that it would have been inappropriate to use the second term. But whether he uses the one term or the two terms to refer to the same thing or the same person, they *never* for Plato have the same meaning. The confusion and misunderstanding has arisen because of a failure to make the necessary distinction between meaning and reference.

The more straightforward of the two terms is eristic. This derives from the noun *eris* meaning strife, quarrel or contention, and, as Plato uses the term, eristic means 'seeking victory in argument', and the art which cultivates and provides appropriate means and devices for so doing. Concern for the truth is not a necessary part of the art – victory in argument can be secured without it, sometimes more easily so. It

5 so already in one of the earliest of the modern discussions of the terms, Excursus V in *The Meno of Plato* ed. E. S. Thompson, London 1901.

follows that eristic as such is not strictly speaking a *technique* of argument. It can use any one or more than one of a series of techniques in order to achieve its aim, which is success in debate or at least the appearance of such success (cf. *Theaetet.* 167e3–6). Fallacies of any kind, verbal ambiguities, long and irrelevant monologues may all on occasion succeed in reducing an opponent to silence and so be appropriate tools of eristic. This is the kind of skill which Plato saw as exemplified by the brothers Euthydemus and Dionysodorus in the dialogue, the *Euthydemus*, of whom he said (272a7–b1) that they have become so very skilled in fighting in arguments and in refuting whatever may be said, no matter whether it be true or false. Consequently as used by Plato the term eristic regularly involves disapproval and condemnation.

Antilogic as used by Plato in a technical sense, differs from eristic in two major respects. First its meaning is different, and secondly Plato's attitude towards it differs from his attitude towards eristic. It consists in opposing one logos to another logos, or in discovering or drawing attention to the presence of such an opposition in an argument or in a thing or state of affairs. The essential feature is the opposition of one logos to another either by contrariety or contradiction. It follows that, unlike eristic, when used in argument it constitutes a specific and fairly definite technique, namely that of proceeding from a given logos, say the position adopted by an opponent, to the establishment of a contrary or contradictory logos in such a way that the opponent must either accept both logoi, or at least abandon his first position. One example has already been considered, namely the application of the term to the method of argument used by Zeno of Elea. A second example is found in the *Phaedo*, in a passage to be discussed shortly, and a third in the *Lysis* (216a). The point has been reached in the argument where it has been suggested that it is the opposite which is most friendly to its opposite. Socrates then says that at this point the *antilogikoi* will tell us, truly, that enmity is most opposite to friendship. And so we have the (Platonically unacceptable) result that it is the enemy which is most friendly to the friend, and it is the friend that is most friendly to the enemy.

What then is Plato's attitude towards this method of antilogic? Quite clearly he does not rate it very highly as a method of philosophical debate. His first objection is its inadequacy – what is wanted is the method of dialectic. While it is possible for people without being aware of it to mistake antilogic for dialectic (*Rep.* 454a4–5) it lacks the essential feature of dialectic, namely the power to discuss on the basis of Division of things by Kinds, and instead it proceeds on the basis of (merely) verbal contradictions. A similar point is made in the *Theatetus* 164c2–d8 where Socrates expresses dissatisfaction with his own preceding refutation of Protagoras on the ground that he was unconsciously acting in an antilogical manner by relying upon verbal coincidences (i.e. to establish the contradictory consequences of Protagoras' position and similarly for that of Theaetetus – 164d5–10). Once again, as in the *Republic* passage, Socrates' lapse into antilogic is unintentional and initially unconscious, and this makes it clear that his action is not dishonest – he is not trying 'to palm off a fallacious argument on his interlocutor',[6] and is not acting eristically. He has simply stopped short of what is required and has failed because his method, though well-meant, is inadequate to the task in hand.

Plato's second point against antilogic is not so much an objection as a constant fear over the danger of its misuse, especially in the hands of those who are young. This fear on his part is indeed not confined to antilogic, it actually extends to dialectic itself which if studied by those who are too young (before the age of thirty) is liable to destroy respect for traditional authority, by asking questions such as What is right (*to kalon*) when the questioner is unable to cope with such enquiries in the proper way and discover the truth *Rep.* 537e1–539a4). 'Young men, when they first taste arguments, misuse them as in a game, appropriating them in every case in order to establish an antilogy, and imitating those who engage in cross-examination, by themselves cross-examining other people, enjoying themselves like puppy-dogs by pulling and tearing to pieces with their argument all those who come near them' (539b2–7). The result of repeated mutual cross-examinations or elenchi conducted in this way, Plato says, is to 'discredit both those concerned and the whole business of philosophy in the eyes of the world. But someone who is older would not be willing to participate in this kind of madness, but will imitate the man who wants to proceed dialectically (*dialegesthai*) and who wants to see the truth rather than the man who is playing about and proceeding antilogically for the sake of amusement. He will be more measured in his approach, and will make the undertaking more deserving of respect than less deserving of it' (539b9–d1). In other words, without dialectic the practice of antilogic is dangerous in the extreme as it can so easily be used for purposes that are merely frivolous. But an attentive

---

[6] correctly seen by Vlastos, *op. cit.* p. 154.

reading of their passage shows, I think, that Plato is not condemning antilogic as such. The process of elenchus is for Plato regularly a necessary part of the process of dialectic (cf. *Phaedo* 85c–d, *Rep.* 534b–c). In the present passage Plato is condemning the abuse of the elenchus when it is used for frivolous purposes, but by implication he is *approving* of it when used for the purpose of dialectic. Now the process of elenchus in the Platonic dialogues takes many forms. But one of the commonest forms is to argue that a given statement leads to a self-contradiction, in other words to two statements which are mutually contradictory.[7] But two statements which are mutually contradictory are the essential feature of antilogic.

Dialectic as understood by Plato is difficult to characterise in detail. Indeed at crucial points he seems almost to shy away from the detailed exposition which the reader is expecting. It has been well said[8] that the word 'dialectic' had a strong tendency in Plato to mean 'the ideal method, *whatever* that may be'. But it regularly involves an approach to the Platonic Forms and it is this more than anything else which distinguishes it from antilogic. Thus in the *Phaedo* it is used to refer to the method of hypothesis, in the *Republic* it is the 'upward' path, and in the *Philebus* it consists of the process of Synthesis and Division.

Once the three terms eristic, antilogic and dialectic are clearly distinguished a good many things fall into place. Plato is wholly opposed to eristic, and is completely committed to dialectic. Antilogic for him comes in between eristic and dialectic. It can be used simply for eristic purposes. On the other hand if it is claimed as a sufficient path to truth it also meets with Plato's condemnation. But in itself it is for Plato simply a technique, neither good nor bad. In the early dialogues especially, behind dialectic and leading up to it, there is the prominent technique of argument known as the elenchus, which constitutes perhaps the most striking aspect of the behaviour of Socrates. It consists typically of eliciting an answer to a question, such as what is Courage, and then securing assent to further statements which are visibly inconsistent with the answer given to the first question. On rare occasions this leads to something approaching an acceptable modification of the first answer. But far more often the Dialogue closes with the participants in a state of *Aporia*, unable to see any way forward or any escape from the contrdictory views in which they are

---

[7] for details see the discussion in R. Robinson, *Plato's Earlier Dialectic*, Oxford 2nd edn. 1953, pp. 7–32.

[8] *ibid.*, p. 70.

enmeshed. This is clearly an application of antilogic.

The essential aspect of this use of antilogic is the setting up of opposed logoi or arguments about the question at issue. But for Plato there is much more to it than this. His basic view of the phenomenal world is that it is always in a state of change and flux, such that it can be described as in a sense rolling about between being something and not being that something. Moreover this is not merely something that happens between two points in time. At any one time 'things which we say are large or small, light or heavy, may equally well be given the opposite epithet' (*Rep.* 479b6–8). This shows two things. First the opposition between logoi can be simultaneous in that the logoi are opposed not one after the other but at the same time. At any one time the same man, for example, is both tall and short, depending on whom he is compared with. Secondly the opposition between logoi which is the starting point for antilogic applies not merely to opposed arguments, but also to the facts of the phenomenal world with which the arguments are concerned.

That Plato himself was aware that his view of the phenomenal world involved antilogic emerges clearly from a famous passage in the *Phaedo* (89d1–90c7), the full significance of which has not always been understood by scholars. This is the passage in which he speaks of the danger of coming to hate logoi or arguments, a condition which he calls Misology. In the case of a human being, if we first trust him and then later find we cannot trust him, and then repeat this experience we are likely to end up in misanthrophy, the hatred and rejection of all human beings. Likewise with arguments – if one first trusts and believes that an argument is true and then subsequently discovers that it is false, one can end up by hating and distrusting all arguments. Then follows the statement to which I want to draw particular attention:

And above all those who spend their time dealing with antinomies [*logoi antilogikoi*] end as you well know by thinking that they have become the wisest of men and that they are the only ones who have come to understand that there is nothing sound or secure at all either in facts or in arguments, but that all things that are, are simply carried up and down like the [tidal flow in the] Euripus and never stay at any point for any duration of time.

Plato is of course going on to suggest both the need, and the methods to be followed, to escape from misology. Nonetheless it is clear that in the above passages he *is* giving expression to his *own* view of the flux of phenomena. Throughout the dialogues it is the instability and changing character of the phenomenal world which makes it for Plato incapable of functioning as the object of knowledge. Knowledge must necessarily be firm and unchanging and it requires objects of the same character as itself. In the *Phaedo* the expression 'up and down' is used again (96b1) to characterise the confusion (100d3) felt by Socrates when attempting to understand and explain the physical world in purely physical terms, *before* he embarked on his 'second voyage' based on the method of hypothesis and the doctrine of the Forms. This provides a method of escape (99e5) from the confusions of the world of the senses. Nonetheless, that from which Socrates is to escape is just this world of the senses, and the reason for his need to escape from it is that it exhibits just those characteristics identified by the people known as *antilogikoi*.

But not only is this so. In an unemphatic phrase Plato actually reveals that he was aware that his own view of phenomena was *anticipated* by those who concerned themselves with *logoi antilogikoi*. This is clearly implied by the statement that such persons 'think they are the *only* ones to have come to understand' – they are being criticised, not for holding this view, but for mistakenly supposing that no one else has come to the same understanding. In other words both Plato and the practitioners of antilogic are agreed on this one point, the antilogic character of phenomena. The only fundamental point on which Plato is going to take issue with them is their failure to understand that the flux of phenomena is not the end of the story – one must look elsewhere for the truth which is the object of the true knowledge, and even for the understanding of the flux and its causes we have to go to more permanent, secure and reliable entities, the famous Platonic Forms. This in turn suggests that the real basis of Plato's enmity towards the sophists was not that they were wholly wrong in his eyes, but that they elevated half the truth to the whole truth by mixing up the source from which things come with its (phenomenal) consequences (*Phaedo* 101e1–3). This made them far more dangerous. Indeed, when elsewhere Plato suggests, as he does repeatedly, that the sophists were not concerned with the truth, we may begin to suppose that this was because they were not concerned with what *he* regarded as the truth, rather than because they were not concerned with the truth as *they* saw it. For Plato, though he does not like to say so, antilogic is the first step on the path that leads to dialectic.

7

The theory of language

Linguistic theory was discussed by the sophists under the headings of 'correct diction', *orthoepeia*, and 'correctness of words or names', *orthotēs onomatōn*. A treatise on *Orthoepeia* is listed among the works of Democritus, and as a subject it was said to have been discussed by Protagoras (DK 80A26). *Onomatōn orthotēs* was also said to have been discussed by Protagoras, and by Prodicus. Hippias was concerned with correctness of letters, which may refer to correctness in the written forms of words (DK 86A12). Plato in the *Cratylus* (391b) introduces his own discussion of the problem of 'correctness of names' with the statement that the best way to commence such an investigation is by seeking the help of those who know, and these are the sophists, patronised by Callias, who spent a great deal of money on them, and so himself acquired a reputation for wisdom.

It is clear, then, that the topic 'correctness of names' was something of a standard theme in sophistic discussions, and it is, as we shall see, the subject of a whole dialogue by Plato, the *Cratylus*. What, we may ask, did the topic involve? It involved first of all much detailed discussion of individual words, and Xenophon tells how on a certain occasion at a banquet conversation turned to names and the specific function of each separate name (*Mem.* III.14.2). Such discussions however also involved the establishment of grammatical categories of various kinds. Thus Protagoras was said to have been the first to divide up discourse (logos), according to one account into wish, question, answer and command, according to another into narration, question, answer, command, reported narrative, wish and summons, while the sophist Alcidamas proposed a different, four-fold, classification, into assertion, negation, question and address (DK 80A1, paragraphs 53–54). In addition Protagoras distinguished the three genders of names, as masculine, feminine and those referring to inanimate objects (DK 80A27).

In drawing these distinctions Protagoras was not merely trying to analyse and describe established Greek usage, his aim was to *correct* such usage, and in order to do so he was prepared to recommend drastic measures. Thus grammatical genders should be revised as part of a process of language correction. The Greek words for 'wrath', *Mēnis*, and 'helmet', *Pēlēx*, which are in fact feminine, should be corrected to the masculine gender. Some have supposed that this is because 'wrath' and 'helmet' are naturally 'unfeminine' in character, being especially associated with the male sex, while others have supposed that Protagoras was simply trying to rationalise usage on the basis of morphology – in this case the word-endings. Both criteria, that of morphological consistency, and that of consistency with natural gender, are found in the satirical passage in Aristophanes' *Clouds* which has a clear reference to the doctrine of 'correctness of names' (DK 80C3), and it seems likely that both considerations were used by Protagoras himself. In support of the view that it was primarily formal considerations that influenced Protagoras may be cited the statement by Diogenes Laertius (IX.52 = DK 80A1) that, when arguing, Protagoras left aside the *Dianoia* (? in the sense of the meaning of a word) in order to concentrate on the name alone. But unfortunately the interpretation of this statement is quite uncertain. A second piece of evidence would be of a more definite character, if only we could accept it as sound. Unfortunately I believe that it cannot be so accepted, but I yield to the temptation to include it because of its interest. I refer here to the fascinating theory of Italo Lana.[1]

According to this theory we might actually have an example of Protagoras' application of his theory when we find the unique form *dunamia* in place of the normal *dunamis* ('power') in two of the manuscripts giving the text of the Proem of the Laws of Charondas. By an audacious conjecture, Lana suggests first that these laws were revised by Protagoras when he was called on by Pericles to provide a constitution for the new colony of Thurii, around 443 B.C., and secondly that Protagoras took the opportunity to alter *dunamis* which on his view ought to be treated as masculine, to the form, which occurs nowhere else in Greek, namely *dunamia*, with the appropriate feminine termination in *-a*. The progression from hypothesis to hypothesis unfortunately makes this speculation rather hard to accept. But if the speculation is modern only, it may nevertheless be accepted as *ben trovato*!

The position is somewhat clearer when we turn to Prodicus. He was

---

[1] I. Lana, *Protagora*, Turin 1950, 56 ff.

famous throughout antiquity for his treatment of synonyms, which must surely have figured in his lecture *On the correctness of names*. But his discussion of synonyms was regarded as a distinctive feature of all his teaching and lecturing. The most conspicuous aspect of his treatment of words was the way in which he distinguished the meanings of sets of words – most commonly two, but on occasion three or more – all of which were similar in meaning. This may best be illustrated from the example of his art supplied by Plato in the *Protagoras* (337a–c = DK 84A13):

Those who attend discussions of this sort ought to listen to both speakers impartially, but not equally. For there is a difference: we should listen to both with impartiality, yet not give equal heed to each, but more to the wiser and less to the less instructed. I for my part, Protagoras and Socrates, call upon you to agree to my request, and to dispute, but not to wrangle, with each other over your arguments: for friends dispute with friends in a spirit of good will, whereas wrangling is between those who are at variance and in a state of enmity with one another. In this way our meeting will have the greatest success, since you the speakers will thus win the greatest esteem, but not praise, from us who hear you. For esteem is present in the hearers' souls, being something genuine and free from deception, but praise is frequently found in the language of those who speak contrary to their real opinion. And we who listened would thus gain the most enjoyment, but not pleasure. For a man derives enjoyment when he learns something and gets a share of understanding purely in his mind, while he is pleased who eats something or has some other pleasant bodily experience.

This passage makes plain the possible rhetorical application of Prodicus' technique. But it is clear that he did not wish his distinctions between words to be merely arbitrary – his aim was to relate each name or *onoma* to some one thing and to no other, just as a person's name is the name of that one person and no other person (cf. DK 84A19), in the belief that it is valuable and important to use only the *right* name in each case. But the examples given in the passage from the *Protagoras* make it plain that *onoma* or name was used for words in general, not simply what we now call names. A large number of his examples are made up of verbs and adjectives. In fact all parts of a sentence, and even a sentence as a whole is treated as a name or *onoma* in Plato's *Cratylus*. But a name, in order to be a name, must be a name of something. The something which is named is regarded as the meaning of the name in question. From this it follows that a name which is not the name of anything at all is not a name in any real sense of the term, and is necessarily without any meaning. So in Plato's *Euthydemus* (283e9–286b6) we find it said that what a sentence or logos asserts is what the sentence is about. To each segment of reality there belongs just one logos and to each logos there answers just one distinct segment of reality.

The results of this way of looking at words are, however, paradoxical, and the paradoxes so generated provide the material for a considerable part of the history of Greek philosophy both in the archaic and in the classical periods.[2] First it deprives all overtly negative statements of meaning, since what is not cannot be named, and this leads to the doctrine that it is not possible to contradict – *ouk estin antilegein* – discussed below, p. 88ff. Secondly there is a more or less acute difficulty that has to be faced in the case of all expressions that involve any degree of denial whatsoever. We feel constrained to say that many statements embodying various kinds of denial are in fact true. But if they are so, what do they mean on the above outlined view of meaning? Heraclitus was prepared to reject much of what people without knowledge ordinarily declare to be the case. But he maintained that his own logos or account was also a correct account of the structure of reality. But this correct account is for him an account of states of affairs that are contradictory – the apparent world that language is about is found to be full of objective contradictions.

To Parmenides however such a view was not acceptable. For a world that is full of objective contradictions is full of negations and so of non-worlds. Such a view can neither be thought nor said. It follows that a world so described cannot be real at all. It was on this basis that Parmenides was induced to sunder the world of appearance from the world of being by treating the first of the two as no more than a piece of fiction. 'For nothing else besides that which is, either is or will be, since Fate fettered it to be whole and exempt from change. Wherefore all that mortals posited in the belief that it was true will be name only, coming into being and perishing, to be and not to be, change of place and interchange of shining colour' (DK 28B8.36–41).

The contrast between the position of Heraclitus and that of Parmenides was clearly established by the middle of the fifth century B.C. and provided the starting point for sophistic discussions of linguistic theory. Parmenides himself however had no followers among the

[2] for what follows see in particular A. Graeser, 'On Language, Thought and Reality in Ancient Greek Philosophy', *Dialectica* 31 (1977) 360–88. I draw considerably on his terminology, though my presentation of Heraclitus differs from his.

sophists when he wished to deny the reality of the phenomenal world. Rather for them the starting point was the phenomenal world itself, regularly seen as constituting the whole of reality and consequently as the only possible object of cognition. Sometimes it was regarded as subject to continuous change. This was notoriously the case with the Heraclitean Cratylus (cf. DK 65.3). According to Sextus Empiricus (DK 80A14) Protagoras had actually described the physical world as in a state of flux, with emissions continually replaced by accretions which made good what was lost. Plato paired Protagoras with Euthydemus and treated them both as holding theories which exclude the possibility that things have some fixed being of their own, but instead mean that they are drawn 'up and down' by their appearing to us (*Crat.* 386c–e, not in DK). In the *Theaetetus* he credits Protagoras with a 'secret' doctrine of perception with similar implications. While the attribute 'secret' probably means that this doctrine was never expressed in writing by the historical Protagoras, the doctrine may nevertheless well represent what Plato regarded as the natural implication of Protagoras' known views. Gorgias went at least some distance in the same direction in that he explained perception of physical objects in the same fashion as Empedocles, namely by positing continuous effluences from objects which enter or fail to enter the various pores in the body (DK 82B4). Plato, as we have already seen, in the *Phaedo* credited the *antilogikoi* and the sophists generally with the view that all the things that are move up and down as though they were in the Euripus and never remain at rest anywhere for any period of time (90c4–6).

More important however were the consequences of sophistic relativism (discussed below in Chapter 9) which was more often than not associated with a form of phenomenalism according to which all appearances are equally true (or at least equally valid as cognitions). With this as their view of the real world, while at the same time remaining fully committed to the view that words must either name exactly the things to which they refer or else be without meaning, the sophists adopted two expedients. Language as a whole must provide formulae for exhibiting reality, and the structure of language must exhibit the structure of things. But the world of experience is characterised by the fact that all or most things in it both *are* and *are not*. Therefore language also must exhibit the same structure. This it must do by giving expression to two opposed logoi concerning everything. But this by itself is not sufficient. We are left with the problem of negation which is in grave danger of becoming something quite meaningless unless some object can be found to which it can be seen to refer.

This problem was tackled in two different ways, seen either as mutually exclusive alternatives, or used so as to supplement each other. The first was to correct language by renouncing negative statements. So the famous linked contentions that it is not possible to contradict, and that it is not possible to say what is false. This would restrict language to true positive statements about the phenomenal world. But to maintain that all positive statements are of equal worth was not going to be very satisfactory, if only because it deprived the sophist of his own claim to superior wisdom. So a second device was considered, according to which amongst opposed logoi one logos in the structure of things was superior, more straight than another and this constituted the *orthos logos*. This situation was to be repeated in speech and argument where once again one logos either was or was to be made to be seen to be straighter and stronger than another.

The art of making one logos superior to another was especially associated with Protagoras, whereas the search for *onomatōn orthotēs* or correctness in names was above all associated with Prodicus. It constituted a second way in which language was to be corrected to bring it into accord with the structure of perceived reality. The significance of this attempt in the history of philosophy is considerable – it represents the first step in the search for what in modern times tends to be spoken of as a single language, called philosophical language, the primary or atomic language, the 'corrected' language of the logician, the ideal which inspired among others the early Wittgenstein in his attempts to restrict and delimit significant language-use to that which depicts the world, and which in its own structure will reflect the structure of reality. But modern attempts are primarily concerned to reform the structure of language in relation to the supposed (logical) structure of reality. Thought in the fifth century B.C. was concerned, not in the first instance with logical structure, but with the search for a one–one relationship between things and names, on the basis that the meaning of any name must always be the thing or things to which it refers.

Yet even so the correction involved could be extremely radical and Plato's *Cratylus* opens with the remarkable statement attributed to Cratylus according to which (383a–b): 'Everything has a right name of its own which comes by nature, and a name is not whatever people call a thing by agreement, simply a piece of their own voice applied to the thing, but there is a kind of constituted correctness in names which is the same for all men, both Greeks and barbarians.' This introduces us to the ideal of a single, natural and above all *universal* language, which ideally might replace all existing languages.

The method by which Prodicus proceeded was not confined to him – according to Plato (DK 84A17) he derived it from Damon, and it was shared in as well by other sophists. The method consisted in the *Diaeresis* or Division of names, and is so regularly labelled by Plato, and by Aristotle after him.[3] We can say that his normal method consisted, as Classen has argued, in setting two names against each other in order to abstract from them the basic sense which they share and to ascertain those subtleties of meaning in which they differ. But words are not defined individually – he is asking not 'what is *x*?', but 'in what respect is *x* different from y?' This serves to distinguish his approach from that of Socrates, whose precursor in all essentials he nevertheless remains, who normally asks simply 'what is *x*?' But we are not justified in attempting to trace a further difference, by suggesting that Prodicus is interested in the proper meaning of words, whereas Socrates is interested in the real thing.[4] As we have seen, for both of them the meaning of a word consists in that to which it refers, and the correct view has been expressed by Classen, when he says that in describing any object or given state of affairs Prodicus will note: this word is appropriate, while that, though almost equivalent and identical in meaning, is not. Socrates pursues the same path, except that, when he asks what is *x*, the *onoma* or name for which he is searching is not usually going to be found to be a single word, but rather a formula consisting of a series of words, a logos or a definition.

The sub-title of Plato's dialogue, the *Cratylus*, is *On the Correctness of Names*. For long it was regarded as a work of rather specialised interest only, an attitude typified by what is said by H. N. Fowler in the introduction written for his translation of the dialogue in the Loeb series in the year 1926, where we read: 'The *Cratylus* cannot be said to be of great importance in the development of the Platonic system, as it treats of a special subject [the origin of language] somewhat apart from general philosophic theory.' Since about 1955 something of a revolution has taken place in the scholarly interpretation of the dialogue, however, and there are probably few

---

[3] cf. DK 84A14, 17, 18, 19, to which should be added Plato, *Prot.* 358a6. See on the technique of *Diaeresis* C. J. Classen, *Sophistik*, Darmstadt 1976, 231–8.

[4] as Calogero, 'Gorgias and the Socratic Principle Nemo Sua Sponte Peccat', *Journal of Hellenic Studies* 77 (1957) 12.

who would now seek to deny the fundamental importance of the themes which it discusses. The subject matter of the dialogue is not the origin of language, but the question how it is possible for names to be correct.[5] Plato's starting point is thus as so often a question arising out of sophistic speculations. The dialogue opens with Hermogenes, the brother of Callias the famous patron of the sophists, first briefly stating the position of Cratylus the Heraclitean, according to which there is a natural rightness in names, the same for all, Greeks and barbarians, and then stating his own view, that the only rightness in names depends on what people agree at any one time to assign as the name of a thing.

Socrates favours, at least at this stage, the theory of natural correctness and suggests (391b–e) that the best way to investigate the question would be to ask those who know, namely the sophists. But as Hermogenes is not in control of his inheritance he cannot afford this, and would do best to ask his brother to teach him the doctrine of correctness in such cases, which he had learnt from Protagoras. Hermogenes refuses on the grounds that it would be absurd for him to make this request since he rejects the *Truth* of Protagoras and so could not regard what is said in that kind of 'Truth' as of any value. Socrates then says that Hermogenes should turn to Homer and the other poets where the doctrine that the gods used different names for things from those used by mortal men is clear evidence of a belief in names that are naturally right. This provides sufficient grounds for us to conclude that in his work *On Truth* Protagoras had in fact discussed the rightness of names, and the natural way to read the passage is to suppose that Protagoras had himself in some sense and in some degree given expression to a belief in the doctrine of natural rightness.

This fits with the evidence cited earlier for his belief that there were right and wrong uses for particular words. In the myth in the *Protagoras* (322a3ff) we are told how mankind proceeded to an articulated distribution of voice and names, and this suggests that some kind of *diaeresis* of names was involved in the process.[6] The fact that the discussion to which Hermogenes was referred by Socrates occurred in the treatise *On Truth* suggests that the doctrine of rightness of names may have been developed by Protagoras in relation to the doctrine of

---

[5] For a very clear demonstration see G. Anagnostopoulos, 'The significance of Plato's Cratylus', *Review of Metaphysics* 27 (1973/74) 318–45.

[6] see P.M. Gentinetta, *Zur Sprachbetrachtung bei den Sophisten und in der stoisch-hellenistishchen Zeit*, Winterthur 1961, 25–6.

making one logos more correct (*orthos*) than the other logos to which it was opposed, but in the absence of details we can only speculate as to how all this was fitted together.

In the remaining part of the dialogue, that is of course in the main part, Socrates proceeds to an extended examination, first of the thesis of Hermogenes that correctness of names depends simply on agreement by the users as to which names are to be accepted as correct, and then of the thesis of Cratylus that there is a natural basis for their rightness. Socrates argues throughout that the correctness of names springs from their function of indicating the nature of the things named (see e.g. 422d1–2), and he supposes that they do their indicating by a process of imitation of the thing in question. But the things that we encounter in our experience are cognitively unreliable in that they always both *are* and *are not*. This makes them unable fully to answer to the names that we use in meaningful discourse – the problem already posed by Parmenides. Plato's solution however was neither that of renouncing language, nor that of abandoning altogether the world of experience, but rather the manufacture of a 'Third World', that of the Platonic *Forms*. These Forms are as it were deliberately devised to satisfy the requirements of being satisfactory objects of linguistic meaning and reference. But while in one way they may be described as deliberately devised, of course in another sense this is false – they are for Plato real entities, the ultimate constituents of reality.

The Platonic Forms were thus intended to serve as the primary designates or referents for names. Perceptible objects in relation to which these same names tend to be used in everyday speech about the world constitute a kind of secondary or derivative realm of reference. The introduction of this distinction between primary and secondary designates has rightly been seen as a first step in the direction of a distinction between meaning and reference. One of the difficulties confronting a referential theory of meaning which posited a one–one relationship between names and phenomenal objects was, as we have seen, that a name for which there was no corresponding object to be found in the phenomenal world could have no meaning because there was nothing to which it could be taken as actually referring. If we can say that the word possesses meaning quite independently of whether or not it is actually used to refer to anything, then we may say either that the problem is solved or that it is at least reduced to more manageable proportions. Just this was indeed what the Stoics partially accomplished with their doctrine of immaterial *lekta* associated as meanings with words and thoughts in a world in which the only actual objects were all material and corporeal.

But it is unlikely that Plato ever went as far as this. Throughout he remained committed, it would seem, to a purely referential theory of meaning. The *Cratylus* concludes with the contention that while names may be given and so may be assigned by a kind of agreement, they will only be rightly given by those who have direct knowledge of unchanging reality, that is to say the world of the Forms, and who frame names in such a way that they are like the things named and are images of them. This is Plato's contribution to the problem which he inherited from the sophists. He resolved the problem of correct language by altering reality to fit the needs of language, instead of the reverse.

8

The doctrine of logos in literature and rhetoric

Some features of life in Athens in the second half of the fifth century B.C. might suggest that what was happening was a fairly fundamental change towards a society in which what people thought and said was beginning to be more important than what was actually the case. In its extreme modern form this leads to the doctrine that there are no facts and no truth, only ideologies and conceptual models and the choice between these is an individual matter, perhaps dependent on personal needs and preferences, or perhaps to be influenced by the thinking of social groups treated as units, but not to be established in any other ways than these. What happened in the fifth century B.C. hardly went as far as this. What did emerge however was a realisation that the relationship between speech and what is the case is far from simple. While it is likely that fifth-century thinkers all were prepared to accept that there is and must always be a relationship between the two, there was a growing understanding that what is very often involved is not simply a presentation in words of what is the case, but rather a representation, involving a considerable degree of reorganisation in the process. It is this awakening of what has been called rhetorical self-consciousness that is a feature both of contemporary literature and of theoretic discussion in the fifth century. It was the widening gulf between rhetoric and reality which led Plato in the *Gorgias* to contrast rhetoric and philosophy, and to condemn the practice of the first, and then later in the *Phaedrus* to argue in favour of a reformed rhetoric based on dialectic and psychology as a possible servant of philosophy.

The power of rhetoric was of course not the discovery of the generation of the sophists – its importance was known already to Homer, and none of the early poets was likely to understate the importance of his own activity in the use of words. But the theory of literature and the rhetorical art was largely the creation of the sophistic period. Our best insight is to be found in the two surviving works of Gorgias that are given the form of rhetorical declamations, but surely have much more

78

serious purposes, the *Encomium of Helen* (DK 82B11) and the *Pala-medes* (DK 82B11a). The aim of the *Helen* is stated to be to free Helen from blame for having done what she did in leaving her home and husband to go to Troy with Paris, to show that those who blame her are speaking falsely, and by indicating the truth to put an end to their ignorance (par. 2). Here the emphasis on truth is emphatic, and shows that there is no denial intended by Gorgias of the existence of that which is the case. Indeed deceit is only possible in relation to that which actually is true. Four possible explanations for Helen's behaviour are then considered, (1) that it was by decree of the gods and of Necessity, (2) that she was carried off by force, (3) that she was persuaded by the power of speech (logos) and (4) that it was all the work of Love. In the first case god is a stronger force than man and it follows that it is god who is to blame, not the weaker human being. In the second case the woman is to be pitied rather than blamed, and it is the barbarian who seized her who is deserving of blame in words, loss of civil rights in law (nomos), and punishment in fact.

Some difficulty however may be felt to arise in the third case, when it is logos that has done the persuading, and the answer is developed by Gorgias at some length. How can it be that persuasion frees from blame the person who has been persuaded to do whatever it is that he has in fact done? Gorgias' reply seems to be two-fold. First of all (pars. 8–10) stress is laid on the enormous power of logos. This is seen in the emotional experiences, both welcome and unwelcome, that are produced both by poetry and by the artistry of prose. But there is a second way also in which logos acts on the human soul (pars. 10–14). The majority of men are unable to recall what has actually happened or to investigate the present or to divine the future. So on most matters they use Opinion (*Doxa*) as an adviser to their souls. Such opinion however is unreliable and liable to make a person stumble and fall with unfortunate consequences to himself. Logos is able to operate persuasively on such opinion because the opinion is not knowledge and so is easy to change. This can be seen in three examples. First is the case of those who discuss the heavenly bodies, the *meterologoi*. These substitute one opinion for another, by removing the one and forming another in its place, and make things which are unseen and lacking in credibility become apparent to the eyes of opinion. The second is the case where logos is in peremptory contest with logos – one would suppose in a debate in the law-courts – here one speech by the skill of its composition, not by the truth of its statements, both delights and persuades an abundant crowd. The third case is that in which philosopher disputes with philosopher. Here the quickness of thought demonstrably makes it easy to change the credibility of the opinion in question.

The result is that the power of logos in relation to the condition of the soul is comparable to that of drugs. For different drugs have different effects on the body in that some cure disease and others bring life to an end. So also with logoi – some cause pain, others delight and others fear, some make their hearers confident and courageous while others drug and bewitch the soul with a kind of evil persuasion. The comparison of persuasion with drugs suggests that Gorgias wishes to distinguish two kinds of persuasion, one good and one bad. It will then be the second kind of persuasion which has been at work in the case of Helen. This fits well with the position attributed to Gorgias in Plato's dialogue named after him (449d–457c) where Rhetoric is in itself for Gorgias simply a technique. As such it can be used to produce either false belief or true belief, though Gorgias, and his defenders in the dialogue all maintain that it ought in fact to be used morally and not for immoral purposes. But there is a particular problem within the *Helen*. At the beginning of the *Encomium*, as we have seen, Gorgias stated that it was his purpose to indicate the truth (par. 2). Yet throughout the discussion of logos (in pars. 8–14) he speaks of the logos that persuades as producing deception (*apatē*), and of persuasion as succeeding because it has first moulded a false logos. This has led to the suggestion that for Gorgias the sole way in which persuasion operates upon opinion is by deception.

This is a matter that has already been extensively discussed,[1] but which has not yet been fully elucidated. What is needed is first to see the doctrine in relation to what is said in the second and third parts of Gorgias' treatise *On Nature* (DK 82B3). There we have, in the second part, the contention that, even if things are, they cannot be known, thought or grasped by human beings, and, in the third part, the argument that even if they could be apprehended, they still could not be communicated to another person. This is so because the means by which we communicate is speech or logos, and this logos is not and can never be the externally subsisting objects that actually are. What we communicate to our neighbours is never these actual things, but only a logos which is always other than the things themselves. It is not

---

[1] especially by Italian scholars, see for a useful discussion and survey M. Migliori, *La filosofia di Gorgia*, Milan 1973, 95–108.

even, says Gorgias, speech that displays the external reality, it is the external object that provides information about the logos.

It follows that Gorgias is introducing a radical gulf between logos and the things to which it refers. Once such a gulf is appreciated we can understand quite easily the sense in which every logos involves a falsification of the thing to which it has reference – it can never, according to Gorgias, succeed in reproducing as it were *in* itself that reality which is irretrievably *outside* itself. To the extent that it claims faithfully to reproduce reality it is no more than deception or *apatē*. Yet this is a claim which all logos appears to make. So all logos is to that extent Deception, and in the case of literature, such as tragedy, the interesting conclusion was drawn that the man who deceives is better than the man who fails to deceive (DK 82B23). This doctrine explains the statement in par. 11 of the *Helen* that if men did possess knowledge, the logos would (visibly) not be similar (to that of which they possess the knowledge). At the beginning of the *Encomium* what Gorgias seems to be saying is that in order to get at the truth it is necessary to indicate the truth or reality itself and not the logos, and this can only be done by applying some kind of process of reasoning to the logos in question (par. 2).

Some further light may result from a consideration of the second of the two rhetorical discourses of Gorgias, the *Defence of Palamedes* (DK 82b11a). Once again we are told (par. 35) that if it were possible for the truth about things to be made pure and clear through the medium of logoi to those who hear, judgment would be easy as it would follow directly from the things that have been said. But this is not the case. What is needed is to attend not to logoi but to real facts. Earlier in the speech Knowledge of what is True is opposed to Opinion (par. 24) and we are told that logos by itself is inconclusive unless we learn also from actual Truth itself (par. 4). Finally (par. 33) Palamedes declares his intention of expounding what is true and of avoiding deceit in the process.

On the basis of these indications it is possible to discern a common conceptual model underlying the argument both in the *Helen* and in the *Palamedes*. On the one side is the real world, labelled truth or that which is true. The cognition of this real world is knowledge. But the commonest cognitive state is opinion, not knowledge, and logos, which is more powerful than opinion, operates upon opinion. Both are deceptive in contrast with truth and knowledge. But it is possible to appeal from the deceptions of logos and opinion to knowledge and truth. The effect of such an appeal, while it provides knowledge, does not remove the incurably deceptive character of logos, since logos can never *be* the reality which it purports to state. Yet there *are* two kinds of logoi – one better, and one worse than the other.

The superiority of one logos to another is not accidental, but depends on the presence of specific features. The study of these is the study of the art of rhetoric, and their successful development is the source of the power of logos over souls which is entitled *Psychagogia*, or the winning of men's souls in Plato's *Phaedrus* (261a). Just a little later on in the *Phaedrus* (267a) we are told that the power of logos makes small things seem large and large things seem small, that it can present things of recent date in an old fashion or recount things of old in a new manner. Both Tisias and Gorgias had argued that things that are probable deserve more respect than do the things that are true, and it is this ability to promote probabilities which is part of the power that is found in logos. Much of what is here said by Plato is stated also by Isocrates in his *Panegyricus* 7–9, and he adds that it is important in oratory to be able to make proper use of the events of the past, and *at the appropriate time* or *Kairos*. Quite a number of references elsewhere stress the importance of the *kairos* or the selection of the appropriate time, in rhetoric, and Dionysius of Halicarnassus not only tells us that Gorgias was the first to write about the *kairos*, but he adds the statements, unfortunately not included in DK, that the *kairos* is not something that is to be attained by knowledge – it belongs rather to opinion.[2] A reference in Diogenes Laertius (IX.52) makes it clear that Protagoras also had written concerning *kairos*. When we put together the doctrines of the Probable or Plausible and the Right moment in Time, in relation to Opinion (or what men think or believe), it is clear that we have already the elements of a theory of rhetoric which can stand comparison with modern accounts of the technique of advertising. Indeed Rhetoric, which is now an old fashioned term, is perhaps best understood as covering in antiquity the whole art of public relations and the presentation of images. It was the theory of this art that the sophists inaugurated.

---

[2] *De Compositione Verborum* 12. For the whole topic of the *kairos* see W. Süss, *Ethos, Studien zur älteren griechischen Rhetorik*, Leipzig 1910, 17 ff.

9

Sophistic relativism

In the discussions in the three preceding chapters the terms logos and logoi have been used repeatedly. In a large number of cases they have been left untranslated, on other occasions they have been variously translated by 'statements', 'arguments' and (in the singular) by 'speech' or 'discourse', and on one occasion at least it seemed appropriate to speak of a logos as occurring 'in the structure of things'. In fact a glance at standard dictionaries immediately reveals that the range of meanings or applications of the one Greek word logos is even wider than might be suggested by the above variety of renderings. What we are confronted with is not strictly speaking one word with a number of different meanings, but rather a word with a range of applications all of which relate to a single starting point. This is a phenomenon which, following G. E. L. Owen, has come to be labelled 'focal meaning', although perhaps 'focal reference' would be a better term, since what is involved is an extra-linguistic reference to something which is supposed to be the case in the world around us.[1] In the case of the word logos there are three main areas of its application or use, all related by an underlying conceptual unity. These are first of all the area of language and linguistic formulation, hence speech, discourse, description, statement, arguments (as expressed in words) and so on; secondly the area of thought and mental processes, hence thinking, reasoning, accounting for, explanation (cf. *orthos logos*), etc.; thirdly, the area of the world, that *about* which we are able to speak and to think, hence structural principles, formulae, natural laws and so on, provided that in each case they are regarded as actually present in and exhibited in the world-process.

While in any one context the word logos may seem to point primarily or even exclusively to only one of these areas, the underlying meaning usually, perhaps always, involves some degree of reference

[1] For this point see Charles H. Kahn, *The Verb 'Be' in Ancient Greek*, Dordrecht 1973, p. 6 n. 11.

to the other two areas as well, and this I believe is as true for the sophists as it is, say, for Heraclitus, for Plato and for Aristotle. Accordingly, in what follows, where for convenience the term 'argument' is frequently used as a translation, it should be remembered that this will be misleading unless it is understood as normally referring in some degree to all three of the areas mentioned above.

Diogenes Laertius opens his very sketchy summary of the doctrines of Protagoras (DK 80A1) with the statement: 'He was the first to say that there are two logoi [arguments] concerning everything, these being opposed each to the other. It was by means of these logoi that he proceeded to propound arguments involving a series of stages,[2] and he was the first to do this.' This doctrine is firmly associated with Protagoras in other sources as well (DK 80A20), and according to Seneca (*Ep.* 89.43) he meant by it that one can take either side on any question and debate it with equal success – even on this very question, whether every subject can be debated from either point of view. Of course there had always been opposing arguments as long as the human race had indulged in argument. But the essential feature was not simply the occurrence of opposing arguments but the fact that both opposing arguments could be expressed by a single speaker, as it were *within* a single complex argument.

This doctrine was indeed well known in the second half of the fifth century B.C., and it was not confined to Protagoras. A fragment of Euripides' play, the *Antiope*, which cannot be earlier than 411 B.C., says 'In every case if one were clever at speaking, one could establish a contest of two-fold arguments' (fr. 189N²), and it is interesting to notice that apparently, according to Aristides, it was one speaker in the play who had himself given expression to both arguments. In Aristophanes' *Clouds* first produced in 423 B.C. there is a famous debate between two personified logoi or arguments – the Just Argument and the Unjust Argument. As we have seen, there actually survives a treatise known as the *Dissio Logoi* or 'Twofold Arguments' (DK 90) probably to be dated early in the fourth century B.C. It begins with the statement 'Twofold arguments concerning the good and the bad are put forward in Greece by those who are pursuing philosophy', and the

---

[2] It has not been generally recognised (as it should have been) that the word *sunerōtēsen*, here translated by 'propound arguments involving a series of stages', is in fact a highly technical term in the Hellenistic period, see Sextus Empiricus, Vol. IV Indices coll. K. Janacek (Teubner Series) Leipzig 1962, p. 220.

three following paragraphs begin in the same way, but discuss respectively the beautiful and the ugly, the just and the unjust, the true and the false. Under each heading antithetic or opposing arguments are set out.

The authorship of the treatise is unknown. It is certainly sophistic in character, and some have wished to attribute it to the school of Protagoras if there was such a thing. But there is a danger of circularity in argument here. The technique of opposed arguments is certainly attributed to Protagoras. But until it has been established that it was confined to him we must not conclude that all other examples spring solely from him. In fact there is evidence that this way of looking at things was very much a feature of the period. In addition to the references given already I would cite the passage in Plutarch's *Life of Pericles* 4.3 according to which:

Pericles was also a student of Zeno the Eleatic, who discoursed on physics, like Parmenides, and who perfected a kind of skill in examining opponents in argument that brought them to a state of *aporia* through opposed arguments [*di' antilogias*]; so Timon of Phlius expressed it, when he spoke of the great power, that failed not in its effect, of Zeno with the two-edged tongue, the man who laid hold upon all things.

Here Timon is correctly identifying the procedure with the method by which Zeno reduced his opponents to silence by showing that their chosen positions were contradictory in that they implied also the negation of themselves. As we have already seen this is the method of antilogic, and it is perhaps the most characteristic feature of the thought of the whole sophistic period.

After his mention of the doctrine of the two opposed Logoi, Diogenes Laertius goes on to quote the famous statement, apparently from the beginning of one of Protagoras' writings: 'Man is the measure of all things, of things that are as to how they are, and of things that are not as to how they are not.' The title of the writing is given by Plato (*Theaetet.* 161c) as *The Truth*, while Sextus Empiricus (DK 80A1) says that it came at the beginning of *The Overthrowing Arguments*, possibly another name for the same work. The interpretation of this famous sentence has been a matter of discussion from the time of Plato right down to the present day. Indeed, it would not be too much to say that the correct understanding of its meaning will take us directly to the heart of the whole of the fifth-century sophistic movement. Certain points that have been the subject of controversy in the past may now be taken as reasonably settled, and I propose simply to list these in order to save space for other matters of controversy. The

ı) man who is the measure is each individual man, such as you and I, and certainly not the human race or mankind taken as a single entity.

ı) Secondly what is measured about things is not their existence and non-existence, but the way they are and the way they are not, or in more modern terms what are the predicates which are to be attached to them as subjects in subject–predicate statements. So Plato in the *Theaetetus* says (152a6–9), immediately after quoting the statement, that this means that 'each group of things is to me such as it appears to me, and is to you such as it appears to you'. The standard later illustration in antiquity was: if honey *seems* sweet to some and bitter to others, then it *is* sweet to those to whom it seems sweet, and bitter to those to whom it seems bitter.

But if this much would now probably be accepted by most scholars, that is about as far as it is safe to go – the rest is a matter of debate and some difficulty. The most controversial question concerns the nature and status of the things for which man is the measure. It will be convenient to summarise Plato's discussion in the *Theaetetus*, where an example is given. Protagoras had said that man is the measure of all things, meaning that each group of things is to me such as it appears to me and is to you such as it appears to you. So in the case of a wind, sometimes when the same wind is blowing it feels cold to one person and to another not. So in such cases Protagoras would say that the wind *is* cold to the one who feels cold, and is not cold to the other. Now it is clear that this theory involves the rejection of the everyday view that the wind in itself is either cold or not cold, and one of the percipients is mistaken in supposing that the wind is as it seems to him and the other percipient is right. But at least three possibilities remain. (1) There is no one wind at all, but two private winds, my wind which is cold and your wind which is not. (2) There is a (public) wind, but it is neither cold nor warm. The coldness of the wind only exists privately for me when I have the feeling of the cold. The wind itself exists independently of my perceiving it but its coldness does not. (3) The wind in itself is both cold and warm – warm and cold are two qualities which can co-exist in the same physical object. I perceive the one, you perceive the other.

All three of these views have found modern supporters, though the major division has been between those who have supported (2) and those who have supported (3).[3] I will call (2) the subjectivist view (though the term subjectivist could also clearly be applied in a still stronger sense to (1)), and (3) the objectivist view. But it must be understood that (2) will embrace the view that perception is causally based on features actually present in the objective world. These causal factors may well, on a commonly held view, be the source of the contents of an individual's perceptions. But what he perceives are the results of these causes, not the causal factors themselves and, as these results are determined by the impact of the causal factors on himself as a subject, and will vary from person to person according to differences in the subject, it will be convenient and not I hope too misleading to continue to include this theory under the heading of subjectivist theories.

After explaining that by the man–measure doctrine Protagoras meant that the wind was cold to the man to whom it seemed cold and not so to the man to whom it did not so seem, Plato continues in the *Theaetetus* (152b9) by saying that in this context seeming is the same as being perceived, and he concludes, Perception then is always of that which is, and is infallible, being the same as knowledge. Now as the expression 'that which is' is almost regularly used in Plato to refer to permanent, objective reality as distinct from the changing patterns of the world of appearances this might seem to favour interpretation (3) rather than interpretation (2). But such an inference is hardly justified in the present case since the man-measure doctrine is not a criterion for existence but rather for determining *how* things are, in the sense of what predicates are to be applied to them. In other words in saying that perception is always of that which is, one should suppose that the meaning is that for Protagoras perception of a white object is always the perception that it is white.

<hr/>

[3] Here some references may be of interest. For (1) I know only A. E. Taylor, *Plato, the man and his work*, London 4th edn 1937, 326. But Gregory Vlastos holds that Plato was not concerned to pronounce on the status of the unperceived wind so that his view bridges (1) and (2), see *Plato's Protagoras* ed. G. Vlastos, New York 1956, p. xiii with n. 26 a. For (2) which has been very widely supported see most recently W. K. C. Guthrie, *History of Greek Philosophy* III, Cambridge 1969, 184. For (3) there may be cited P. Natorp, *Forschungen zur Geschichte des Erkenntnisproblems*, Berlin 1884, V. Brochard (1889) reprinted in his *Etudes de Philosphie*, Paris 1926, H. Gomperz, *Sophistik und Rhetorik*, Leipzig 1912, 200 ff., Cornford, *Plato's Theory of Knowledge*, London 1935, H. Cherniss, *Aristotle's Criticism of the Presocratics*, Baltimore 1935, Von Fritz, *Real-Encyclopädie* s.v. Protagoras 916 f., E. R. Dodds, *The Ancient Concept of Progress*, Oxford 1973, 95–6. I gave my support to this view in 'Plato's Account of the Relativism of Protagoras', *Durham University Journal* 1949, 20ff.

More important for our present purposes is the claim that
✶ perceptions as such are infallible. This means that each individual
perception in each individual person and on each individual occasion
is strictly speaking incorrigible – it can never be corrected by being
compared with a perception by someone else which differs from mine,
nor by another act of perception by myself on another occasion, even
if only a moment later than my first act of perception. If something
seems to me sweet, then it is sweet for me, and this is not to be refuted
by someone else's experience who perceives it not as sweet but as
bitter and so on. This contention is of considerable philosophical
significance and the fact that it was put forward by Protagoras is
surely clear enough evidence that in putting it forward Protagoras was
philosophising. For it constitutes the doctrine that all perceptions are
true.

But the consequences of such a philosophical position are not
inconsiderable. If all perceptions are true it follows that no
perceptions are false. If all perceptions are incorrigible then they are
not to be corrected, nor are they to be refuted by opposing to them
further acts of perception either by the same person or by another.
That these consequences were in fact drawn in the sophistic period can
now, I believe, be established in the following way. The starting point
must be the argument in Plato's *Euthydemus* 283e–286d. There it is
✶ maintained that 'it is not possible to contradict', meaning by this that
it is not possible for one person to contradict another (*ouk estin
antilegein*). This paradoxical doctrine is based on a second
paradoxical contention, namely that it is not possible to say what is
false. This second paradox is supported in the following way.

Anyone who speaks the truth is saying what is the case about that
which is the case. A person who is speaking untruthfully is saying
what is not the case about that which is not the case. But that which is
not the case is simply not there. So a person who says what is not the
case is not talking about anything at all. He is using words but they
refer to nothing because what they might seem to refer to is simply not
there. From this, it is argued, it follows that if two people make
statements, either (1) they say the same thing, in which case there is no
contradiction, or (2) one person is saying what is the case, i.e. what is
true because the thing about which he is speaking is as he says it is, and
the other person is saying something different from what the first
person says. This also is the case and so is true, but because it is true it
will be about something different from that about which the first

person was speaking. So the two persons are speaking each about different things. Their apparently conflicting statements do not constitute a contradiction because they are not talking about the same thing, or (3) one person is saying what is the case i.e. what is true because the thing about which he is speaking is as he says it is. The other person is saying something verbally different, of the kind which is ordinarily spoken of as untrue. But because it is untrue it is not about anything at all, and so certainly not about what was referred to by the statement made by the first person. He is using mere words that refer to nothing and so is not contradicting the true statement made by the first person.

This, or something like it, is the argument deployed in the *Euthydemus*. Both contentions, that it is not possible to contradict and that it is not possible to say what is false have a long subsequent history. Aristotle (*Met.* 1024b32, *Top.* 104b21) attributed both to Antisthenes, though he does not say that they originated with him. Antisthenes was apparently still alive in 366 B.C. and on the basis of this it has been common to deny that either of the doctrines had anything to do with the sophistic movement. The evidence against this view was, however, always considerable, as immediately after the account in the *Euthydemus* outlined above Plato goes on to make Socrates say (286c1) that he has 'heard this argument from many people on many occasions – for Protagoras and those associated with him used to make great use of it, as did others even earlier than him'. If this were not enough, we also have a statement in the *Cratylus* (429c9–d3) that there are many both now and in the past who say that it is completely impossible to say things that are false. No doubt on the basis of evidence such as this Philoponus in the sixth century A.D. had no doubt that the doctrine did belong to Protagoras (*in Cat.* 81.6–8).

Even so the position might have seemed to some still a matter of doubt, in default of fresh evidence. Unexpectedly, just this did arise. In 1941 part of a papyrus commentary on *Ecclesiastes* probably by Didymus the Blind (fourth century A.D.) was discovered. From this a passage of great interest and importance became generally available in 1966 when it was published by two scholars, G. Binder and L. Liesenborghs.[4] What it says is the following:

A paradoxical statement by Prodicus is transmitted to us to the effect that it is

---

[4] *Museum Helveticum* 23 (1966) 37–43, reprinted with important revisions in C. J. Classen, *Sophistik* (Wege der Forschung 187), Darmstadt 1976, 452–62.

not possible to contradict (*ouk estin antilegein*) ... this is contrary to the thought and opinion of all men. For all men contradict both in their everyday transactions and in matters of thought. But he says dogmatically that it is not possible to contradict. For if two people contradict, they both speak. But it is impossible for both of them to be speaking with reference to the same thing. For he says that it is only the one who is saying the truth and who proclaims things as they really are who is speaking of them. The other, who is opposing him does not speak of the thing, does not speak the truth.

Prodicus was spoken of in the doxographic tradition as a pupil of Protagoras (DK 84A1) and the passage vindicates completely the attribution of the doctrine that it is not possible to contradict to the sophistic period in general and in particular to Protagoras and his followers.

We may now return to the man–measure doctrine and the illustration given in the *Theaetetus*. In the case of perceptual disagreements between two or more people it is not possible for any of the statements they make to involve false descriptions of what is being described. For the man to whom the wind seems cold, it is cold, and for the man to whom it seems warm it is warm. Both statements are true and there is no possibility here of falsity. But likewise there is no contradiction – the two statements are not about the same thing, since each man is speaking only about either his own experience or what is referred to by his own experience. He has no access to the other man's experience or what is being referred to in the other man's experience, and cannot make any meaningful statement about it.

If then something like this was involved in Protagoras' doctrine of perception as expressed in his man–measure doctrine, how is it to be related to his statement 'concerning everything there are two logoi each opposed to the other'? Two difficulties arise. First if each man's perceptions are true and these constitute logoi it might seem that concerning every thing there would be not two logoi, but a number very much greater, namely as many as there were different perceptions by different people, either now or in the past or in the future. The answer must be that the great variety of perceptual experiences will always reduce to two only, when one is taken as a starting point. All colours other than red are always necessarily not-red, all tastes other than sweet will always necessarily be not-sweet. So the two opposed logoi should be understood as A and not-A respectively. But this leads to a more serious objection. A and not-A are clearly contradictories. If there are in fact for Protagoras always two opposed logoi concerning every thing and all logoi are true, what has happened to the doctrine that it is impossible to contradict? This is a problem that did not arise quite so sharply on the older interpretation of Protagoras, since on the older view he did not hold that it is impossible to contradict. But it was a problem that was always there, since the man-measure doctrine seems to require that there are never opposing logoi about the *same* thing, they are always about different things, e.g. my experience and your experience and these are two different things, not one and the same thing. If, as we have now seen reason to suppose, there is strong evidence that in fact Protagoras held that contradiction is impossible, we seem to have a direct conflict with the two-opposed-logoi doctrine.

But there is a possible answer. What is needed is to recognise that there are two different levels involved. As the Didymus passage stated, people do contradict one another in the sense that they oppose one statement to another negatively, both in every day life and in philosophic argument. There is probably no situation in which this is, at least psychologically, impossible, and this was recognised in the quotation from Euripides' *Antiope*. What we need to say is that at the verbal level contradiction is possible, but that this does not apply at the level of the things about which we are speaking. For when we set up apparent contradictions, at the level of words, these are apparent only, and if both statements are meaningful it will be because they are about different things, they are not about the same thing.

This explanation has the advantage of enabling us to make sense of a historical statement which unfortunately has not been regularly included in collections of passages relating to the sophists. At the commencement of his composition on *Helen* written perhaps about 370 B.C. Isocrates speaks of 'men who have grown old asserting that it is impossible to say things that are false, or to contradict, or to oppose two arguments (logoi) concerning the same things' and he opposes these men as a group to others (who sound like Platonists) who maintain the unity of the virtues. He goes on to say that unfortunately such developments are not merely recent – everyone knows that Protagoras and the sophists of his time have left us writings exhibiting things of this kind – and he then mentions Gorgias, Zeno and Melissus. First of all it should be noticed that this passage does bring together the three principles – the two-logoi doctrine, the impossibility of falsehood and the impossibility of contradiction, in relation to a single group of men. But it speaks of the *impossibility* of the two-logoi doctrine, whereas Protagoras was credited with its positive assertion. Does this mean that the reference cannot be to Protagoras after all?

Not so. The traditional formulation of the two-logoi doctrine said that there are two logoi concerning every thing. What Isocrates says is that 'they' held that it is impossible for there to be two logoi concerning the same things (in the plural). In other words, when there are two logoi, these concern not the same thing but different things. Could it not be that Isocrates is correct in that he is preserving the answer given in the circle of Protagoras to just the difficulty that we have now been discussing?[5] We do know that in some sense Protagoras had attacked the doctrine that reality was One (DK 80B2).

But if there are two logoi concerning everything, how is it possible to hold at the same time that, when there are two logoi, these concern not the same thing but different things? Indeed in the *Theaetetus* had not Socrates actually said (152b2) 'when the same wind is blowing it feels cold to one person and to another not' – surely this suggests that the wind is one thing, not two things? To this the answer must obviously be yes. But if so, what has happened to the suggestion that there are two things involved, rather than one? The answer can only be that the one thing is what functions as the subject, and the two logoi are what are expressed by predicate terms applied e.g. to the wind as subject. This would explain why Aristotle regularly treats Protagoras' man-measure doctrine as involving a denial of the law of non-contradiction. For Protagoras the same one wind is hot and not hot (= cold). This involves two contradictory statements, namely 'the wind is hot', and 'the wind is not hot', and to that extent those who make these two statements are talking about the same, one, thing. Yet to the extent that the wind is regarded as containing at the same time two qualities, or substances, namely hot and cold, it is also true that the statements 'the wind is hot' and 'the wind is cold' are about two different things, namely the hot in the wind and the cold in the wind. They can then both be true, without contradiction, since the two statements are statements about *different* things. Here it is appropriate to mention the chance survival from Protagoras' book *On that which is* quoted by Porphyry (DK 80B2) according to which Protagoras argued at considerable length using a series of demonstrations against those who introduce being as one. We may infer that Protagoras insisted that that which is is not one but a plurality on all occasions.

---

[5] It is perhaps significant that some manuscripts of Isocrates *corrected* 'concerning the same things' to 'concerning all things' as if aware that this was needed to bring the statement into accord with the better-known formulation of the two-logoi doctrine.

Clearly some of the detailed interpretations suggested here are open to challenge. What I want to suggest is that the evidence is overwhelming in favour of the attempt to interpret Protagoras' doctrine as a seriously intended contribution to a serious philosophic problem. I turn next to the question how far this was something to be associated with Protagoras only, and how far it represents an approach that was shared also by other sophists, or even by the sophistic movement as a whole. We have already had occasion to consider the startling new evidence which makes it clear that Prodicus was associated with just these problems. But what of others? Here the available evidence is not new. But it does, I believe, cry out, as so often is the case with the study of the sophists, for a fresh approach, not blinkered by traditional assumptions.

The most important single piece of evidence is the treatise of Gorgias, entitled according to Sextus Empiricus 'On that which is not or on Nature'. We have two separate summaries of this work, one preserved by Sextus (see DK 82B3) and the other in the third section of a piece of writing in doxographic style, wrongly attributed to Aristotle and so included in the corpus of his writings under the title 'On Melissus, Xenophanes and Gorgias' – or *De MXG* for short. In this treatise Gorgias presented his argument in three stages: (1) nothing is, (2) even if it is, it cannot be known to human beings, (3) even if it is and is knowable, it cannot be indicated and made meaningful to another person.

The interpretation of what Gorgias is saying is difficult, and we are certainly not yet even in sight of an agreed understanding of its overall significance, let alone its detailed arguments. Yet its importance can hardly be overestimated. It is, after all, probably the nearest we have or will ever have to a complete technical presentation of an articulated sophistic argument from the fifth century B.C. It is both more technical and more organised than the *Dissoi Logoi*, with which otherwise it might be compared. Its treatment by scholarship in many ways epitomises the problem of the scholarly approach to the sophistic movement as a whole. There have been in essentials three stages.[6] For long the view was held that it was not meant seriously, but that it was composed simply as a parody or joke against philosophers, or was at best a purely rhetorical exercise in argument. On the whole it is probable that this view no longer obtains, though it still has supporters. Thus

---

[6] see for a fuller summary with references, H. J. Newiger, *Untersuchungen zu Gorgias' Schrift über das Nichtseiende* Berlin 1973, 1–8.

Guthrie can write of the argument presented in the first of the three sections of the work: 'It is all, of course, engaging nonsense.'[7] A second stage was reached by those who were prepared to take it seriously and who took it as a full scale and carefully orchestrated attack on the philosophic doctrines of the Eleatics, and to a subordinate extent on the doctrines of certain physical philosophers among the Presocratics. This kind of interpretation takes the verb 'to be' in Gorgias' treatise to mean 'exist'. The first part then contends that Nothing exists, and proceeds to establish this by arguing that Notbeing does not exist, nor does Being exist. This is directed against the contention of Parmenides that only Being exists and Gorgias by his arguments achieves a position of philosophic Nihilism. Parmenides had destroyed the manifold world of appearances but retained the unitary world of True Being, Gorgias cleared the slate completely, and was left with simply – Nothing.

One of the attractions of this second stage in the interpretation of Gorgias' treatise was that it placed Gorgias firmly, even if rather destructively, within the main stream of the history of philosophy. I believe that this does remain a requirement for a correct interpretation. But in the meantime there have been some rather fundamental changes, as a result of which we may be in sight of an improved understanding of the general course of the history of Greek philosphy. Briefly, our approach to Parmenides and the Eleactics tends to be now rather different from what it was a century or even half a century ago. This springs partly from a closer examination of the surviving fragments and the doxographic tradition for Parmenides, and partly from a more general re-assessment of the philosophical interpretation of the verb 'to be' in Greek, both before and after the sophists. In a major investigation starting with Homer, Charles Kahn noted the difficulty in making any firm syntactical distinction between the use of the verb absolutely, i.e. without any further predicate, as in 'X is', and its predicative construction, as in 'X is Y, and argued against taking the first or absolute use as 'existential'. Both uses he inclines to treat basically as in effect assertion signs, reducing both the 'existential' use and the 'predicative' use to a more ultimate use which is far nearer to the 'predicative' than to the 'existential'.[8] Then in an article of fundamental

[7] in his *History of Greek Philosophy*, Vol. III 197 n. 2.
[8] see his 'The Greek Verb "To Be" and the Concept of Being', *Foundations of Language* 2 (1966) 245–65, and his book *The Verb 'be' in Ancient Greek*, Dordrecht 1973.

importance G. E. L. Owen[9] argued that in Plato's dialogue the *Sophist* the argument neither contains nor compels any isolation of an existential verb, and that it turns out to be primarily an essay in problems of reference and predication. Thirdly this new approach was applied directly to Parmenides, above all by A. P. D. Mourelatos,[10] with the conclusion that Parmenides, was not concerned primarily with existence and non-existence, but rather with distinguishing between two routes, one positive in which we say '*x* is *F*', and one negative in which we say '*x* is not-*F*'. It is the second route which Parmenides is condemning in favour of the first as the only possible route.

All this amounts to a massive shift of emphasis, away from the view that much of Greek philosophy was concerned primarily with problems of existence, and towards the view that it was rather in such cases concerned with what we would call problems of predication, but which they tended rather more to regard as problems of the inherence of qualities and characteristics in objects in the real world around us. This leads me to what I would like to regard as the third stage in the approach to Gorgias' treatise, namely its interpretation in the light of problems of predication. Such an approach is relatively new, and is controversial. I cannot attempt here to justify it by detailed argument and analysis.[11] But after some reflection I have concluded that it might be best simply to present my interpretation of the treatise as a whole without further apology, for what it may be worth. I will simply say that even if I should be judged to be entirely wrong in this matter, this would in no way conflict with the antilogic character of the treatise. The disagreement would not be about whether Gorgias' argument is built about inferred contradictions and opposing logoi – it clearly is – but about the nature and applications of the opposing logoi only.

On this view it is primarily the predicative use of the verb 'to be' with which Gorgias is concerned, and the contradictions which this is

---

[9] 'Plato on Not-Being', which is Chapter 12 in G. Vlastos, *Plato, a collection of critical essays*, Vol. I – Metaphysics and Epistemology, New York 1971.

[10] *The Route of Parmenides* New Haven 1970, also 'Determinacy and Indeterminacy as the Key contrast in Parmenides', *Lampas* 8 (1975) 334–43.

[11] I attempted to apply this approach to the first part of the treatise in what I would like to regard as a pioneering article, 'Gorgias on Nature or that which is not', *Phronesis* 1 (1955/56) 3–25. In general terms, the first attempt to look at the treatise in this way is to be found in G. Calogero, *Studi sull'eleatismo* Rome 1932, Ch. 4, German translation *Studien über den Eleatismus*, Hildesheim 1970.

felt to generate. He is arguing that there is no way in which the verb 'to be' can be applied to a subject without contradictions arising and he is thinking primarily of statements about phenomena. These contradictions the Eleatics had been able to identify in the case of negative statements, for Gorgias they apply also to positive statements.

For the first part of the treatise it is probable that the text of *De MXG* is a more faithful representation of the original than the version given by Sextus. On either version the first part opened with the claim that nothing is. In *De MXG* we are given a special argument to establish this, devised by Gorgias himself – it is not possible for anything either to be or not to be. Suppose that it is able not to be, the fact that it is (so able), means that it is. But if it is (taken as the alternative to supposing that it is able not to be), then we will be confronted with a series of options – either it is one or it is many, either it is ungenerated or it is something that was generated. Arguments, derived in part from Zeno and Melissus, are adduced to show that none of these four options is possible. If it is neither one of the paired alternatives, it is equally certainly not both alternatives taken together. If it is none of these three possibilities it is not anything at all, since these are the only three possibilities.

What is the it that is here being talked about? There seem to me clear indications that what Gorgias is concerned with is each and every thing no matter what, including above all phenomenal objects. This is strongly suggested by the use of the word *pragmata* ('things') in the plural (979a27–28), supported by two more general references in Isocrates who says in the *Helen* (X.3): 'For how could one surpass Gorgias who dared to assert that none of the things that are is', and in the *Antidosis* (XV.268) where he names Gorgias as the last of a whole series of the 'old sophists, of whom one said that the sum of things is made of an infinite number of elements, Empedocles of four ... Parmenides and Melissus one, and Gorgias none at all' (both passages in DK 80B1).[12] This last passage, especially, strengthens the view that Gorgias was concerned not merely to attack the Eleatics but also the pluralists among the Presocratics as well.

The second part of the treatise argues that even if we were to say of something that it is, it would be unknowable and unthinkable by any human being. The way in which this is argued is philosophically of

---

[12] For a very good exposition of this point, see most recently H. J. Newiger, *op. cit.*, 21–2.

considerable interest and the question of its actual validity is only part of this interest, perhaps a relatively small part. We cannot say that things being thought are – if we were to say this we would have to say that all things being thought are, and that they are as they are thought, e.g. possess the qualities present to them in thought. So if one thinks of a man as flying or of chariots running races in the sea it would follow that a man is in fact flying or that chariots are in fact racing in sea. So, generally, if we suppose that whatever a man thinks is, then there would be no falsehood. So, we conclude, we cannot say that what a man thinks is. From this it is argued that what is is not capable of being thought. So if anything is, it will not be thinkable.

Perhaps the main interest of this argument is the way in which it opens up a contrast, indeed a gulf between cognitive mental acts (thoughts, perceptions and so on) and the objects about which they are or purport to be cognitive. It seems to be being held that for anything to be known or thought it must have (i.e. repeat or reproduce and so *itself* possess) the appropriate characters of the object cognised. White objects, if thought, require white thoughts, and objects that are require, if thought, thoughts that are. The implications of, and the objections to such a view are of considerable interest but this is not the place to pursue them. What is more relevant for my argument are certain other considerations. It has been argued in Part I of the treatise that nothing is. Now, hypothetically, we are asked to consider the consequences of supposing that in fact things are. These consequences are said to be unacceptable because of what would follow about things and our thinking about them. There is no attempt to abolish thinking, only to deny that we can say of thoughts that they are – likewise there is no attempt to abolish things. Indeed the whole argument depends completely on the retention of both thinking and things. Moreover it is even implied that thoughts can be true (as well as false). This means that Gorgias is *not* accepting the view I have earlier attributed to Protagoras, that it is not possible to say what is false. Secondly the whole of Part II of the treatise is concerned with thought about phenomena. It begins by supposing that phenomena are. This supports the suggestion made earlier that Part I also is concerned with phenomena.

The view that there must be a correspondence between the characters of thought and the characters of the objects of thought is repeated and developed further in the implications of Part III of Gorgias' argument. Here it is argued that even if something is, and it is knowable, it cannot be communicated to another person. The sole method of communication selected for discussion is speech (logos). The method of transmission of logos from one person to another is by vocal sounds or utterances. Clearly these are audible and equally clearly they are not visible. So if we are concerned with communication concerning things visible, for example colours, such things cannot be transmitted by non-visible colourless sounds. There is thus a fundamental gulf between the logos and the things or *pragmata* which come to us from outside ourselves. This gulf is not to be regarded as bridged by the fact that the logos, at least when expressed in audible, vocal sounds, is itself something in the same category as *pragmata* – it comes to us from outside ourselves, it is true, but through a different sense organ than that through which we receive visual impressions.

But perhaps the gulf might be bridged in a different way. There is a sense in which the logos does come to us from the *pragmata* outside us. For logos *is* formed from them when they are perceived by us – so from our encounter with flavour there arises in us the logos which is the expression that accords with this quality, and from the incidence of colour the logos which is in accord with the colour. But this will not do either. The logos does not have the function of displaying the external object, it is the external object which provides us with information about (the meaning of) the logos. Here we seem to have the beginnings of two different senses for logos, (1) as something generated in our minds as a result of our perceptions, and (2) as an audible phonetic sound, i.e. a 'spoken' word. That a distinction of this kind was being made is supported by the language used in *De MXG*, where we are told that it is impossible for a person to convey to another by words or other signs something which he himself does not possess in his own thought. This suggests a three stage analysis – the object itself together with its qualities, what we acquire from such an object, and the spoken words with which we attempt, but according to Gorgias inevitably fail, to pass on (knowledge of) such an object to someone else.

It should be stressed that the above account of Gorgias' treatise is open to challenge in many of its details, though it does represent fairly precisely what I myself believe Gorgias to have been saying. But the condition of the text, especially in the version of *De MXG*, is so bad, and the difficulties of interpretation in the case of the version of Sextus as well as in *De MXG* are so great that much more work needs to be done before we can hope to arrive at any secure understanding in detail.[13] This does not matter too much, however, for my present purposes. For whatever corrections and refinements or even fundamental alternations from the above account are still to be made, the philosophical interest and importance of what Gorgias had to say hardly needs further stressing. First, looking backwards in time, it is clear that he was pulling apart and separating three things which Parmenides had identified in his fragment 8.34–36, namely being, thinking and saying. On the traditional interpretation of Parmenides these lines read: 'Thinking and the thought that it is are one and the same. For you will not find thinking without the being wherein it is expressed.' In the first part of his treatise Gorgias had denied being to phenomena, in the second and third parts he had argued that even if being were to be conceded to phenomena one must still separate being from thinking and the words in which thinking is expressed either to oneself or to another.

So much for the retrospective significance of Gorgias' doctrine. Far greater is its prospective significance. For Gorgias is raising, by implication and, I would say, to a considerable degree consciously, the whole problem of meaning and reference. Let us not worry too much about the inadequacies of his treatment of the question, the important thing is that he was beginning to see that there is a question and a very serious one. If words are used to refer to things, and it seems obvious that this is the primary purpose for which they are used, how is it that a word is accepted as referring to the things to which we say it does refer, and not to other things to which we say it does not refer? It would be convenient if we could say that it is something about the word itself, and it would be simplest if there were something in the word which mirrors or reproduces within the word itself the distinguishing features of the things to which it refers. But, except perhaps for words that are specifically onomatopoeic and by their own sounds reproduce the sounds of the things to which they refer, no such features are apparent in words, and we are driven to attempt to develop a doctrine of the meaning attached to words, in virtue of which meaning they can then be understood to refer to the things to which we suppose them to refer. But this meaning will have to be something distinct from the mere sounds of the words concerned. This is Plato's starting point in

---

[13] The best and fullest treatment to date is in the book by Newiger, for which see above p. 93 n. 6 (I judge it superior to that in M. Migliori, *La filosofia di Gorgia,* Milan 1973), but much remains to be done.

the *Cratylus*, and some would say for the whole of his philosophical career. A similar question arises for the cognitive acts, the thoughts and perceptions which, as we say, we express in words. Words, thoughts and things, what is the relationship between them?

Nor does it end there. Once we have separated these three things each from the other, while still insisting that there needs to be some kind of correspondence maintained between all three as a requirement for truth and knowledge we are confronted with the problem of the best way to understand logos in relation to just these three things. For, as was said at the beginning of this present chapter, logos seems to have, indeed must have, a kind of foot planted in each of the three areas. The logos of a thing is (1) the principle or nature or distinguishing mark or constituent elements of the thing itself, it is (2) what *we* understand it to be, and finally it is (3) the correct (verbal) description, account or definition of the thing. All three raise the question of being. For the logos of a thing under heading (1) is what that thing is, under (2) it is what we understand it to be, and under (3) it is what we say it to be.

So far we have seen that in the sphere of perception Protagoras had argued that all perceptions are true and so are of things that are, as they are, whereas Gorgias maintained that we ought not to say of anything that it is. Did neither Gorgias nor Protagoras then make any distinction between conflicting perceptions purporting to be of the same thing? Contrary to what might have been expected of him Gorgias clearly did retain a distinction between true thoughts and false, though how he analysed the difference between them we are not told, except that he seems to have supposed that perception involves the reception of appropriate 'effluences' from physical objects (DK 80B4). For Protagoras there can be no distinctions in terms of truth between varying and conflicting perceptions. But for him also there clearly were distinctions none the less and these must now be considered.

It will be convenient to begin with the evidence of a substantial passage in Aristotle's *Rhetoric B*.24.10–11 (1402a5–28, of which a small extract only is given in DK 80A21):

In Dialectic it is argued that that which is not *is*, for that which is not *is* that which is not, and also, that the unknown can be known, for it can be known of the unknown that it is unknown. Similarly in Rhetoric, an apparent enthymeme may arise from that which is not absolutely probable but only in particular cases. But this is not to be understood absolutely, as Agathon says:

100

'one might perhaps say that this very thing is probable, that many things happen to men that are not probable', for that which is contrary to probability nevertheless does happen. If this is so that which is improbable will be probable ... [further examples] ... Here both alternatives appear equally probable, but the one is really so, the other not probable absolutely, but only in the conditions mentioned. And this is what 'making the worse appear the better argument' means. Wherefore men were justly disgusted with the promise of Protagoras; for it is a lie, not a real but an apparent probability, not found in any art except Rhetoric and Sophistic [trans. Freese].

The promise of Protagoras 'to make the weaker argument [logos] stronger' became notorious in later writers. But there must already be a reference to this doctrine in Aristophanes' *Clouds* (DK C2) where he makes Strepsiades declare that in the house of Socrates 'they keep both logoi, the stronger, no matter what it is, and the weaker, and of these two they say the weaker is victorious while giving expression to what is more unjust'. It looks as if Aristotle also is giving us actual fifth-century examples – notably the 'is not *is*' argument which was used by Gorgias, and the quotation from Agathon, whose first tragic victory was gained in 416 B.C., so that what he says about the probable could conceivably be taken from Protagoras' own writings. The rhetorical application of a doctrine concerned with making the weaker argument into the stronger is obvious, and it is sometimes treated as if it had a purely rhetorical application only. Thus according to Eudoxus (80A21) as an exercise in its application Protagoras taught his pupils to praise and blame the same argument.[14] But Aristotle, who of course does regard such arguments as rhetorical and sophistical only, says that people are disgusted with Protagoras' promise 'because it is false'. This may suggest that Protagoras claimed that his doctrine was not merely rhetorical, but somehow involved a degree of validity or truth. As we have seen (above, p. 85) the treatise in which he gave expression to the man–measure doctrine was apparently known both as *The Truth* and as *The Overthrowing Arguments*.

But if all perceptions and moral judgments are to be accepted as equally true how is it possible for any one logos giving expression to perceptual and moral judgments ever to be described as superior to another logos? Are not all truths simply equal in respect of their truth? Maybe, but perhaps there are other ways in which logoi may be ranked as inferior or superior. One obvious way is in terms of their

[14] usually, but less correctly I think, translated 'the same person', but see e.g. J. P. Dumont, *Les sophistes fragments et témoignages*, Paris 1969, p. 37: 'la même chose'.

relative persuasiveness, and the fairly elaborate doctrine of persuasion developed by Gorgias has already been considered. But persuasion consists in making one view appear preferable to another in at least some respect. One way was to class the preferred argument as *orthos* – 'upright', 'straight', 'right' or *orthoteros* 'straighter', 'more correct' and so on, and it is clear that the concept of *orthotēs* and of an *orthos logos* was important. So we are told that when Pericles spent a whole day discussing with Protagoras the case of the athlete accidentally killed by a javelin at the games the argument turned on whether it was the javelin, or the man who threw it, or the organisers of the games who were to be judged to blame 'according to the most correct argument' – the *orthotatos logos* (DK 80A10), i.e. which is the most correct of the three logoi mentioned. When Antiphon wants to reject the view that painful things are beneficial to nature more than pleasant things he defends his view as being according to the *orthos logos* (DK 87B44 fr. A. Col. 4).

This way of talking about things was familiar, it would seem, both to Socrates and to Plato. In the *Crito* when Crito has appealed to Socrates to save himself by escaping from prison, Socrates replies (46b):

My dear Crito, your eagerness is worth a great deal, if it should prove to be accompanied by *orthotēs*, but if it is not, the greater it is the more difficult it is to endure. So we must examine the question whether we ought to do this or not. For I am not only now but always a man who follows nothing else but the logos which on consideration seems to me best [*beltistos*]. And I cannot now cast aside the logoi that I used earlier.

Taken in isolation the reference to the need to follow the *beltistos logos* may seem merely casual and general in its formulation, though I suspect that those are justified who suppose that behind its general character there is a fairly specific reference at least to terminology that was sophistic.[15]

However that may be, there should not be much doubt about the fuller discussion of the problem put into the mouth of Socrates in the *Phaedo*. This is the famous discussion of the 'new method' and it occupies the whole section from 89c11–102a1. Only certain points can be selected here, as our immediate purpose is not with the in-

---

[15] see G. Calogero, 'La regola di Socrate', *La Cultura* 1 (1963) 182–96, A. Szabo & G. Calogero, Beltistos Logos, *ibid*. 607–30. G. Giannantoni, *Dialogo e dialettica nei dialoghi giovanili di Platone*, Rome 1963, 73 ff., 179–80, 200, Burnet ad *Crito* 46b5 in his *Plato, Euthyphro, Apology and Crito*, Oxford 1924.

terpretation of Plato, so not with the relation to the theory of Platonic Forms, but with the relation between what Socrates is saying and the sophistic debate with which he is intimately concerned throughout the whole passage. The opening part of the passage has been summarised already in the course of our earlier discussion of the *antilogikoi*. To re-capitulate, Socrates distinguishes himself from those who simply oppose one argument to another – this leads to misology, a hatred of all logoi, while at the same time he accepts that at the phenomenal level there is in fact nothing sound or reliable but that all things are in process of being turned up and down as in the Euripus, and do not abide in anything for any duration of time.

What is needed, Socrates says, is the proper skill in dealing with logoi (90b7). For it may be that not all logoi are of the fluctuating kind that are incapable of being grasped intellectually (90c8–d7). Lacking this skill, in the period when he was concerned with physical science Socrates found himself moving up and down (96b1) just like the phenomena. After all attempts at reaching the truth by the direct contemplation of phenomena had failed, he decided to take refuge in logoi and in them to examine the truth of the things that are (99e4–6). So he proceeded along this path. On each occasion he laid down as a starting point (the Greek says 'hypothesised') the logos which he judged to be the strongest and posited as true the things which seemed to him to accord with this logos. What he had in mind is explained by a series of examples. In the case of things that are beautiful we must hypothesise the existence of the Form of Beauty as the source, explanation and cause of the many beautifuls. This procedure is the safe path for an inexperienced person to follow and this avoids the confusion in which the *antilogikoi* are involved. Their mistake is to try to discuss without distinguishing between them both the source and the consequences that proceed from the source (101e1–3 cf. *Rep.* 476d2–3). What the *antilogikoi* do, in Socrates' view, is to mix up 'causes' with effects, by confusing Forms with phenomena, and 'higher' Forms with 'lower' Forms. By so doing they generate a plurality of logoi, each opposed to the rest. The safe way avoids the contradictions involved in the two-opposed-logoi doctrine, which, it should be stressed, on Plato's view applies only to phenomena. The contradictions do not apply to the Forms, and the contradictions found in phenomena disappear when we move from phenomena to the Forms.[16]

[16] for a substantially correct understanding of this point see *Plato, Phaedo* trans. R. S. Bluck, London 1955, pp. 171–2 with note 1 on p. 172.

This then is Plato's answer to the *antilogikoi* on the subject of the two-opposed-logoi doctrine. As it is expressed in terms of the theory of Forms it is not likely to have been expressed, at least in anything like this developed fashion, by Socrates himself. But the phrase, 'the logos judged to be the strongest' (100a4) is strongly reminiscent of the best or straightest logos in sophistic discussions. Plato represents Socrates as always searching for satisfactory logoi or accounts, above all of the various virtues, and Aristotle attributes as we have seen the search for *epactic* logoi specifically to the historical Socrates. Certainly he was an active participant, we may reasonably conclude, in the sophistic search for the better or stronger logos in cases of a conflict of logoi.

But it is time to return to the doctrines of Protagoras as he was in so many ways expressing not simply his own views but was also acting as a leader for the sophistic movement as a whole. When we turn to the *Theaetetus* we find that his man-measure doctrine is required to face a most interesting objection. As Socrates points out (161d3–e3):

> If whatever any man supposes on the basis of perception is indeed to be true for him, if just as no one is to be a better judge of what another experiences so no one is more authoritative in investigating whether another's opinion is right or false, but as we have said more than once every man will have his own beliefs for himself alone, and they are all right and true, then, my friend, where is the wisdom of Protagoras, to justify him in thinking that he is fit to be a teacher of others and to be handsomely paid for it, and where is our comparative ignorance so that we must go to him for instruction, when each of us is the measure of his own wisdom?

To this charge Protagoras replies in due course, through the mouth of Socrates (166d1–8):

> I maintain that the truth is as I have written. Each one of us is the measure of the things that are and the things that are not; but there is all the difference in the world between one man and another in just this, that what is and appears to one is different from what is and appears to the other. And as for wisdom and the wise man I am very far from saying that there's no such thing. By a wise man I mean precisely the man who works a change and where bad things are and appear for any one person makes good things appear and be for him.

This is followed by an example: to the sick man his food appears and is bitter, to the healthy man it is and appears the opposite. Both conditions are equally true, but the second condition is better than the first, and the physician changes the first condition into the second so that the food which previously seemed and was bitter now seems and is sweet. In education the sophist does with words what the physician does with drugs, and substitutes not true for false, but better for worse opinions. Here the example given is bad things, that seem and so are just, needing to be replaced by good things which will then seem and so be just. This applies not merely to the individual but also to whole communities – for them also the educational function of the sophist can be most helpful and beneficial (167c4–7). A joke made by Socrates makes it clear that Plato was well aware that the substitution of one experience for another was regarded by Protagoras as substituting one logos for another, in fact the logos that had been weaker has now become stronger (172b8–9).

The implications for the man-measure doctrine of this way of looking at things are however considerable. In its unrestricted form the man–measure doctrine seemed to involve that if something seems F to someone, then it is F for him, and this is the case for all values of F. We have now been told however that some people are wiser than others on the question of what is better or worse, and this in turn leads to the inescapable further proposition that at least some judgments *are* false, namely judgments about what is advantageous and not advantageous. The need for this modification to the generality of the original position ascribed to Protagoras is fully recognised by Socrates (172a5–b2) and is presented by him as the kind of thing which Protagoras himself might have said if he had been able to return from the underworld and pop his head up through the ground as far as the neck and speak before he sank out of sight once again. I have no doubt that this defence must be taken seriously – just how far it was authorised by what Protagoras had actually written may remain a matter of debate, but I believe it is a clear indication that this is what Plato considered to be the historically correct interpretation of Protagoras' doctrine.[17]

However that may be, the modified doctrine is of considerable interest. The famous story told by Herodotus (III.38) shows that something like what we would call a kind of sociology of knowledge was already beginning to be applied to moral values: If all men were asked to name the best laws and customs each would choose his own, and Euripides (fr. 19) made a character say that no behaviour is shameful if it does not seem so to those who practise it. For many at the present day, views about values are not matters of objective fact like views

---

[17] for the view opposed to mine see e.g. Plato, *Theaetetus* tr. John McDowell, Oxford 1973, pp. 172–73.

about the physical world, and what Protagoras' doctrine (in its modified form) provides is a way of comparing judgments about matters of
value, not in terms of their own truth or falsehood but in terms of their
social consequences. That this view was not confined to Protagoras
but was far more widely held, presumably within the sophistic movement, is clear from Plato's statement that it was also held by those who
did not completely affirm the doctrine of Protagoras (*Theaetet.*
172b6–7).

But acceptance of the modified view does raise further questions. So
far we might say that the formula 'if something seems F to someone,
then it is F for that person' will apply in cases where F is interpreted as
meaning 'hot', 'sweet', 'just', 'beautiful' and so on, it will not apply
where F is interpreted as meaning 'good', 'healthy' or 'advantageous'.
But what about other cases? If Protagoras says that whatever seems to
a person is so for that person, this might well be understood as
meaning that every judgment whatsoever is true for the person whose
judgment it is, not merely judgments about perceptual and moral
qualities. Just this unrestricted interpretation of the man–measure
doctrine was attributed to Protagoras by those of his critics who used
it as a basis for the counter-attack, known later as the *peritropē* or
turning-of-the-tables. This was already well known when Plato wrote
the *Theaetetus*, as we are told it had been brought against Protagoras
also by Democritus (DK 68A114).

The objection goes like this (171a6–9): Protagoras, admitting as he
does that everyone's opinion is true, must acknowledge the truth of
his opponents' belief about his own belief, where they think he is
wrong. It is immediately in reply to this argument, in fact, that
Socrates suggests that Protagoras might stick his head up above the
ground if he could. But Plato does not actually provide such an
answer, and this is unfortunate. For the application of the *peritropē*
involves the claim that there is an internal contradiction in Protagoras' position, and the nature of this supposed internal contradiction
is important for the interpretation of Protagoras' man–measure doctrine. According to one formulation of this doctrine Protagoras had
maintained, for example, that when the wind seems cold to Protagoras it is cold *for him*. When the (same) wind seems warm to his opponent then it is warm *for that opponent*. But provided the italicised
qualifying phrases are retained in each case, there is in fact no contradiction between the two contentions – the statement that something
appears to be the case to one man is clearly not contradicted by the

statement that the same thing appears not to be the case to another man. If 'appears' is replaced by 'is' there is still no contradiction, provided the qualifying phrases 'is for *a*' and 'is not for *b*' are retained in each case. If Protagoras held the view that the wind in itself exists independently of my perceiving it, but that its coldness only exists privately for me when I have the feeling of cold, and its warmness only exists privately for another when that other has the feeling of warmth, no contradition is involved, and the *peritropē* fails.

This *may* have been the answer which Socrates supposes Protagoras would have made if he had been able to stick his head up above the ground. But against this view there are a number of objections. First the answer is so obvious that one might have expected that it would have prevented the very formulation of the *peritropē* objection right at the start. The *peritropē* objection is only plausible, it would seem, if the qualifying phrases are removed or disregarded and Protagoras' position is taken as involving the contention that the wind in itself both is and is not cold, and that this is so objectively and not merely as a matter of appearance to different observers. Secondly, virtually the whole of the later tradition[18] about the meaning of Protagoras' man–measure doctrine does in fact interpret it objectively, i.e. as involving the view that the wind in itself is both cold and warm – warm and cold are two qualities which can co-exist in the same physical object. I perceive the one, and you perceive the other. This makes the *peritropē* objection entirely understandable. Thirdly in this later tradition the *peritropē* objection is attributed both to Democritus and to Plato in its objectivist form. Thus Sextus Empiricus writes (DK 68A114): 'One cannot say that every presentation is true, because this refutes itself, as Democritus and Plato taught in opposing Protagoras; for if every presentation is true, the judgement that not every presentation is true, being based on a representation, will also be true, and thus the judgement that every presentation is true will become false' (translation by Bury). This fits exactly with the objectivist view of Protagoras' doctrine given elsewhere in Sextus Empiricus (DK 80A14):

He says that the logoi of all the appearances subsist in matter, so that matter,

---

[18] This is in fact conceded by M. F. Burnyeat, 'Protagoras and Self-Refutation in later Greek Philosophy', *Philosophical Review* 85 (1976) 44–69, although he differs from me in supposing that Plato attributed to Protagoras what I have called the subjectivist position, and that this interpretation was mistakenly altered by Aristotle, and those who came after him, into an objectivist interpretation.

so far as depends on itself, is able to be all those things which appear to all. And men, he says, apprehend different things at different times owing to their differing dispositions; for he who is in a natural state apprehends *those things subsisting in matter* [my italics] which are able to appear to those in a natural state, and those who are in a non-natural state apprehend the things which can appear to those in a non-natural state. Moreover, precisely the same account applies to the variations due to age, and to the sleeping or waking state, and to each several kind of condition. Thus, according to him, Man becomes the criterion of things that are; for all things that appear to men also are, and things that appear to no man, also are without being.

If the objectivist interpretation enables us to make sense of the *peritropē* objection, how are we to suppose that Protagoras would have replied to it, if he had been able to stick his head up above the ground? Regrettably, we are not told. But we may conjecture that his reply might have consisted of two parts. First in the case of perceived qualities, taken here as including moral and aesthetic qualities as well as the normal qualities perceived by the several senses. Here his answer would be to admit that he is positing contradictory situations. The same wind *is* both warm and cold, and this is so because it is capable of possessing contradictory qualities simultaneously. This is just the way things are. Plato was prepared to accept this as a correct description of phenomena, but supposed that such a situation is only possible if beyond and above the phenomena there are also further entities, the Forms, which are exempt from the distressingly contradictory situation which obtains with phenomena. Protagoras, on the other hand, was not prepared to posit any entities other than those that were phenomenal. Secondly, in the case of characteristics such as good, bad, advantageous and not advantageous, wise and not wise, here Protagoras simply held that such characteristics were not subject to the man—measure doctrine. Here there is only one truth, not the two logoi which apply in the earlier case. Indeed there is a sense in which Protagoras held that the second class of characteristics, good, bad, advantageous, etc. apply to the first class of characteristics where the two-logoi doctrine is fully at work. For while two people may have opposed sensations, one perceiving the wind as warm, another as cold, and these two qualities are of equal status so far as regards their truth, yet they are not of equal status with respect to their value. As the quotation from Sextus makes clear, one perception will be that of a man in a healthy or natural state, and the use of the term 'natural state' implies that such a perception will accordingly be preferable to the other perception which arises in the case e.g. of illness or a non-natural state in the percipient.

Protagoras' restriction of reality to phenomenal reality is seen not only in the last sentence of the account by Sextus Empiricus that has just been quoted, but also in the interesting statement preserved by Aristotle in *Metaphysics* B (DK 80B7) where he says:

> It is not true that land-measurement deals with perceptible and perishable magnitudes; for then it would have perished when they perished. And likewise astronomy will not be found to be dealing with perceptible magnitudes, nor with this heaven above us. For perceptible lines are not the kind of lines of which the geometer speaks, for no perceptible thing is straight or round in the way in which he speaks of straight and round. For a perceptible circle does not touch a straight edge at a point, but does so as Protagoras used to say it did in his refutation of the geometers.

In other words, according to Protagoras, the tangent touches a circle not at a geometrical point, but as it does in the visible world, that is over a segment of a certain dimension. Simplicius (DK 29A29) preserves what seems to be a passage from a dialogue between Zeno and Protagoras. It does not matter for our purposes whether, as is probable, the dialogue is entirely fictitious, since it certainly presents a correct application of Protagoras' doctrine. Zeno asks Protagoras whether a single grain of millet or the ten thousandth part of a grain of millet makes any sound when it falls. Protagoras replies that they do not, but admits that a bushel (*medimnos*) of millet seed does make a sound. Zeno then concludes that a single grain must make an appropriate fraction of the sound made by the bushel. The point so far as concerns Zeno may very well relate to the problem of infinitesimals. But for Protagoras the point is much more likely to have been simply the denial of unheard sounds, i.e. the denial of anything other than sounds which are actual phenomena because they are audibly so. At least on this point he had Aristotle on his side, in that Aristotle argued that there was no reason why such a part of a bushel should not, in no matter what length of time, simply fail to move the air that the whole bushel moves in falling.

The doctrine that there are not entities other than phenomenal entities involves the denial that there are any non-phenomenal objects for the understanding. So we are told by Diogenes Laertius in his summary of Protagoras' doctrines that Protagoras left aside the *dianoia* ('understanding', here presumably in the sense of the significance or meaning of the word) and paid attention only to the actual wording, or name, the *onoma* (IX.52 = DK 80A1). But if there are no objects for the understanding, then the understanding has no distinguishable function, it might be argued, in the soul. And this is presumably the explanation of the remarkable statement made by Diogenes Laertius, in the paragraph immediately preceding the one just cited, that the soul was nothing apart from its sensations. We know that Protagoras had a physical doctrine of the soul, and that he located it in the chest (DK 80A18), so it is unlikely that he meant that the soul had no existence apart from the *content* of its sensations. Rather it is probable that he meant that it has no function to perform apart from that of perceiving, a doctrine apparently found also in Democritus (DK 68A112) and subsequently in Strato and Aenesidemus, though they identified understanding with perception and did not deny the existence of understanding (Sextus Empiricus, *Adv. Mathematicos* VII.350).

10

The nomos–physis controversy

It has long been recognised that two terms, *nomos* and *physis*, were of great importance in much of the thinking and arguments in the second half of the fifth century B.C. The term *physis* is usually translated by 'nature'. It was the term which the Ionian scientists came to use for the whole of reality, or for its most abiding material source or constituents. But it also came early to be used to refer to the constitution or set of characteristics of a particular thing, or class of such things, especially a living creature or a person, as in the expression 'the nature of a man'. In each case the term, at least by implication, involved a contrast between the characteristics appropriate to a thing as such, that it possessed in its own right, or of its own accord, on the one hand, and acquired or imposed characteristics on the other hand.

Central to the meaning of the term is the static concept of 'the way things are'. But a range of terms in Greek that were visibly cognate carried the meaning 'to grow'. This probably had the result that the word *physis* was quite often felt to have a kind of overtone as a result of consciousness of a certain pull in that direction, and so it is frequently used of things that are the way they are because they have grown or become that way. Just occasionally the word is actually used to mean something like 'birth, genesis or growth', but such cases are quite rare, and Aristotle's philosophic lexicon in *Metaphysics* △.4 is no doubt to be followed when Aristotle there suggests that there is something a little odd about this sense, as if one were to lengthen the quantity of the first vowel which is what one would expect if it were to be related directly to the verb meaning 'to grow'. Whatever the reason it is certainly the case that in most contexts and in most applications the term *physis* retained a kind of dynamic aspect, and it is not accidental that Aristotle can conclude his discussion of varying senses of the term by declaring (*Met.* △.1015a13–15) 'now from what has been said nature [*physis*] in the primary and strict sense is the substance of things which have in themselves as such a source of movement'.

111

Nomos, traditionally translated either as 'law' or 'convention' or 'custom' according to what seems best to fit the context, is perhaps a rather more subtle term than these translations would suggest. Both the meaning and the history of the word have been much discussed, often without pointing to any very clear conclusions. But I believe that the matter can be stated simply. The term *nomos* and the whole range of terms that are cognate with it in Greek are always prescriptive and normative and never merely descriptive – they give some kind of direction or command affecting the behaviour and activities of persons and things. The nearest modern term for *nomos* is 'norm' – the establishment or promulgation of *nomoi* is the setting up of norms of behaviour. So *nomos* as law is legally prescribed norm, and *nomos* as convention is norm prescribed by convention; in each case what is being said or prescribed is that something is to be done or not done, or is to be or not be the case or is to be accepted as being the case. So when we come eventually to the expression *nomos physeōs*, the norm of nature (first actually in Plato, *Gorgias* 483e3, but anticipated in Thucydides V. 105. 2), this is what nature urges or requires us to do, never simply what actually happens at the level of description. It follows that 'custom' is only *nomos* in those cases, admittedly frequent, where it carries with it the implication that it is approved custom, or custom regarded as normative in some way or to some degree. The cognate verb '*nomizo*', traditionally 'I think', should perhaps be taken as meaning 'I accept' or 'I approve' (that it be so, etc.), *nomizetai* as meaning 'it is accepted as right', while *nemetai* means 'is assigned as the right portion' and *Nemesis* means either the assignment of the right portions or where necessary the correction of a wrong assignment of portions.

Human laws, norms and habits of behaviour vary from community to community, and the more widely Greeks travelled in the ancient world the more apparent this became. Herodotus, himself a considerable traveller, seems to have set himself the task of collecting and describing the customs of Scythians, Persians, Lydians, Egyptians and others. He was not the first to do so, being preceded by Hecataeus of Miletus early in the fifth century. The second chapter of the *Dissoi Logoi* at sometime after the end of the fifth century uses systematic oppositions between the customs of different peoples, and references to a lost work of Aristotle testify to a continuing interest in *Nomima Barbarika*, the customs of the barbarians. Heraclitus of Ephesus, perhaps about 500 B.C., after castigating the folly and blindness of the

112

majority of men, which led them to live as though they each had their own private understanding, argued <u>that all human laws are nourished by one divine law</u>, and that it was this that they should follow (combining DK 22B2 with 114, as Marcovich, *Heraclitus* Merida 1967, fr. 23).

In appealing from ordinary laws to a higher reality Heraclitus was appealing from what varies and is subject to change and so challenge, to what was permanent, unvarying and not open to challenge. He was in fact seeking for something from which to derive human laws, and in the process to justify some of them while rejecting others as not in accord with the higher law. By implication he was also providing a criterion or standard in the light of which ordinary laws might be corrected or improved. Historically this is so, whether or not Heraclitus understood that this was what he was doing. All this was well understood by Aristotle when he wrote in the *Rhetoric* (137b4–11):

There are two kinds of law, one particular and one common. By particular laws I mean those determined by each people in relation to themselves, and these again are divided into written and unwritten; by laws that are common I mean those in accordance with nature. For in fact there is a common idea of what is just and unjust in accordance with nature, which all men divine to some extent, even if there is neither sharing in it nor agreement between them. This is what Antigone in Sophocles evidently means, when she declares that it is just, though forbidden, to bury Polynices, as being naturally just.

In fact in the *Antigone* nature is not mentioned as a criterion of justice – what Antigone appeals to are unwritten, divine *nomima* contrasted with laws determined among men, and it is Aristotle who here equates the universal or common law with what is just by nature.

Who first introduced this equation we do not know. But we do have a useful historical statement by Aristotle when he tells us in the *Sophistici Elenchi*, 173a7–18:

A widespread *topos* causes men to utter paradoxes in the application of the standards of nature and law, as Callicles is represented as doing in the *Gorgias*, and which *all the ancients* regarded as valid; for according to them Nature and Law are opposites, and justice is a fine thing according to law, but not so according to nature. So to a man who has spoken in terms of nature you must reply in terms of law, and when he speaks in terms of law you must lead the argument in terms of nature; for in both cases the result will be that he utters paradoxes; in the view of these people what accorded with nature was the truth, while what accorded with law was what was approved by the majority. It is, therefore, clear that they also like the men of today, were trying either to refute the answerer or make him utter paradoxes.

Here is it possible that the reference to 'all the ancients' in contrast to 'the men of today' is not simply to sophists other than Callicles or to some of such sophists, but is intended to have a more general application and to include those who were properly presophistic as well as members of the sophistic movement itself. But the reference to paradoxes, the statement that justice is good by *nomos* but not by *physis*, and above all the advice to appeal to the other of these two opposed terms when your opponent has argued on the basis of one of them, suggests, with its clear reference to the two-logoi doctrine, that it is above all the sophists whom Aristotle has in mind.

Whenever and however it be that the antithesis of *nomos* and *physis* first arose, it did regularly involve a recognition of *physis* as a source of values and so as itself in some way prescriptive. Sometimes the appeal was simply to the nature of things, essentially to the nature of the phenomenal world. That is what is done by Hippias in the *Protagoras* (337c6–e2) when he addresses those present in the house of Callias with the words, 'I for my part regard you as all kinsmen and as belonging together and as fellow-citizens, by nature and not by law: for like is akin to like by nature, whereas law, a tyrant over human beings, in many things constrains us contrary to nature. We who know the nature of things must act in accordance with what is expected of us as a result.' Here Hippias is appealing to what is, in his view, really the case. Men *are* alike, and to treat them differently, namely as if they were not alike, is to apply a principle that is not in fact true. His starting point is here not different from that of Democritus when he claimed (DK 68B9 & 125) that it is by *nomos* that there is sweet, bitter, hot, cold, or colour, but in reality there are (merely) atoms and void.

But it is not easy to infer prescriptions simply from what is the case, and indeed some philosophers would dismiss the whole attempt as involving a fallacy – the so-called naturalistic fallacy. But in the ancient world the attempt was easier, or might seem to have been made so, because of the dynamic and often quasi-biological aspect of the meaning of Nature. And in many of the applications of the antithesis in the sophistic period the appeal is not to Nature in general, but to the nature of man or human nature, and this must have made the appeal easier still, since the urgency of many of the demands that spring from our own natures seems to give them a clear prescriptive force.

We stand at the latter end of a tradition which began with the

114

sophists and we are familiar with the major constituents in this tradition. So it is easy for us to underestimate the magnitude of the achievement of those who first clearly posed the problem of the relationship between laws and the requirements of human nature. Yet in another way we are perhaps well placed to understand, since we live in a world in which frequently it is not the validity of some state-maintained laws which is being challenged, but of all such laws either because of the restrictions they place on the individual, or because they stand in the way of political or other preferred overall objectives. Hippias had said that law constrains us contrary to nature *in many things*. But in Antiphon's treatise *On Truth* this has become 'the majority of the things which are just by *nomos* are in a state of open warfare with nature'. How then did Antiphon proceed to discuss the antithesis?

The answer lies in the papyrus fragments discovered earlier in the present century. But their interpretation faces us with considerable problems, not merely in relation to what Antiphon says elsewhere, but also problems of internal consistency or the lack of it. Progress in understanding these problems has not always been linear and straightforward. But there has been progress. The key to the first part of the first fragment (DK 87 A44) lies, as I have argued elsewhere,[1] in recognising that initially Antiphon is not stating his own view but is posing problems which he is proposing to investigate. This is after all what he himself says, as is clear once the correct reading is established in column 2 line 24 in the first papyrus fragment: 'it is for all these reasons that we are making our investigation'. What this means is that Antiphon is providing us with a discussion of the opposition between *nomos* and *physis* which is quite invaluable as giving us an insight into the way in which such themes could be discussed in the sophistic period.

The papyrus opens, at least where it begins to be readable, with the words 'Justice is therefore not to transgress the *nomima* (observances) of the city in which one lives as a citizen.' But, as the most recent commentator has well pointed out,[2] 'the opening statement can hardly represent a view of justice held by Antiphon, who immediately proceeds to recommend ignoring the laws when one can get away with

---

[1] 'The moral and political doctrines of Antiphon the Sophist, a reconsideration', *Proc. Camb. Philol. Soc.* 184 (1956–57) 26–9.

[2] T. J. Saunders, 'Antiphon the Sophist on Natural Laws (B44DK)', *Proc. Aristotelian Soc.* 78 (1977/78) 219–20.

it, and later has harsh things to say about laws and legal procedure actually in force. He is presumably stating a view of justice held by the man in the street' (cf. Xenophon, *Mem*. IV, IV.12). Antiphon's conclusion on this point is clearly stated: if one follows this view of justice in ordering one's life the results are contrary to nature.

The first step is thus to set up an antithesis: that which is required by law is contrary to that which is required by nature. We are then told that the advantages which are prescribed by the laws are fetters on nature, whereas the advantages which are prescribed by nature make for freedom. This might suggest that whatever is prescribed by nature is to be preferred to what is prescribed by the laws. This might seem to be supported by the statement that comes near the beginning of the papyrus, namely that a man would employ justice best for his own interests if he were to regard the laws as important when witnesses were present, but, when no witnesses are present, he were to regard the demands of nature as important. But there is some evidence that for Antiphon the matter was not to be regarded quite so simply. Life and death, he says, both belong to nature, and life results from things that are advantageous and death from things that are disadvantageous. Death then is disadvantageous, it would seem, even though it is instituted by nature. In other words not everything coming from *physis* is advantageous and it is the advantageous which is desirable.

This accordingly suggests that Antiphon, in attacking the norms set by society, is operating with a new criterion according to which right and wrong are identified with 'benefit' and 'damage'. These are of course 'natural' benefit and 'natural' damage. What is advantageous or beneficial helps nature and what helps nature is advantageous, and the expression 'helping nature' suggests that it is human nature rather than nature in general which is being helped or harmed as the case may be. It is what advantages man and his nature that is being treated as good, and it is argued that the provisions of the laws and norms of society do not help nature, but on the contrary are fetters and bonds imposed on it which prevent rather than contribute to what is required. This leaves open the question whether, exceptionally, some laws may actually help nature, a question which has become a matter of controversy,[3] since, whatever be the answer, the overriding *general* viewpoint of Antiphon's discussion is that 'a morality enforced by law

---

[3] Yes, T. J. Saunders, *op. cit.* and C. Moulton, 'Antiphon the Sophist *On Truth*', *Trans. Am. Philol. Ass.* 103 (1972) 329–50. No, E. A. Havelock, *The Liberal Temper in Greek Politics*, London 1957, Chapter 10.

and custom is contrary to nature and nature's way is to be preferred'.[4] Particularly scathing is the attack made on the inability and ineffectiveness of the law-courts and the legal system either to restrain the doer of injustice or to protect the victim or even to protect the person who is merely acting as a witness. All this is not helpful but harmful to nature and nature's way.

But if we ask what *is* nature's way, what we have of Antiphon's writings does not provide us with an answer. For answers to this question we must go to other sophistic sources, and I turn first to the views expressed by Callicles in Plato's *Gorgias* 482c4–486d1. The argument in the dialogue has reached the point where Socrates has secured an admission from Polus that to do wrong is more shameful than to suffer wrong. Callicles is not satisfied with the way the argument has developed, because, he says, it ignores a fundamental distinction, that between *physis* and *nomos*. Indeed it is interesting that he accuses Socrates of using what we have seen Aristotle was to call a widespread *topos*, that of moving in argument from one to the other without warning and so generating misleading contradictions in one's opponent's argument in order to discomfort and refute him.

Callicles then proceeds to argue that for the most part nature and *nomos* are opposed to each other. By nature everything which is worse is more shameful, and so suffering injustice is more shameful than doing it. Polus had argued that suffering injustice was worse for a person, but that doing injustice was more shameful, meaning by this more shameful by *nomos*. But Socrates improperly treated Polus as conceding that doing injustice was more shameful by nature. Callicles wishes to argue that this is most certainly not the case. Conventional laws are made by the majority who are weak. They make them in their own interests, and, through fear of stronger individuals than themselves getting a greater share than they can, they condemn getting more, and, being themselves inferior, they are happy to settle for equal shares for all alike. Consequently by this *nomos* or norm it is called unjust and shameful to seek to have more than is possessed by the majority. But by nature it is right that the better should have more than the worse, and the abler than the less able.

This is something which nature herself indicates, according to Callicles, in many ways, in the animal world, in relations between states and communities where human judgment has come to this conclusion, and in the behaviour of Heracles, mentioned in a famous passage of Pindar, when he carried off by force the cattle of Geryon. When a really strong and noble personality arises he will break out of the bondage of convention. He who was our slave rises up and becomes master, and there dawns the full light of natural justice. Two points are fundamental for the correct understanding of Callicles' position. The appeal to the evidence of what happens in such cases has been described by Paul Shorey as 'the most eloquent statement of the immoralist's case in European literature', but against this E. R. Dodds in his commentary on the passage was right to protest. The position held by Callicles is not immoralist – it involved the rejection of conventional right in favour of natural right as something claimed to be higher, better and morally superior. Secondly in appealing to what happens in nature Callicles is not guilty of arguing that simply because it happens that way in nature it is therefore better, in other words he is not guilty of simply reducing 'ought' to 'is' as the answer to the question what is right. Plato's language is clear and careful. The evidence from what happens is evidence that clear thinking people have come *to judge* that what is right by nature is superior to 'our' laws – it is the *nomos* or norm of nature because it is what nature *prescribes*.

After the conclusion of Callicles statement at 486d1 there follow a series of elaborate and important discussions and objections. The greater part of these are designed (of course by Plato) to give Plato an opportunity to introduce some of his own distinctive contributions to the debate. But Callicles' position is either clarified or some would say modified in certain directions. The man who for Callicles is the superior person is wiser, braver and more manly, and as a result it is appropriate that he should be a ruler. But only a ruler over other people, not over himself. This last would require that he should exercise self-control. Callicles insists that the freedom which is the prescription of nature involves the absence of any restraint on his desires – these are to be permitted to be as great as is possible and to be provided with whatever objects are desired. Luxury, lack of restraint and freedom coupled with the means of supplying the objects of desire, these are what constitute virtue and happiness (*aretē* and *eudaimonia*). The prescription of nature is to seek the maximum gratification of all desires.

This doctrine of sensual indulgence as the ideal for man is something to which Callicles gives his assent after long argument with Socrates. To what extent it represents the real direction of his thinking may be doubted. Certainly it was not this interpretation of Callicles' doctrine which appealed so strongly to Nietzsche when he uses his doctrine as to some degree a model for his own vision of the man who is above other men.[5] Nor is it a necessary consequence of Callicles' own earlier account of the behaviour of the superior man. This points rather in the direction of the Homeric hero's ideal of power and success. What we must remember is something which the greatness of Plato's art encourages us to forget. I believe that it is reasonable to conclude that Callicles was a real, historical figure. But *inside* a Platonic dialogue the characters are not real persons. In varying degrees Plato is taking account of the views and personalities of the real person lying behind the characters. But the actual arguments in the dialogues with hardly an exception are composed and manipulated by Plato himself. He is the producer, stage-manager and script-writer for the whole performance, and this will include in the present instance both the part played by Socrates and the part played by Callicles.

Accordingly it is probable that Plato here features the development of Callicles' doctrine in the direction of the maximum gratification of all desires not so much in order to discredit Callicles' position, but rather to give himself an opportunity to say where he himself parted company with Callicles. For Plato in fact agreed with Callicles in wishing to get away from conventional justice in order to move to something higher. For Plato Vulgar Justice must be replaced by Platonic Justice, the justice appropriate above all to the ruler and the philosopher. Both Plato and Callicles accept that *aretē* must involve the fulfilment of the needs of individual human beings. Such fulfilment is *eudaimonia*. But for Plato fulfilment involves a pattern of restraint in the satisfaction of desires, a pattern based on reason, whereas for Callicles neither reason nor restraint have anything to do with the matter. This is the fundamental point at which Callicles' Natural Justice departs utterly and absolutely from Platonic Justice.

But while Plato in the *Gorgias* found it, perhaps, not too difficult to refute the life-ideal of desires gratified without restraint, he had not really touched the hard core of Callicles' teaching. This was not simply that one must move away from vulgar justice on the grounds that it is inadequate and incomplete, but that it is to be rejected outright in favour of selfishness and seeking to get as much as possible for oneself.

[5] see E. R. Dodds, Appendix to his edition of Plato's Gorgias, and A. H. J. Knight, *Some aspects of the life and work of Nietzsche*, Cambridge 1933.

This is condemned indeed by popular morality, but Callicles had argued (483b4–c1) that such condemnations spring from the self-interest of others, the weak. Callicles is making a definite suggestion here that this involves an internal contradiction – selfishness is condemned in order to promote selfishness. Would not clear-headed selfishness lead to the outright rejection of everything prescribed by vulgar justice? This is a question not answered in the *Gorgias*, and this is no doubt one of the reasons why the whole issue is taken up again by Plato in the *Republic*.

By far the greater part of the first book of the *Republic* is devoted to expounding and criticising the views of the sophist Thrasymachus. As a result it forms a kind of unit by itself and this has led some to suppose that it was originally written, and perhaps published as a separate dialogue, the *Thrasymachus*. But the case for this view is not very strong, and the intimate relation of the first book to the rest of the *Republic* makes it on the whole unlikely. It has never been doubted that the opening statement by Thrasymachus represents the position actually held by him as a historical person. But it is followed, as so often in Plato, first by discussion and criticism, then by a new statement of Thrasymachus' position. Here there is a problem and three main views have been taken. First it can be supposed that Thrasymachus is merely muddled and confused. When his first position has been undermined or even demolished by Socrates he shifts his ground, quite improperly, to take up a new position. Secondly it is possible to suppose that Plato has manipulated Thrasymachus' position in a way that suits his own purposes. The second statement, on this view, will be unhistorical – it may represent in part a drawing out by Plato of what he regarded as the most significant of the implications of the earlier position, in part it may represent an outright substitution of a new position. Thirdly, the view which I myself advocate, namely that the second statement represents a reformulation of the position adopted right at the outset, without fundamental change, and above all without any inconsistency between the two positions except at the most superficial and trivial level, perhaps mainly and simply because Thrasymachus does not state all that he thinks right at the beginning.[6]

Whichever of these views be judged correct there can be no doubt

---

[6] For these views see e.g. my article, 'The doctrine of Thrasymachus in Plato's *Republic*', *Durham University Journal* 40 (1947/48) 19–27, and J. P. Maguire, 'Thasymachus–or Plato?', *Phronesis* 16 (1971) 142–63, both reprinted in C. J. Classen, *Sophistik* (Wege der Forschung), Darmstadt 1976, 545–88.

that the two positions ascribed to Thrasymachus (if they are two and not one) are of great historical interest and importance and their roots are planted deeply in the soil of the sophistic movement. It is the second position with which Plato is concerned most of all, and the whole of the rest of the *Republic* can be regarded as his answer to the question it raises, so that a fairly extended analysis is, I think, justified.

When he first enters the discussion (338c1–2) Thrasymachus says that Justice is the interest of the stronger or superior. When asked for further elucidation he declares that in each city it is the ruling body which is the stronger or superior, and whether this be a tyrant, a democracy or an aristocracy, in each case it makes the laws in its own interest, so that in all cities one and the same thing is just, the interest of the ruling body (338d5–339a3). But Socrates points out that rulers are liable to make mistakes as to their own interests, and if these mistakes are expressed in laws which it is just for the subjects to obey, it will follow that it will sometimes be just for them to seek the opposite of the interest of the rulers. Forced to choose between two positions, that justice consists in obeying the laws, and that justice consists in seeking the interest of the rulers, Thrasymachus refuses to accept the first and so, at least by implication, gives his assent to the second, by arguing that true rulers never make mistakes as to their interests, even though actual rulers do on occasion make mistakes as to their own interests.

Socrates then argues that to every Art there is a specific object and it is the whole nature of an art to seek to promote the interests of that object. Hence in the case of ruling the ruler qua ruler is concerned solely to promote the interests of those over whom he is ruling. To this Thrasymachus replies that Socrates is completely misrepresenting the true situation. The correct analogy is that of the shepherd and his flock. In the exercise of his art the shepherd may in a sense be said to be seeking the good of the flock, but it is only with the ultimate end of promoting his own interest or that of his master. This leads on to Thrasymachus' long speech in which he provides the second and more extended statement of his position. He now states that justice consists in pursuing another's good – so a ruler is just, it follows, if he seeks the interests of his subjects, whereas a subject is just if he seeks the interests of the stronger who is his ruler. Injustice on the other hand consists in seeking one's own good, and so for the ruler the interest of the stronger who is himself, and for the ruled the interest of the weaker, who are themselves, namely the ruled.

I believe that this identification of injustice with seeking one's own good and justice with seeking another's good is entirely consistent with the earlier claim that justice consists in seeking the interest of the ruler, provided one thing is accepted, namely that the statement that justice is to seek the interest of the ruler was made by looking at the matter from one viewpoint only, namely the viewpoint of the ruled. Once we ask what about justice from the viewpoint of the ruler, we can no longer say that justice consists in seeking the interest of the ruler, we must say that it consists in seeking the interest of the ruled.

However this may be, it is the last stated position of Thrasymachus, the equation of justice with seeking the interest of another, and injustice with seeking one's own interest, that Plato wishes to examine. Also it is the contention which is the more important from a historical point of view. For Thrasymachus claims two things in relation to his view when it has been stated in this second way. First the just ruled are foolish in seeking the interest of the ruler and the just ruler is foolish in seeking the interest of the ruled. A sensible and wise man seeks only his own interest. In all circumstances and for all persons justice is folly and unwisdom. Secondly it is injustice which is the true virtue for man since it is by pursuing injustice that men achieve *aretē* and so *eudaimonia*, since it is by this path alone that they fulfil their needs.

Thrasymachus does not actually use the terminology of the *nomos–physis* antithesis. But he is rightly to be placed among those who employ it, since in rejecting vulgar justice in favour of vulgar injustice he is elevating vulgar injustice to the status of what is right by nature, and what is right by nature is, in the language of the *nomos–physis* antithesis, natural justice. This is recognised early in Book II (359c3–6) where Glaucon does not hesitate to express the problem raised by Thrasymachus in the actual terms of the *nomos–physis* opposition. What we have in the *Republic* is a restatement of the position assumed by Callicles in the *Gorgias* without the complication of alliance with the doctrine of fulfilment of desires. It was significant from a number of different points of view. In a period of considerable social change it gave expression to the felt need to shake off what was felt to be the overly restrictive and inappropriate heritage of traditional moral norms and requirements. The revolt against nineteenth-century values in the present century may serve as an analogy. Secondly it raised the banner of freedom, by asking the question why should we have to submit ourselves to frustrating controls upon our natural behaviour.

But it was not merely negative and did not proclaim a programme of simply dropping out and yielding to unguided and purposeless drift. It advocated an alternative policy for living, the rational pursuit of one's own interest. Finally it raised a point of considerable philosophical interest, familiar to us since Kant as the requirement for the autonomy of the will and the rejection of heteronomy. This is the point taken up by Plato. Thrasymachus has raised the question why should I restrict the pursuit of my own interests for the sake of others, and, ever since, this has been one of the central questions in ethics. For the first answer, that it is because this is the duty prescribed for men, raises the further question why should I need to pursue a duty imposed on me from outside me, and so prescribed heteronomously. Plato in the remainder of the *Republic* offers his own answer. To many it has seemed less than satisfactory and certainly he has not disposed of the question for all time. But at least the path that he followed was the right and perhaps the only possible one to follow with any chance of success. For he proceeds by an analysis of the structure and functioning of the individual human soul, to argue that the source of what is right is indeed not a heteronomous prescription, but autonomous because it is a prescription arising from within our own natures. To that extent Plato accepts the challenge of Thrasymachus, and I have no doubt that that is why he placed the statement of Thrasymachus' views where it is, namely right at the beginning of the *Republic*.

This I believe is the real significance of the doctrine of Thrasymachus. Nonetheless we must not forget that it also had a much more subordinate, practical and indeed political role to play. For the doctrine of the rightness of the pursuit of self-interest could be applied not merely to and by individuals, but also to and by communities. And that it was so applied we learn from Thucydides who was clearly very well aware of its importance and chose to develop the theme at some length in his History.

First the Mytilenaean debate (III.38–48). Mytilene, a non-subject ally of the Athenians on the island of Lesbos, revolted in the fourth year of the Peloponnesian War, in 428 B.C. So outraged were the Athenians that when the revolt had been crushed they decided that the whole adult male population should be put to death, but on the day after this decision there was a fresh debate about it in the Assembly at Athens. Cleon argues in favour of maintaining the original decision, by claiming that the decision taken satisfies the claims both of justice and self-interest, the first because the gravity of the Mytilenaeans' crime makes the punishment appropriate, and the second because such a deterrent punishment is needed to safeguard the interests of the Athenian domination. But he seems to admit that there might be room for debate on the score of justice, for example if the Athenian rule itself was wrong. He then goes on to say (40.4) 'but if you propose to hold power all the same in spite of its not being proper, then I want you to realise that you must in your own interest punish them though it be contrary to what is right, or else you must give up your empire and cultivate honesty without danger'. Despite the fact that this follows some rather rude remarks made by Cleon about sophists, he is obviously arguing that the claims of expediency or self-interest must override those of conventional morality. So convincing is this approach that Diodotus in his reply argues on the basis of the self-interest of the Athenians (III.44.1) and it is on this basis that he comes to the opposite conclusion from Cleon. Such an approach is often called non-moral or even immoral. And so it inevitably seems to someone committed to a belief in traditional norms. Yet the way in which it is put forward shows that for those who were putting it forward such a view was itself moral, representing a different morality, that of nature, in contrast to the vulgar justice of traditional morality.

The second occasion relates to the island of Melos which had refused to join the Athenian confederacy like the other islands, and in 416 B.C. was attacked by an Athenian army, besieged and forced to surrender. All the adult males were put to death. By what has been called a curious device Thucydides constructed a colloquy between Athenian envoys and the Melian government which constitutes the famous Melian Dialogue (V.85–111). The Athenians begin (89) by saying that they do not wish to deal in fine words about alleged rights and wrongs between the two sides, for the Melians know as well as the Athenians do that right only comes into question in cases where there is equality of power whereas the strong do what they have the power to do and these things are accepted by the weak. The Melians accept that the Athenians are appealing to the standard of interest rather than that of (conventional) justice, and the debate turns (90) to the question of whether it is really in the interests of the Athenians to deny conventional justice to those in danger. It is not altogether easy for the Melians to make this argument convincing until they come to their conclusion, namely that the Athenians are likely to forfeit divine support once they abandon (conventional) justice. To this the Athenians reply (105.2) that what they believe about the gods and what they know about men lead them to conclude that it is a general and necessary law of nature to rule in cases where one possesses the power. 'This is not a *nomos* that was made by us nor were we the first to use it when it had been made. We are merely acting in accordance with it after finding it already in existence, and we shall leave it to exist for ever in the future. We know that you or any one else with the same power as us would act in the same way.'

All the theories so far summarised have in one way or another been critical of traditional *nomoi* and have given their preference to *physis*. But this was by no means the whole of the story. Already in antiquity three quite distinct ways came to be formulated for the interpretation of the overall course of human history, culture and civilisation. Although clearly distinguishable, however, such views were presented in many different forms by different writers at different times, and their earliest appearances take us back into the period of myths. The first of these has come to be known as the Theory of Decline, more familiarly referred to as the myth of a Golden Age which is followed by increasing degeneration. This view is found in a fairly developed form in the myth of the five Races succeeding each other in time in Hesiod's *Works and Days*. The second is the Cyclical Theory of History or the myth of Eternal Recurrence, which may also have been known to Hesiod.[7] It was probably oriental in origin, based on Babylonian astrology and the doctrine of the Great Year, and was given physical expression in a number of Presocratic cosmologies. The third view was the Theory of Progress, according to which there has been and will continue to be an overall improvement, even if subject to interruptions, in the human condition.

Sophistic theories of the nature of society must be discussed later on. But one aspect of the Theory of Progress is directly relevant to the *nomos–physis* controversy. For on this view man began in a state of nature and then proceeded to one of increasing civilisation. This progression is expressed in a particular way in the famous Myth put into the mouth of Protagoras in Plato's *Protagoras* (320c8–322d5), which in all probability is based to some extent on doctrines of the historical Protagoras as published in such works as his treatise 'On the Original State of Man'. When the first men came up to the light of day, they were sufficiently equipped with innate qualities to enable them to house, feed and clothe themselves. But they lived separately from each

[7] *Works and Days* 174–5, on which see E. R. Dodds, *The Ancient Concepts of Progress*, Oxford 1973, 3 n. 4.

other and because of their physical inferiority they were dangerously vulnerable to attacks by wild animals. For self-protection they tried coming together to form groups. But when they did they proceeded to act unjustly towards one another – the groups broke up and they continued to be destroyed. So Zeus sent the two moral virtues, *aidōs* and *dikē* – mutual respect and right or justice to be distributed so that all should have a share in them.

This means that nature alone is regarded by Protagoras as insufficient – it is a necessary condition for the maintenance of effective communities that there should be added to man's innate equipment the requisite political virtues. And in the explanation and further interpretation which follows the myth it is made plain that the justice of which Protagoras is speaking consists of the *nomima* of the community. In other words Protagoras has produced a fundamental defence of *nomos* in relation to *physis*, in that *nomos* is a necessary condition for the maintenance of human societies. Just what *kind* of *nomos* Protagoras contemplated will be considered further below.

A more explicit and conscious defence of the claims of *nomos* as against *physis* is found in the so-called *Anonymus Iamblichi* which provides a manual of advice on how to succeed in life.[8] First it is necessary to be born, but this is not sufficient. The natural qualities possessed from birth require to be supplemented and developed by a desire for things that are good and noble (so this is not innate in us), by hard work, practice and instruction over a long period of time, and the lack of any one of these will prevent the achievement of the final goal. In other words, we might say, nature needs to be developed by nurture if man is to achieve *aretē*, a doctrine already found in Protagoras (DK 80B3) for whom the whole of human life was a process of ethical and social education. Stress is laid by the *Anonymus* on the need for the programme of education and training to be continued over a long time, and this includes training in the art of speaking fluently as well (*Euglossia* cf. 88A17) which is regarded as part of the prolonged process. In contrast a certain *technē* concerning *logoi* can be acquired quickly, a phrase which suggests a direct reference to the art of the two opposed Logoi, and while it is said to be learnable quickly, it is not said, *pace* some interpreters, that it is to be excluded altogether from

---

[8] for the best analysis see A. Levi, in his posthumous *Storia della Sofistica* Naples 1966, Ch. 6 which was first published separately in 1941 and is translated into German in C. J. Classen, *Sophistik*, (1976) 612–26.

the processes of education. What is being stated is probably simply that education involves far *more* than merely the formal technique of antilogic.

The talents so acquired and developed must be used only for purposes that are good, and this will be achieved if a man gives his support to the laws and to what is just. From this one is justified in inferring that the end for man has a social and juridical basis (so Adolfo Levi), but it certainly does not mean what was maintained by Richard Roller, namely that the whole treatise is designed to exalt the position of the State. For the *Anonymus* goes on to say that the reason why one should subordinate self-seeking to respect for the laws is because men cannot live alone and are required to associate in order to survive and flourish, and communal life is impossible without submission to law. Even if, what is not possible, there were to be a man who did not himself need the help and support of society, submission to law would still be necessary for his survival, since all other men would be his enemy, and with the help of their own laws and in virtue of their numbers they would be too strong for him. In fact the strength of the laws is itself something that is based on nature. This provides, at least indirectly, a refutation of the principle proclaimed by Callicles. It is not in fact the man who scorns vulgar justice who is going to be strong, intelligent and successful, it is rather the man who exercises control over himself and co-operates with the society in which he lives who will best achieve these qualities.

The treatise closes with praise of communities where law is observed – these are in a condition of *eunomia*, in contrast with states where law and justice have departed and *anomia* prevails with the consequences that follow, of which the worst is anarchy leading to tyranny by a single ruler. Under *eunomia* those who have good fortune can enjoy it in safety and without fear of attack, while those who are unfortunate receive help from those who enjoy good fortune because of their association in common and the trust which arises from the *eunomia*.

A similar set of ideas is found in certain chapters of the speech No. XXV attributed to Demosthenes. Though it is possibly a mistake to try to identify this as an extract from a separate treatise, it nonetheless does preserve arguments from the same kind of source as the *Anonymus Iamblichi*. The whole life of human beings, it maintains, in cities great and small is governed by nature and by laws. But nature is a thing lacking in order, and varies with the individual, whereas the laws are universal, constitute an ordered whole, and are the same for all. Nature when bad frequently seeks bad ends, and men in such cases will be found to be doing wrong. But the laws seek what is just, noble and advantageous (par. 15–16). They secure the good government and safety of the city – if they are removed, and each man is given the power to do what he wishes, then not only is constituted society abolished, but our life would differ in no way from that of wild animals (par. 20). Four grounds are selected from the many as to why all should obey the law – it is a discovery and gift from the gods, it is something decided upon by men of wisdom, it is a correction of wrong actions both voluntary and involuntary, and it is an agreement common to a city as a whole according to which it is appropriate that all in the city should conduct their lives (par. 16).

These grounds have been criticised as giving a series of three mutually exclusive accounts of the origin of *nomoi*, due to divine origin, individual legislations, and social contract.[9] But the criticism is misplaced, there are not three grounds but four, and these are selected from still more, they are not theories of the origin of law, but reasons for accepting laws in a city, and they are cumulative not mutually exclusive. Two of them were in fact combined by Aristotle in Aristotle's reference to the sophist Lycophron (DK 83A3) when he says that *Nomos* on one view becomes an agreement and a guarantee of things that are just between citizens, but not something that is capable of making citizens good and just. The attribution to Lycophron of the theory of a social contract is not justified by the actual words used by Aristotle, despite assertions frequently made to this effect. We do however find the doctrine that the laws are agreements referred to by Glaucon in Plato's *Republic* Book II (359a3) in such a way as to suggest that the doctrine may already have been well known (see further below, pp. 147ff.)

The appeal from *nomos* to *physis* was in one of its aspects intended to be destructive of Nomos in the sense of traditionally accepted norms of behaviour. But it was probably never (or at least hardly ever!) intended to be *merely* destructive. Its real object was to substitute a more satisfying and satisfactory set of norms in place of those that were no longer fully acceptable. No doubt the real reason why many of the traditional norms came under attack was the process of social and political change that was in fairly full flood in Athens in the

<hr />

[9] Pohlenz followed by Untersteiner, *I sofisti*, 2nd edn Milan 1967, Vol. II p. 210.

later part of the fifth century B.C. But the actual attack was in part intellectual, and the intellectual attack had as its starting point the contention that traditional norms if accepted without critical examination involved internal contradictions and inconsistencies. What was being called for was their replacement where necessary, but only where necessary, and replacement by something that would be intellectually satisfactory, in other words something that would be rational and internally consistent, as well as taking due account of the actual natures of human beings. Once the matter is stated in this way, it should begin to be clear how much there is of common ground between Socrates, Plato and the major sophists. First all of them are asking how a man should live. Secondly they agree in expecting that any answer will be expressed in terms of *aretai* or virtues such as manliness (*andreia*, traditionally rendered as 'courage'), wisdom and so on. But none of them is completely satisfied with ordinary or current accounts of such virtues, and they are united in the wish to go behind such accounts to some more adequate account. Neither Socrates nor Plato are concerned simply to preserve ordinary beliefs.[10] Thirdly they assume that the sum of virtues will constitute virtue (in the singular) or *aretē* understood as meaning fulfilment of function, and, in the case of human beings, fulfilment of a man's function, this function being regarded as something rooted in his nature. This means that virtue and the virtues are always beneficial to the person practising them. Yet ordinary or current accounts of the virtues suggest that their exercise does not always produce benefit to the practitioner. The need to resolve this problem gave added urgency as Plato saw it to the need to go behind ordinary accounts of the virtues.

Earlier in this chapter it has been argued that Protagoras was not one of those who regarded nature as a sufficient principle for the maintenance of ordered political communities. He supposed that in addition to nature *nomos* was essential. Does this mean that unlike Plato, Socrates and the majority of the sophists he saw no need to criticise or go behind the actual laws and norms of any particular community? Just this has indeed often been suggested, but I believe it to be mistaken as an interpretation of the position ascribed to Protagoras by Plato.

The interpretation which I believe to be mistaken goes like this. In the myth and the logos that follows it in the *Protagoras* the sophist has

---

[10] for a defence of this statement see now T. Irwin, *Plato's Moral Theory* Oxford 1977, 208–9 with note 33.

maintained that political *aretē* is not something which comes to men by nature, but is something which is learnt as a result of a continuing process of instruction inside each and every community. This is a process to which all in the community are inescapably subjected. Nonetheless within the community there are some men, like Protagoras himself, who have a special and superior ability for teaching goodness, and as a result their pupils make exceptional progress (327e1–328b5). Now it has been maintained[11] that Protagoras is simply identifying goodness with the actual traditions of an existing civilised state – there is no moral standard more ultimate than the standard of respectability current in a given society. What Protagoras on this view is claiming is simply an exceptional ability to discern and to teach the actual traditions of any particular community. This has seemed to fit well with the doctrine ascribed to Protagoras in the *Theaetetus* according to which whatever practices seem just and laudable to each city are so for that city as long as it holds them. But I believe this cannot be a correct interpretation. For this doctrine has as a corollary that while whatever seems just to any city is so, in place of practices which are harmful the wise man (the sophist) substitutes others that are beneficial (*Theaetet.* 167c4–7) and these must be actually, objectively, beneficial and not merely those which seem so. As has already been seen, the man—measure doctrine does not apply to terms like 'good', 'healthy' or 'advantageous'. Thus Protagoras neither accepts the standards of respectability of any particular society as an *ultimate* moral standard ... nor does he simply impart a medley of traditions lacking any theoretical basis.[12] He like Socrates and Plato is committed to moving from vulgar justice when this is shown to be inadequate to something superior and more beneficial.

[11] e.g. by A. E. Taylor, *Plato, the man and his work* London ⁴1937, 245–7.
[12] for a good statement and development of this point see *Plato Protagoras*, trans. C. C. W. Taylor, Oxford 1976, pp. 100–2.

11

Can virtue be taught?

The discussion of the relationship between nature and *aretē*, leads directly to what was one of the major themes of discussion both in the second half of the fifth century B.C. and in very nearly all of the earlier dialogues of Plato, namely the question whether *aretē* or virtue can be taught. The traditional translation of *aretē* by 'virtue' is in some danger of obscuring the importance of this debate. In general terms, the virtue denoted by *aretē* comprised all those qualities in a man which made for success in Greek society and which could confidently be expected to secure the admiration of a man's fellow-citizens, followed in many cases by substantial material rewards. If all this can be taught this was bound to have a fundamental influence on the functioning and structure of the society in which the teaching took place. As has already been briefly mentioned in Chapter 4 (above p. 37) the acquisition of this kind of learning makes it possible for *anyone* to rise to any heights in a given community. It is thus a key to social mobility. An incidental result is that those who are able to develop such qualities in others, that is those who teach, have a particularly important part to play in promoting social change, or at least in helping to make it possible. Under Pericles Athenian society was changing greatly and it is no accident that it was he above all who favoured and encouraged the sophistic movement at Athens.

The question whether virtue can be taught is the subject-matter of chapter VI in the *Dissoi Logoi*, a chapter which provides a convenient if not very profound summary of some of the arguments involved. It has been maintained, we are told in the opening paragraph, that wisdom and virtue can neither be taught nor learned. This logos, it is stated, is neither new nor true, and the chapter concludes with the statement 'I do not say that wisdom and virtue are teachable, but only that the above-mentioned proofs are sufficient for me.'[1] The purpose

---

[1] The standard text here is regularly emended to say 'but the above mentioned proofs are *not* sufficient for me'. But this destroys the antithesis, and the reading of the manuscripts should be retained, as e.g. Untersteiner, *Sofisti, Testimonianze e Frammenti*, fasc. III p. 182.

of this final statement is presumably to maintain an element of scepticism about the objective validity of statements of this kind – its meaning will then be '*I* am quite satisfied as to their teachability whatever others may say.' Indeed we can well understand that the ✱ sophistic profession as a whole simply could not accept the doctrine that virtue cannot be taught, and Protagoras was quite forthright on the point, as represented to us in Plato's *Theaetetus*. We could not expect any sophist to disagree, any more than we would expect a modern teaching profession to accept the view that teaching is impossible.

Some five arguments are mentioned in the *Dissoi Logoi* in support of the unpalatable doctrine that virtue cannot be taught. The first is that it is not possible, if you were to hand something over to someone else, that you should still retain that thing. An argument of this kind can only have arisen inside the sophistic movement rather than from outside it. It suggests the view expounded by Gorgias in the third part of his *On Nature* that it is not possible to communicate what one knows to anyone else. The compiler of the *Dissoi Logoi* has no difficulty in dismissing it as 'merely silly', since he knows, as does everyone else, that there are teachers who teach reading and writing, while each such teacher continues to possess knowledge of what he teaches, and likewise with those who play the lyre. This suggests that whoever it was who compiled the *Dissoi Logoi*, he was not speaking as a supporter of Gorgias, just as the conclusion of the chapter suggests equally that we are not dealing with a disciple of Protagoras.

The remaining four arguments however do certainly have affinities with those which Protagoras was concerned to answer. They are that there would have been recognised teachers of virtue as of music, if virtue could be taught, that wise men would have handed on their wisdom to their friends and their families, that some pupils have been to sophists and have gained no benefit from them, and many persons have risen to eminence who have *not* associated with sophists. It will be convenient to consider these arguments in their more extended form as seen in the argument in Plato's *Protagoras*; Protagoras at the opening of the dialogue is presented with a new pupil, Hippocrates, and he states what he proposes to teach him 'such prudence in domestic affairs as will best enable him to regulate his own household, and such wisdom in public affairs as will best qualify him to speak and act in affairs of state' (318e). Socrates asks is this the art of politics and is Protagoras undertaking to make men good citizens, and Protagoras agrees (319a). Socrates replies that he had supposed that his art could not be taught, and he gives two grounds: (1) the Athenians are agreed to be wise men, yet, while they call in experts in the assembly to advise them on technical matters, they regard all citizens alike as capable of advising them on matters pertaining to the city (319b–d); (2) the wisest and best of the citizens are not able to hand this virtue on to others. So Pericles educated his sons well in all that could be taught by teachers, but he did not try to teach them, or have them taught his own wisdom, but left them to pick it up unaided (319d–320b).

Now Protagoras, it has been pointed out, is in a difficult position. He is apparently confronted with the choice of admitting that virtue cannot be taught and that his profession is a fraud, or of declaring that the theory of Athenian democracy is false, and his patron, Pericles, is ignorant of the true nature of political virtue. His reply takes the form of a myth, followed by a set argument (logos).

The myth proper extends from 320c8 to 322d5. It is followed by an explanatory passage 322d5–323a4, and this in turn is followed by what might seem to be a series of independent arguments down to 324d1. Then Protagoras says one difficulty still remains (that of the sons of good men). 'For this point, Socrates, I shall not now tell you a myth, but a logos.' This sentence makes two things plain: the logos begins here only and not earlier at 323a4, and in some sense the discussion of the myth is regarded as continuing right down to this point, 324d1. As the myth proper clearly ends at 322d5, this can only mean that the whole section 322d5–324d1 is regarded as an explanation and application of the myth. The last sentence of the section then, 324c5–d1, must be regarded as summarising the contents of the myth.

The myth proper (320c8–322d5) describes how, before the fated day on which mortal creatures were to come up to the light from inside the earth, Epimetheus distributed the various 'powers' among the animals on an equalising principle, to secure them protection both against one another and against the elements (320d–321c). But human beings received none of these powers and so lacked protection. Accordingly, Prometheus stole for them skill in crafts together with fire, thus enabling them to live. Clearly all this takes place *before* men come up to the light of day for the first time. On reaching the earth's surface, men develop religion, speech, and the material elements of civilisation. For defence against wild animals they founded fortified posts (*poleis*), but as they lacked the art of politics injustice prevented them from living together and they soon scattered again (322a–b). Accordingly, Zeus sent Hermes to give men *aidōs* and *dikē* to secure their protection. The crafts had been distributed among men in the same way as the powers among the animals, namely different crafts to different people. But *aidōs* and *dikē* are to be given to all men, and all men are to share in them. Any man who is unable to share in them is to be killed, as being a plague to the city.

Having shown in this way that all men are regarded as possessing some share in justice and political virtue, Protagoras immediately goes on to declare that this share is not *by nature*, nor is it acquired of its own accord, but from instruction and by practice (323c3–324d1). Men do not punish others for natural or chance defects, but they do punish them for failure to learn. In fact, in civilised societies punishment is a sort of teaching. Punishment is inflicted for deficiencies in justice and virtue. So on both grounds justice and virtue are regarded as teachable. So much Protagoras bases on his myth, and before leaving it he sums up the two main conclusions once again: virtue is shared in by all and can be the product of teaching (324c5–d1).

At this point Protagoras abandons the myth and proceeds with his logos. Three main points remain to be dealt with: (1) how all men get their share in virtue if not by nature; (2) why good men on the common view do not teach their sons virtue; (3) why the sons of outstanding men so often fail to show the excellence of their parents. He answers that as virtue is the basis of all activities, so it is taught in all the standard forms of teaching – by parents, nurses, school-teachers, music-teachers, and gymnastic instructors. In addition, it is taught by the whole community through laws and punishments. It is important to notice that Protagoras is not simply saying that people absorb the traditions of the community in which they live unconsciously – it is no chance matter, it is an essential part of the formal teaching all receive. It was Socrates who had suggested the unconscious view of moral education. Protagoras' answer is quite definite: good men do have their sons educated in virtue, and take great trouble over it (cf. especially 325d7–9). His point is that the teaching of virtue is universal throughout the community and that those who teach it have no special *names* as teachers of virtue. It is the same point he made earlier in the dialogue when he said there had been many sophists before himself who lacked only the name (316d3–e5).

Finally, the difference between parents and children in virtue is to be explained as due to variations in natural aptitude in the persons concerned. This will always show itself when all people have practically the same teaching and the same opportunities to learn. In addition, some people get more schooling than others (326c3–6) and some teachers are better than others. Such a teacher Protagoras considers himself to be (328a8–b5).

The logos which so concludes is not a continuation of the myth, it is rather an alternative to it. So Protagoras claims that the logos and the myth each show that virtue can be taught and explain the difference in virtue between sons and fathers (328c3–6). Both likewise clearly offer explanations of how all men share in virtue. Accordingly, the universal instruction in virtue in the logos should be regarded as an alternative statement of the conferring of *aidōs* and *dikē* by Zeus in the myth. The two are the same thing, the one expressed in mythical form, the other in rationalised form. The conferring of *aidōs* and *dikē is* the teaching which all people receive in the community.

So interpreted, Protagoras' reply to Socrates' objections is consistent throughout. To recapitulate, Socrates objected that virtue could not be taught, because all men are regarded as sharing in it, and those pre-eminent in virtue do not hand on their pre-eminence to their sons. Protagoras replies that all men share in virtue *because* they are all taught it, and the difference between parents and sons is due to differences in natural aptitudes for learning.

Protagoras' account of the way in which education proceeds in a community is plausible and extremely persuasive. It is certainly not faulted by Socrates in the elaborate discussions that constitute the remainder of the dialogue. Yet at the conclusion Socrates maintains (361a–c) that both Protagoras and himself have now moved to the opposite position from that at which they started. Socrates had begun by denying that virtue can be taught while Protagoras maintained that it could. At the conclusion however Socrates holds that virtue can be taught, and claims that the implication of Protagoras' position is that it cannot be taught. Socrates was able to arrive at this contention only as a result of the elaborate series of discussions about virtue with which the dialogue is concerned from 329b onwards. There Socrates maintains two things: (1) that the only thing that can be taught is knowledge, and (2) that virtue is knowledge, and that the various virtues are ultimately identical with each other and so constitute a single unitary virtue, which in turn results from the application of some kind of unitary knowledge constituting what might be called the knowledge of how to be a good man.

In fact Protagoras' position was consistent throughout the dialogue, and the suggestion that by the end he has reversed his stand is based on no more than illusion and mystification. Socrates in his conclusion (361b3–5) claims that Protagoras is now trying to say that virtue is something other than knowledge. But it is necessary to understand that knowledge can be of a number of different kinds. One now familiar modern distinction is that between knowing *how* to do something, and knowing *that* something is the case. Again we can know something by acquaintance when we are or have been directly confronted by it, and this will be different from the knowledge which is based on descriptions. Socrates is proceeding on the standard Socratic argument, according to which one can only be said to know what one is talking about when one is in a position to give a definition or other verbal specification of it, and it is this concept of knowledge which underlies all the arguments about the virtues from 329b onwards. And he insists on the supposition that in the case of the virtues this will be a single universal knowledge of what virtue is.

Protagoras simply does not accept this. As has been excellently said by C. C. W. Taylor,[2] what Protagoras is committed to explaining is (a) that it is possible to teach someone how to be a good man, in a broad sense of 'teach' which includes conditioning in social mores as well as instruction in specific techniques such as rhetoric, and (b) that the settled states of character which produce the conduct specified as appropriate to the various particular virtues (e.g. just or courageous actions) are not identical with one another.

Plato returned to the problem in the *Meno*, which was very probably composed somewhat later than the *Protagoras*. It opens with a direct question by Meno: 'Can you tell me, Socrates, whether virtue can be taught? Or is it not teachable, but something acquired by practice. Or if it is neither to be obtained by practice or by learning, does it come to human beings by nature [*physis*] or in some other way?' The answer, Socrates replies, requires an answer to the question what is Virtue. No satisfactory answer is in fact reached in the dialogue, but eventually it is agreed that one can perhaps proceed on a basis described as hypothetical. By proceeding in this way we can say that, if virtue can be taught, it is knowledge, but if it cannot be taught it is not

---

[2] *Plato, Protagoras translated with notes* by C. C. W. Taylor, Oxford 1976, p. 214.

knowledge. Meno is, then, perhaps rather too easily, brought to agree that, as there are no clearly identifiable teachers of virtue, it follows that virtue is not something that is taught. It may be noticed incidentally that the sophists are dismissed as certainly not teachers – they make their pupils worse, and are a visible plague and corruption of those who frequent them (91c).

But at this stage in the *Meno* (96d) Socrates has second thoughts. It is not only under the guidance of knowledge that human actions are done well and rightly. Virtue may indeed be directed by knowledge, but this is not the only way. Right opinion (*orthē doxa*) can be as good a guide as knowledge for the purpose of acting rightly. Both knowledge and right opinion are acquired and do not come by nature. Both statesmen and others act on the basis of opinion not knowledge when they act rightly and the very expression *orthē* for right in the case of opinion suggests at least a consciousness of the sophistic doctrine of the *orthos logos*, an expression which is also used by Plato himself on occasion (cf. *Phaedo* 73a10, *Laws* 890d7, *Critias* 109b2). The conclusion that might have been expected is that since right opinion is acquired it also is acquired by teaching, and it seems likely that Plato was well aware that this would be the standard sophistic conclusion. But he will not accept this conclusion. Right opinion is acquired, yes, but not by teaching since teaching is to be related only to knowledge. It remains that the position of statesmen acting on right opinion must be no different from that of prophets and tellers of oracles, who under divine inspiration utter many things that are true but have no knowledge of what they are saying. Plato, of course, cannot bring himself to say that the *sophists* are acting under any such inspiration, but the implication of the discussion in the *Meno* is that, to the extent that they possess right opinion, if they ever do, in his view, possess it, they have somehow or other acquired some degree of insight. To the extent that they are able to communicate this insight it would follow that they would be performing a function of value to the community.

From Socrates' insistence that virtue is knowledge it follows that vice and wrongdoing can only be due to ignorance. This in turn leads to the famous Socratic contention that 'no one sins deliberately', taken as meaning that if one possesses knowledge of what is good and bad one invariably does what is good. Rather to the surprise of commentators, we find Protagoras in the dialogue that bears his name giving his assent to just that proposition (*Prot.* 352c8–d3). Yet both Protagoras and Socrates are well aware that this is not the ordinary view. As Socrates says (352d): 'You are aware that most people will not listen to you and me, but say that many while knowing what is best are not willing to perform it, though they have the power, and do other things instead. And whenever I asked them what was the reason for this, they say that those who act so are acting under the influence of pleasure or pain or some one of the things mentioned just now' [namely inbuilt impulsiveness or anger (*thumos*), pleasure, pain, sexual desire, and frequently fear]. The result is that they look upon knowledge as a slave who is dragged about by all the rest (352b–c).

The surprise at Protagoras' agreement with Socrates at this point is perhaps in part the product of concentration on the positive aspect of Socrates' teaching, namely that virtue is knowledge and that wrong-doing is consequently a matter of intellectual failure. There is certainly no evidence that Protagoras himself held the doctrine that no one does wrong voluntarily. Yet at a fundamental level there is no need for surprise. Both Socrates and Protagoras believe in education as the key to all social and political problems. They differ radically about its content, but that is all. They believe that if only people could be brought to understand the wrongness of their actions they would not do them. Neither Socrates nor Protagoras is prepared to accept the doctrine, clearly as well known in their day as in ours, that people cannot be expected to resist their own impulses.

The doctrine that virtue can be taught leads naturally on to the celebrated theory of punishment developed by Protagoras. This is best stated in the words which Plato assigns to him (*Prot.* 324a–c): 'No one punishes those who do wrong, simply concentrating on the fact that the man had done wrong in the past, unless he is taking blind vengeance like a wild animal. Someone who aims to punish in a rational way does not do so because of the wrong action that has been committed – for that would not undo what is past – but he does so for the sake of the future so that neither the wrongdoer himself nor anyone else who sees him punished will do wrong again. A man who holds this view considers that virtue can be taught by education. For at the very least he is punishing in order to deter'.

12

The theory of society

It has often been said that political thought begins with the Greeks, and of all the political writings that survive from antiquity the first and most famous is surely Plato's *Republic*. Neither its greatness nor its originality can possibly be questioned. Yet concerning it Diogenes Laertius reports a strange tradition (III.37 and 57), namely that according to Aristoxenus (who was writing in the later part of the fourth century B.C.) almost the whole of the *Republic* was to be found written in the *Antilogica* of Protagoras. An attempt was made to emend the text so that it would be only the *beginning* (so perhaps Book I) against which Aristoxenus was levelling his charge. But the story was cited also by Favorinus of Arles in the second century A.D. without any such restriction so that it looks as if the surviving text correctly preserves what Aristoxenus had said.

What then is its significance? It goes without saying that no one in modern times has believed for a moment in the literal truth of the allegation. It is part of a series of charges of plagiarism brought against Plato by hostile critics and many are satisfied to dismiss it simply as a malicious invention. Yet however malicious the charge may have been, it could only have been made if there was at least some slight basis for comparison, however superficial. In other words it *is* evidence that Protagoras treated at least some of the themes which concerned Plato in the *Republic*. Naturally, this is the point at which speculation begins. Possibly Protagoras had outlined his own version of the ideal State, or at least something parallel to the first stage of Plato's ideal State, the 'City of Pigs' in *Republic* Book II. Others have thought of the emancipation of women in the *Republic* as something that might have been anticipated by Protagoras. This is not disproved by the statement in Aristotle's *Politics* (1266a34ff., cf. 1274b9–11) that no other thinker than Plato had proposed such novelties as community of wives and children or common meals for women, since Aristophanes, as we shall see, had already attempted to ridicule what must have amounted to a kind of Women's Rights movement which was known already in fifth-century Athens. In the absence of further evidence it is simply not possible to say what may have been the themes actually treated by Protagoras. But it is likely that these were substantial and were not simply confined to the application of the two-logoi principle to political matters.

The only positive indications that we have concerning Protagoras' views about the nature of human societies are to be found in the myth put into his mouth in the *Protagoras* 320c onwards (DK 80C1), of which I have already made considerable use in earlier chapters. The logical starting point for human societies is the same both for Protagoras, for Plato, and for Aristotle, namely the fact that the individual human being is not self-sufficient. But the operative lack of self-sufficiency is different in each case. For Plato the first needs are for food, shelter and clothing (*Rep.* 369d), for Aristotle the first coming-together of individuals is for the purpose of procreation, in the myth of Protagoras (322a–b) it is in order to secure protection against the attacks of wild animals. It was for this that men needed to come together and establish cities (*Poleis*), perhaps in the primary sense of that term, namely a town or citadel fortified for defence against attack.

Before such comings-together men had lived scattered and dispersed. They had however already discovered dwelling places, clothes, shoes and bedding, they had learnt to talk and had begun to worship the gods, and possessed sufficient skill with their hands to provide themselves with food. On the basis of these statements it has been argued[1] that 'there is no suggestion that in the pre-political phase men lived as isolated individuals, since the development of such institutions as language and religion presupposes at least a rudimentary form of community'. But the inference should be rejected. Neither language nor divine worship were necessarily social in origin, as the ancients saw the matter. And the phrase translated 'scattered and dispersed' (*sporadēn*) is used elsewhere in contexts very similar to that found in the myth of Protagoras, and in these cases it clearly does refer to individuals living in isolation.

These other, similar, passages constitute an interesting problem, since they clearly have some relation to what Protagoras says, but it is not possible to establish whether they are derivative or anticipatory. All that can be said with safety is that they form part of a tradition

---

[1] by C. C. W. Taylor in his commentary on 322b1.

which points to a very active debate on such matters in the second half of the fifth century B.C. In the fragment from the drama entitled the *Sisyphus*, often attributed to Critias (DK 88B25), but most probably composed by Euripides (see above pp. 52–3), we read that there was a time when the life of men was disorderly and beastlike, at the mercy of violence, when the good were unrewarded and the bad without punishment, this being before men established laws. In Euripides' *Supplices* 201 ff. (about 421 B.C.) we find Theseus saying that he praises that god who brought our way of life into order, when it had been confused and beastlike.

Both these passages do little more than establish the one point, that originally the life of man was no different from that of the animals. But it is probable that both are related to a third passage, which is of major importance. This is the account found in Diodorus Siculus (I.8.1–7). It was attributed by Reinhardt to Democritus, and was accordingly inserted by Kranz in DK 68B5. But the complete absence of any references to atomism makes this unlikely. A contrasted view would suppose that the material was worked up into a whole out of earlier elements, perhaps only in the time of Diodorus himself, in the first century B.C. Even on this view, however, it is conceded[2] that many *elements* in the account go back to the period of the fifth century.

The essentials of the account are the following. The first men to be born lived a life that was disorderly and beastlike. They used to go out, scattered and dispersed, to their feeding grounds, taking as their foodstuffs the most attractive of the plants and the fruits that were supplied of their own accord by the trees. As they were warred upon by wild animals they were taught to help one another by the advantage that resulted. So they kept coming together because of their fear and gradually came to know their mutual characterisations. Speech was articulated and was then developed on the basis of agreements as to the meanings of words, apparently differing for different groups in different parts of the world. Originally the physical side of men's lives was burdensome as none of the things useful for living had as yet been discovered. Gradually, with need as a teacher, the arts were discovered as well as the things that were useful. This was possible, because man was well endowed by nature, and was further assisted by his hands, his power of speech and his shrewdness of intelligence.

While not everything in this account accords with that in the myth

---

[2] by its chief proponent, W. Spoerri, *Späthellenistische Berichte über Welt, Kultur und Götter*, Basel 1959, 160 ff.

of Protagoras, nor indeed with any one other account, what is remarkable is the number of words and phrases that are common to more than one account. Thus the identical word 'beastlike' is found in the *Sisyphus* passage, in Euripides' *Supplices*, in Diodorus, and it reappears in a fragment quoted by Stobaeus from the dramatist Moschion (fr. 6 Nauck) whose date is uncertain. The word 'war' in relation to wild animals is found both in the myth and in Diodorus. The same verb for 'coming together' is found also in the myth of Protagoras and in Diodorus, as was the unusual verb 'to articulate' used of the development of speech. The expression 'scattered and dispersed' is used of primitive man in the Protagoras myth, in Diodorus, and in a later passage in Isocrates, *Panegyricus* 39, which refers to Greeks, before Athens came to their help, as living without laws, scattered and dispersed. It is probably going too far to suggest that these are all part of a *single* tradition, but at least it is likely that each of the passages cited was written in full consciousness of the doctrines found in some or all of the others.

According to the myth of Protagoras, when men did 'come together' the result was continued acts of injustice between them, all because they lacked the *technē* of living together in a city, the art of politics, which meant that they soon scattered again (322a–b). So Zeus sent Hermes to give men *aidōs* and *dikē* to be ordering principles of cities and bonds drawing people together in friendship. This clearly means that for Protagoras the prerequisite for human society is something more than mere need, however urgent. What is required is an acceptance of a principle of justice in human relations by the human beings in such relationships. Earlier in the myth, skills in the various arts and crafts had been distributed among them by the activity of Prometheus in their defence, not the same crafts to all men, but different crafts to different people. The present distribution arranged by Zeus is on a different basis in that *aidōs* and *dikē* are to be given to all men, and all men are to share in them. Any man who is unable to share in them is to be killed, as being a plague to the city. Henceforward men are all equipped to be social or rather political animals, capable of participating in the human societies of which they find themselves members.

A proper understanding of Protagoras' theory of society requires a rather careful consideration of the nature and basis of distribution of this new social cement introduced under the name of *aidōs* and *dikē*. First does Protagoras mean, as has often been asserted, that all men possess *aidōs* and *dikē* by nature? It seems clear that the powers of the animals are regarded as possessed by nature. It is possible that the skill in crafts is also so possessed by human beings. It was given to mankind before they began their life on this earth, and it is to man what the powers are to animals. But *aidōs* and *dikē* are in a different position – they are something acquired after man has been living in the world. Zeus commands that all men should share in them and makes provision for dealing with those who are unable so to share. It is true that the provision is death, but this suggests that their natures can't be altered, not that Zeus is adding something to the nature of man as such. The fact that all men are regarded as sharing in *aidōs* and *dikē* is not in itself sufficient to show that they do so *by nature*. We have in fact the strongest possible reason for supposing that Protagoras does not regard them as shared in by nature. He himself is made by Plato to say in the explanatory statement at the end of the myth (323c3–8): 'these then are the reasons I gave why they [the Athenians] rightly allow everyman to offer his advice regarding [matters involving] political virtue, because they believe that every man has a share in it; but that they consider it to be not by nature nor of spontaneous growth, but in whomsoever it is present the result of teaching and practice, this I will next endeavour to demonstrate'.

Secondly it is important to realise that it is not the view of Protagoras that all men are to be regarded as sharing *equally* in *aidōs* and *dikē*. This is often stated to have been his view, but there is no evidence for it whatsoever. It is certainly not implied by the Greek verb for sharing. Even if *aidōs* and *dikē* were by nature, it would not follow that they were shared in by all equally. Upon the conclusion of the myth, Protagoras proceeds to apply and expound its meaning. Since all men share in political virtue, the Athenians and others rightly allow all citizens to advise them on political questions. It is not, of course, suggested that all men are equally qualified to give advice, only that no one is without some qualifications. In the case of the other skills, if anyone says that he is proficient as a flute-player or at anything else when he is not, people either laugh at him or are angry. But in the case of justice and the rest of political virtue the position is different. All men are expected to assert that they are just, whether they are or not, as everyone necessarily shares in justice to some extent or other, if he is to be in the company of human beings, and should a man actually declare that he is unjust he is regarded as out of his senses.

All this is expressed in a long sentence (323b2–c2) which has caused some difficulty to commentators. It may well be that it is compressed in summary form from a much longer passage of argument that had appeared in one of Protagoras' writings. But the difficulties disappear when it is realised that Protagoras' position involves both the contention that all men do have a share in justice, and the contention that this sharing is to an unequal degree. So it is perfectly possible for a man to act unjustly in any particular case. But social expectations differ in the cases of justice and of the special skills. In the case of the latter no one individual is expected necessarily to possess any share of his own, and when he lacks the skill he is expected to admit it. But in the first case he necessarily does possess a share, and so has the capacity of acting justly in the particular case in question, whatever it may be. So when he fails, there is a social expectation that he will endeavour to conceal his failure by claiming that in fact he has been acting justly. This social expectation does not mean that his injustice is condoned – quite the contrary. But Athenians were already quite as familiar as we are with the distressing but frequent situation in which a person who has behaved very badly still claims that he has been entirely justified in what he has done.

The importance of this doctrine of Protagoras in the history of political thought can hardly be exaggerated. For Protagoras has produced for the first time in human history a theoretical basis for participatory democracy. All men through the educational process of living in families and in societies acquire some degree of political and moral insight. This insight can be improved by various formal programmes in schools and under particular teachers and also by the operation of laws deliberately devised by the *polis* in order to supplement the earlier education of its citizens. So all have something to contribute to the discussion of moral and political questions, whereas in matters involving special skills and special knowledge the *polis* will naturally turn for advice only to those who are experts. But in moral and political questions it is not the case that all opinions and all pieces of advice are of equal value. It follows that in a Protagorean democracy the operative principle concerning advice will be 'from each according to his capacity', and somehow or other it will be necessary for the community to *choose* between conflicting advice. In order to do so it will require advice about advice, i.e. what advice it should accept, and presumably the same principles must apply here also.

Thus an ideal Protagorean society is not ultimately egalitarian – it is to be guided by those with the most wisdom on each and any occasion.

Will such people be somehow separately identifiable and so constitute a ruling élite of wise advisers who can provide what is known as 'a led democracy'? This has sometimes been said. And in the *Protagoras* there is an extended passage which has been quoted in support, the logos which follows the myth which Plato puts into the mouth of Protagoras (324d2–326e5). Here Protagoras stresses the very extensive provision made for the education of their sons by 'good' fathers. This is provided above all by those who are described, in an ambiguous phrase (326c3–4), as those most able – the phrase can also mean those who are the most powerful or socially influential – and he adds 'those are most able who are the richest'. So, it has been speculated, Protagoras may have intended that there should be a *corps d'élite* able to serve the state in positions of trust, such as the ten *stratēgoi* at Athens, or to be wise and persuasive advisers on matters affecting law and morality. Such a view, if held by Protagoras, would certainly increase the similarity between his position and that of Plato in the *Republic*, and it is worth recalling that it was through the strategiate or generalship that Pericles was able to exercise the power at Athens which Thucydides described (II.65.9) as in name a democracy but in fact in process of becoming the rule of a single individual.

On the other hand, it is more probable that the real point of Protagoras' doctrine was that virtue can be taught. This means that it is not dependent on noble birth, and that all can learn who can afford it. This might mean that the reference to the richest as those most able to secure such education may be simply a reference to their ability to pay the relatively high fees of the sophists. While it is true that Protagoras is reported to have said (80B3) that teaching needs both nature and practice, and that it is necessary for learning to start already in youth, there is nothing to suggest that there was any inherited natural superiority in the children of the 'most able'. Natural ability for Protagoras was not distributed on a hereditary basis. This emerges very clearly from what he says about flute-players (327b6–c3): 'wherever a son happened to be born with a high natural talent for flute-playing, with appropriate education he will be found to have advanced to distinction ... But often the son of a good player would turn out to be a bad one, and often the son of a bad flute-player would turn out to be good'. The application of this doctrine to the case of virtue (328c5–8) explains for Protagoras why bad sons are born of good fathers and good of bad, even in the case of Paralus and Xanthippus, the sons of Pericles.

It is perhaps worth noting at this point that a kind of feeble echo of this doctrine of Protagoras is incorporated in Plato's *Republic*. For Plato some men are by nature fitted for philosophy and political leadership. Those who are not should follow their lead and should not attempt to lay their hands upon philosophy (474c1–2). For the most part children will resemble their parents in this respect (415a8), and this resemblance will clearly receive very strong reinforcement from the fact that differentiated education appropriate to the ability of the child is to commence at the earliest possible stage. But sometimes (415b1) children will be born with different abilities from those of their parents. In such cases the appropriate demotion or promotion is to be applied ruthlessly in order to maintain unimpaired the differentiating characteristics of members of the respective classes or categories of citizens in the state.

This concession by Plato to the principle of social mobility was perfectly genuine – it is repeated at 423c6–d2 and is not negatived at 434a3–d1 where interchange between classes is forbidden, as this clearly applies to cases where there are no *grounds* for any transfer.[3] In view of modern educational controversies, it is interesting to note that in the *Timaeus* 19a Plato regards review for possible promotion or demotion as a continuing process, going on until children have grown up, and not something to be done once and for all. Graded tests, at least for the Guardians, are to continue throughout the whole of their period of education both as children and as adults, and success is to be called for right through the process of testing before they can actually assume the functions of state Guardians; all those who fail at any point are to be rejected (413c7–414a4). Finally it should be said that while Plato accepted as genuine the fact of natural variation in ability at birth, he seems to have hoped that a programme of scientifically based eugenics would either eliminate or at least considerably reduce its occurrence (459a1–461e6).

In all this it is likely enough that Plato's thinking was moving under a kind of general inspiration acquired from Protagoras. But it is also probable that what he is doing is radically to transform the position first developed by Protagoras into something which in political terms was very near to becoming its exact opposite. For Protagoras' theory involved a *defence* of the behaviour of Athenian democracy, and it

---

[3] so J. A. Faris, 'Is Plato's a Caste State based on Racial Differences?', *Classical Quarterly* 44 (1950) 38–43, against Karl Popper, *The Open Society*, 5th edn, London 1966, Vol. I, 225 n. 31.

rested on the contention that *every* citizen had something that was at least potentially of value to contribute to debates on moral and political questions. For Plato the reverse is the case. Only in exceptional cases has an ordinary citizen anything even conceivably worthwhile to contribute. In all normal cases his contributions will be so ill-informed that they would endanger the maintenance of justice in the state, and they must accordingly be suppressed with all possible firmness (*Rep.* 434b9–c6).

Some further implications of Protagoras' doctrine will be considered below. But first it will be convenient to describe some other models for the structure of human societies which also originated in the sophistic period. One of these concerns the doctrine of the social contract which was to become so famous and important in the seventeenth and eighteenth centuries through its development by Hobbes, Locke and Rousseau. In its standardised form the theory of the social contract maintains that human societies rest upon an implied and so non-historical, or on an actual and historical agreement to establish an organised community. Sometimes it was supposed that prior to such a contract there were no social obligations binding one man to another, and that the contract itself, being based on consent given rationally on the basis of individual self-interest, was the logical source from which all the rights and duties of citizens were to be deduced. Others supposed that independently of such a contract there were rights that flowed e.g. from god or from natural law, but that the obligation to obey civil government had no other source than the social contract on which that government rested. In either case it was supposed that government must rest on the consent of the governed, either given once and for all, or subject to some continued affirmation.

Thus the essence of the theory is the view that political obligation flows from actual or implied contractual agreement. The attempt to ascribe any such view to Protagoras must be dismissed as misconceived, as when Guthrie writes 'since Protagoras did not believe that laws were the work of nature or gods he must have believed, like other contemporary progressive thinkers, that they were formulated as the result of a consensus of opinion between the citizens who henceforth considered themselves bound by them'.[4] Clearly no such inference is possible, since the rejection of god or nature does not leave only the possibility that society is based on a contract. Did Thrasymachus for

---

[4] *History of Greek Philosophy*, III 137.

example hold a contract theory? More important than the invalidity of the inference is the complete absence of any suggestion in the surviving evidence that this was the way in which Protagoras was looking at the matter.

But such theories *were* known in the period with which we are concerned. According to Xenophon (*Mem.* IV.4.13) Hippias spoke of laws as written statements of what must be done and not done following upon agreements made between the citizens of a state, but he went on to minimise the obligation that results. His own view, as we have seen, was that nature is to be preferred to law, and that it is nature which is the real source of human obligations. In the second book of the *Republic*, Plato's brother Glaucon purports to state (358c1) what men say is the nature and origin of justice. What they say (358e3ff.) is that it is by nature good to do wrong, and to be wronged is bad, but that the disadvantages of suffering wrong exceed the advantages of inflicting it. After a taste of both therefore, men who are unable to escape the one and achieve the other decide that it is to their advantage to make an agreement one with another on the basis that no wrong is to be inflicted and none is to be suffered. They accordingly proceed to make laws and agreements of their own, and they give the name lawful and just to what the law prescribes. This is the origin and nature of justice. Not dissimilar is the position outlined in the fragment from the *Sisyphus* (DK 88B25) according to which the absence of rewards and punishments for the good and the bad in the original state in which men first found themselves led them to establish laws in order that justice might rule. Though the term 'agreement' is not included, the implication points towards just such a basis.

Rather more discussion has centred round the *Crito*, where Plato represents the laws of Athens (50a6 ff.) as pleading earnestly with Socrates not to run away from prison on the ground that he has freely agreed with the laws to abide by the legal verdicts pronounced by the city. This agreement is stated to have been made by Socrates not in word but by his action in spending all his life to date voluntarily in the city of Athens (52d5), and is not then to be violated by him. Much later, Plato's treatise the *Laws* proceeds to add still other considerations which need not concern us here, but it is likely that the historical Socrates was at least interested in the view that the basis of the obligation to obey the laws lay in an implicit agreement.

The view that the laws are the product of a kind of contractual agreement is found in the list of encomiastic expressions applied to them in the so-called Anonymus *Peri Nomōn* (Ps. Demosthenes XXV.16) and it is spoken of with disapproval by Aristotle in the *Politics* (III.9.8 = DK 83.3) in what may possibly, but far from certainly, be a reference to the sophist Lycophron, a pupil of Gorgias. What Aristotle certainly does attribute to Lycophron is what has come to be known as the protectionist view of the state, according to which the state exists merely to guarantee men's rights against each other. On this view its function is to be a kind of co-operative association for the prevention of crime, in anticipation of the modern conception of the state as a laissez-faire institution, instead of being, as Aristotle would wish it to be, such as to make the members of the polis good and just.

The protectionist view of the state, which would reduce its function to within definite limits, would make political association rest upon consent over a limited range. A few scattered references suggest that a more positive concept was also known and discussed in the period, namely that of a kind of political consensus based on the like-mindedness of all citizens concerning patterns of living, subsumed under the term *homonoia*. This was a term which denoted what was to become a very important political ideal among the Stoics and in the theory of Hellenistic kingship from the time of Alexander the Great onwards, and was to be equated in due course with the Latin word *concordia*. It is consequently a matter for regret that it is simply not possible to recover the history of the term in fifth-century thought. What we can say is first that it occurs in two fragments of Democritus, namely in DK 68B250 where we are told that it is only as a result of *homonoia* that cities can accomplish great works, including wars, a theme that forms part of Socrates' criticism of injustice, as a source of disabling disagreement, in the first book of the *Republic*, and in DK 68B255 which has been described, perhaps with some exaggeration, as the most remarkable single utterance of a political theorist in Hellas. This is the fragment where we are told that on the occasions when the powerful have the courage to advance money, to serve and provide benefits for the have-nots, then there is pity and an end to isolation, and there is also friendship and mutual aid. The citizens become like-minded and other blessings result such that no man could enumerate them. We know also that Gorgias spoke on the subject of *homonoia* at Olympia (82 B8a). It was the title of a work by Antiphon (DK 87B44a), the contents of which however remain enigmatic. Finally we have one general statement from Xenophon (*Memorabilia*

IV.4.16) put into the mouth of Socrates, where it is said that *homonoia* is the greatest good that a city can possess, and that when it is present the laws are obeyed, the city is a good city.

It is generally admitted that there were definite sophistic influences at work upon the historian Herodotus. It is extremely likely that he knew Protagoras, who was responsible for drafting laws for the colony of Thurii, since Herodotus himself took part in its foundation. In III.108 of his *History* it seems certain that Herodotus either drew on what Protagoras had written, or at least upon the source used by Protagoras, when he mentions the prolific nature of animals liable to destruction in contrast with strong and courageous animals such as lions which produce relatively few offspring. This fits exactly with what we are told in the myth of Protagoras (*Prot.* 321b) about the activities of Epimetheus intended to secure the preservation of the various species of animals.

Equally sophistic in inspiration, though not certainly based on Protagoras, is the famous political debate given in Herodotus III.80–82. The scene is set in Persia and seven Persian nobles who had freed Persia from the magi are presented as discussing which of the three political forms, democracy, oligarchy and monarchy, is the best. But it is perfectly clear that Herodotus is taking the opportunity to dramatise for Athenian ears a constitutional struggle which was being fought out at Athens at or just before the time at which he was writing, and that he is presenting us with a dialogue that both in manner and content belongs not to Persia in 522 B.C. but to the sophistic debates in fifth-century Athens. First, in manner, it involves the opposition of one argument to another in such a way that it suggests the technique of the two-opposed Logoi. But the content also is both contemporary and sophistic in character. First Otanes proposes the abolition of the Persian monarchy on the grounds (1) that a sole ruler can do what he likes and is not answerable to anyone, and (2) that anyone elevated to that position finds his outlook changed even if he be the best of all men. He becomes the victim of insolence in addition to the jealousy and suspiciousness to which all men are subject, and the combination produces in him all the vice that there is. Instead what is wanted is the rule of the many. This has the fairest of all names, *isonomia*, and is free of the vices of monarchy. Magistrates are chosen by lot, and must render an account of all their actions, while all policy decisions are referred to the common assembly of the people.

Megabyzus then speaks in favour of oligarchy. He agrees with the criticisms of a tyranny expressed by Otanes but argues that the rule of the many is no less insolent and hybristic and is at the same time ignorant and lacking in education. He argues in favour of oligarchy on the ground that only men of knowledge and education are fit to rule. It follows that what is needed is a banding together of the best men 'for it is likely that the best decisions proceed from the men who are best'.

Finally Darius argues in favour of the rule of one man – nothing could be better than the one best man. Oligarchy leads to civil disorders because each man in the oligarchy wishes to be himself the leader and to have his views accepted when it comes to decisions, whereas democracy leads to conspiracies in the practice of wickedness. By a majority vote of the seven it is this third view that prevails and Darius in fact becomes king.

The reference to the selection of magistrates by lot and the requirement that they should render an account of their actions as magistrates, upon laying down office, before public auditors (*euthunoi*) is a clear reference to the practice of Cleisthenic democracy at Athens. It is just this practice of selection by lot that aroused the irony of Socrates, who was said by his accuser at his trial, according to Xenophon (*Mem.* I.2.9), to have taught his companions to despise the established laws on just this point. He asserted that it was silly for the rulers of the city to be appointed by lot when no one would be willing to employ the services of a pilot or a carpenter or a flute-player chosen by lot, nor any other craftsman for work in which mistakes are far less damaging than mistakes made in statecraft. It is worth repeating that Pericles exercised his leadership at Athens, not by securing offices chosen by lot – hardly possible in any case without fraud if the office was held repeatedly, but by being elected as *strategos* or general, thus enabling him to satisfy Socrates' requirement on this point, as well as the argument presented by Megabyzus.

In the debate between the three Persians in Herodotus, the term *isonomia*, 'the fairest name of all', is clearly associated with the rule of the many. The precise significance of the term has however been the subject of much debate.[5] The first part of the compound noun means 'equal' and the second part refers to laws or *nomoi*. Consequently some supposed that the word *isonomia* meant no more than 'equality before the law.' This means that there must be equal civil rights where

---

[5] For discussion and survey see in particular Gregory Vlastos' essay in J. Mau &. E. G. Schmidt, *Isonomia, Studien zur Gleichheitsvorstellung im griechischen Denken*, Berlin 1964, 1–35.

isonomia prevails, but there need not be equal political power or equal access to or equal rights to participate in the process of government. Those who have held this view have tended to draw attention to Thucydides III.62.3 where we find a reference to an 'isonomous' oligarchy, in contradistinction to a democracy on the one hand, and a power-group consisting of a few men, this last being that which is most opposed to laws and the ideal of restraint. But the passage in Thucydides cannot support the inference that therefore the phrase means no more than 'equality before the law' since the reference is probably to the rights exercised internally by the members of the oligarchy – in Richard Crawley's translation 'an oligarchical constitution in which all the nobles enjoyed equal rights'. This leaves entirely open the question what was the range of rights that is being considered, i.e. there need be no exclusion of 'equal rights to govern or rule' alongside other equally held rights.

Some further help may perhaps be derived from the famous and much discussed passage in Pericles' Funeral Speech (Thuc. II.37.1) of which a possible translation might be as follows: '[Our form of government] is called a democracy because its arrangement favours the many instead of the few. If we look to the laws there is an equal share for all so far as concerns individual differences between citizens. But in public esteem, when a man is distinguised in any way he is more highly honoured in public life, not on a sectional basis but in recognition of merit. Again if we consider poverty, a man who is able to do something of benefit to the city is not debarred by the obscurity of his recognised status.' Unfortunately no translation of this vital passage is possible without introducing into the translation itself a considerable element of interpretation. But it seems fairly clear that Pericles wishes to maintain that Athenian democracy in his day has two aspects. It does rest on the principle of *isonomia*, but it also makes full provision for men of exceptional ability (no doubt intended to include himself!) to make a far greater contribution than others to the conduct of the affairs of the city. This in turn requires that the principle of selection for office by lot shall not apply in his case. In other words, Pericles, like Protagoras, is combining a principle of some kind of political equality with that of preference for superior people. What is being proposed here is government *for* the people, without involving also government *by* the people.

What then of the meaning of the term *isonomia*? Some of the complications that have arisen in the discussion of its meaning do so because more than one question is involved – in particular the question to whom or what does the term refer, and the question what is its sense or meaning when it does refer to any determinate entity. To the first question a clear answer can be given. Despite a few special applications, in the overwhelming majority of cases the term refers to democracies understood as regimes in which government is regarded as basically entrusted to the many in the community. The second question is more difficult. It is certainly a mistake to treat the term as synonymous with democracy – it does not *mean* the same, and it is consequently possible for it to be used on occasion to refer to non-democratic groups or regimes when it is wished to assert that these possess the qualities regularly attributed to democracies. What then does the term *mean*? To say that it means no more than 'equality before the law' is both anachronistic and is also too narrow. It should be noted that as an epithet *isonomos* applies not to citizens or to individuals, but to cities and communities. This is so in its earliest occurrence, the *skolion* which celebrates the occasion when Harmodius and Aristogiton made, not the Athenians but, Athens isonomous by killing Hipparchus, and it is the usual way of using the term throughout. Its meaning then is likely to be, not 'possessing equal rights as citizens', but something more like 'conferring equal rights as a matter of prescription by the city'. Once this is accepted it becomes probable that *isonomia* does not, as part of its *meaning*, determine either the nature or the limits of the rights which are thus prescribed.

However that may be, the importance of the term for my present purposes is that it does introduce at least some aspects of the concept of political equality into the arena of political discussion in the fifth century B.C. Naturally, once introduced, the concept of political equality was capable of a number of different applications, and it will be appropriate to take some of these one by one. First economic or financial equality. The importance of differences in wealth as a source of political dissension was of course a commonplace. But it was commonly treated as a moral problem rather than as one to be solved by abolishing inequalities. Plato however did suggest that the philosophic guardians should possess no property of their own in order to free them as far as possible from being objects of suspicion on this score to the remainder of the citizens. After criticising Plato for this doctrine, Aristotle proceeds to treat another thinker whom he clearly regards as earlier than Plato.

What he tells us is that there were some who held that the proper dispositions in relation to property were politically more important than any other disposition, because these were the source of all political dissension. So Phaleas of Chalcedon, who was the first to suggest the introduction of property regulations, proposed that all citizens should have equal amounts of property. He supposed that this would not be difficult to achieve at the foundation of a new colony, but much less easy in established communities. Even there, however, it could be accomplished if the rich gave marriage dowries to the poor and the reverse applied in the case of those who were poor, i.e. they received dowries but did not give dowries to the rich (*Politics* II.7.2–3 = DK 39.1). The reference to colonies makes it certain that what is here in question is property in land, and not other forms of wealth. The call for a re-distribution of land within existing cities, often accompanied by the demand for a cancellation of debts owed to private citizens would appear to have become almost a standard part of attacks on property-holders, and both such demands were condemned in the Helliastic oath taken by jurors at Athens, preserved in a speech in the collection that has come down to us under the name of Demosthenes (XXIV.149).

Compared with such battle-cries the approach of Phaleas is indeed moderate and reformist in character. Though he is not named as a sophist in the sense of a professional teacher, Phaleas belongs fairly certainly to the later part of the fifth century B.C., and so is to be regarded as part of the sophistic movement. That he was interested in education is shown by Aristotle's statement (*Pol.* II.7.8) that he proposed not merely equality in property, but also equality of education. Unfortunately we are not told how he supposed this last was to be arranged. It may have been based on the practice at Sparta, but more probably it envisages free universal state education. If this was regarded as extending as far as the education provided by sophists, it would involve a change in the situation envisaged by Protagoras where it is the rich who can procure the best education for their sons (Plato, *Prot.* 326c3–4). In modern terms this would be the equivalent of non-fee-paying state financed university education for all.

The solvent of the idea of equality however had a greater impact in other areas than the economic. Perhaps the most important was in the area of claims to superiority based on birth and family origins. If we can trust the rather uncertain restoration of a papyrus passage it would appear that Antiphon said that we respect and look up to the sons of illustrious fathers, but those from a non-illustrious home we neither respect nor look up to (DK 87B44, II p. 352). If the restoration is correct it is to be related to what he says in the lines immediately following, namely that by nature all of us are of the same nature in all respects (for the passage as a whole see below, p. 158). The sophist Lycophron (DK 83.4) is reported to have said that 'nobility of birth is completely worthless. For he said that its beauty is not something that can be seen, its grandeur is a matter of what men say (*logos*) – preference for it is related only to opinion. In truth those who are ignoble differ in no way from the well-born.' Here the references to truth and opinion suggest that Lycophron is not merely making a social and political statement, but is attempting to support it by an appeal to the sophistic opposition between *physis* and *nomos* as well.

Our information about Lycophron comes from the dialogue *On good birth* composed by Aristotle. If we had more than the very few fragments from it that survive it is likely that it could be seen to have summarised much of what took place in sophistic discussions on the subject. As it is, we can probably gain more insight from a remarkable passage in Plato's *Theaetetus* (174e–175b), where Socrates praises the insight of the true philosopher. Despite its length it is worth quoting as a whole.

When people sing praises of lineage and say how noble someone is because he can point to seven rich ancestors, he thinks the praise is coming from people whose vision is dull and short-sighted, people who because of their lack of education are unable to keep their eyes fixed upon the whole, and cannot calculate that every man has had countless thousands of ancestors and forebears, among whom there have been innumerable instances of rich men and poor, of kings and slaves, of barbarians and Greeks. When people give themselves airs over a list of twenty-five ancestors and trace their descent back to Heracles the son of Amphitryon, this strikes him as showing a strange pettiness of outlook. He laughs at those who cannot calculate that it was just a matter of chance what kind of person the twenty-fifth back from Amphitryon was, and the fiftieth for that matter. In all these cases it is the philosopher himself who is laughed at by the many, for appearing to be arrogant and for his failure to understand the [accepted] facts of everyday life.

Similar in its implications is the statement of the chorus in a fragment of Euripides' *Alexandros* preserved by Stobaeus (fr. 52N) where we read: 'Our *logos* goes too far, if we praise good birth among mortals. For, when long ago we first came into existence, and Earth who had given birth to mortals then separated one from another, the land by its process of upbringing impressed upon each a like appearance. We have no special marks. Well-born and low-born are the same stock. It is time that by *nomos* makes good-birth a matter of pride.' Here it is perhaps worth saying that this passage is *not* saying that all men are of equal merit, only that merit is not to be found related to good birth.

Much more tentative was the criticism of the institution of slavery. Indeed it is doubtful if anyone in the fifth century went further than to suggest that many actual slaves were only so by accident of circumstances. But while this much was accepted by Aristotle, his conclusion was that in an ideal world slavery would be confined to 'natural slaves' and all those who were not slaves by nature would be free. No text survives from the fifth century which actually condemns all slavery as such. It *may* be an implication of the opposition developed by Antiphon between *nomos* and *physis* that all slavery is contrary to nature, but we have no record that he drew out the implication, and it is not sufficient to argue that he did so condemn it because 'he must have done so'.[6] Such a conclusion was indeed eventually reached and Aristotle was aware of it when he wrote *Politics* I.3.4. There are many who would dearly like to be able to assign this view to the fifth century. But in fact the first person who is attested to have held it is Alcidamas, a disciple of Gorgias, who in his Messenian Oration said 'God has left all men free, Nature has made none a slave.' But the date of the Oration may well be 362 B.C. or later, and it is only with the Stoics that we find the doctrine that no man is a slave by nature given full theoretic backing.

We are just slightly better off for evidence concerning Greeks and barbarians. In general the Greeks had a very strong sense of their superiority to other men. According to Hermippus as cited by Diogenes Laertius (I.33) there were some who used to say Socrates was in the habit of declaring that there were three things for which he owed thanks to Fortune, first that he had been born a human being and not a beast, secondly that he had been born a man and not a woman, and thirdly that he had been born a Greek and not a barbarian. Hermippus himself supposed that the story really related to Thales of Miletus. In either case it correctly embodied the traditional Greek view both of barbarians and of women.

In discussing first the comparison beween Greeks and barbarians it will be convenient to commence with the position adopted by Plato in the *Republic*. He distinguishes between the two quite fundamentally.

---

[6] as in effect W. Nestle, *Vom Mythos zum Logos*, 2nd edn 1942, 377–8.

The natural relationship between Greek and Greek is one of kinship and belonging together. So they are by nature friends. When they fight one another this means that Greece is sick and torn by civil war. It follows that strict limits must be imposed on what things may be done when they are fighting each other. In particular it is entirely wrong for Greek states to sell Greeks into slavery. Quite the opposite is the case when Greeks are fighting barbarians. For Greeks and barbarians are enemies by nature. When they fight they are involved in war, and it is appropriate then that Greeks should treat barbarians as Greeks now (wrongly) treat other Greeks (*Rep.* 469b–471c). From this it is clear that Plato accepts and approves the institution of slavery even in his ideal state. His reason for doing so is his belief that barbarians are by nature inferior to the Greeks, who alone are fitted to be masters by their good intellect and love of learning. Aristotle is only following Plato when in the *Politics* (1252b7–9) he cites with approval the view of the poets that it is right that barbarians should be ruled by Greeks, because barbarians are by nature slaves.

The essentials of the Platonic position seem to have been anticipated by Gorgias (DK 82B5b), who, in his efforts to unite the Greeks and turn their energies against the barbarians, declared that victories over barbarians called for hymns of praise, while those over Greeks called for dirges. A different view may have been held by Hippias in the *Protagoras* (337c–d) when he declares to those present that he regards them as 'kinsmen who belong together and as fellow-citizens by nature, though not by *nomos*. For like is akin to like by nature whereas law which is a tyrant over human beings often forcefully imposes constraints that are contrary to nature.' All 'those present' are in fact Greeks so that it is possible that he means no more than what Plato had said in the *Republic*, namely that Greeks constitute one family and kin. The needs of the context in which Hippias is speaking would indeed be satisfied if he was claiming no more than that there is a natural affinity between wise men wherever they occur, Greek or barbarian, or perhaps merely wherever they occur among Greeks. But the universality of the second sentence quoted above, according to which by nature like is akin to like, suggests that he probably wished to go further and to argue for the universal kinship of all human beings who share *any* specific likeness, e.g. all children, all women, all wise men or all beggars, and so on.

A more definite statement, still unfortunately hard to interpret precisely, is to be found in the papyrus fragment of Antiphon (DK

87B44, II pp. 352–3) of which the first sentence has been cited already in connection with the question of the respect accruing to men of superior birth.

We respect and look up to the sons of illustrious fathers, but those from a non-illustrious home we neither respect nor look up to. In this we have become barbarianised in relation to one another. *For we are all by nature alike fully adapted to be either barbarians or Hellenes.* This can be seen from the things which are by nature necessary to all human beings. These are open to all to be procured in the same way, and in all these none of us is distinguished either as barbarian or Greek. For we all breathe out into the air with our mouth and nostrils, and we all eat with our hands.

Here there is some uncertainty about some of the actual words of the Greek text translated in the last two sentences. But the overall sense of the passage is not in doubt. What he is saying is that there is no ultimate distinction fixed by nature between Greeks and barbarians, or between well-born and low-born. Less clear is the sequence of the argument and the particular conclusion which Antiphon wishes to reach. On the translation usually adopted for the third sentence of the passage, in place of the words italicised above we have something like 'For by nature we are made to be alike in all respects, both barbarians and Greeks.' We then have a very strange logical sequence, as Guthrie points out, namely 'We pay great attention to high birth, but this is to behave like barbarians for in reality there is no difference between barbarians and Greeks.'[7] This simply does not make sense, nor is it an accurate translation. What is needed, as Guthrie saw, is to revert to the translation provided by the first publishers of the papyrus, Grenfell and Hunt, namely the words given in italics: For we are all by nature alike fully adapted to be either barbarians or Hellenes. With this translation a different overall interpretation of the sequence of the argument is required, and failure to understand what this could be is no doubt the reason why a less accurate and less likely translation has come generally to be substituted.

I believe that a clue to the correct interpretation can be found in a passage in the Hippocratic treatise *On Airs, Waters and Places* Ch. 12. The treatise as a whole is concerned with the effects of differences in climate and environment upon health and character. In Chapter 12 the comparison is between Asia Minor and Europe (i.e. Greece proper), and we are told that conditions are such in Asia Minor that

[7] *History of Greek Philosophy*, III, 153.

158

courage, industry and the impulse to action could not arise there either among the natives or among immigrants, but pleasure rules supreme. Clearly the contrast is with Greeks who live on the mainland and who do possess these qualities. But if they emigrate to Asia Minor they become like the native Asiatic Lydians whom the Athenians regarded as effete and luxurious in comparison with themselves.

On the basis of this text, which itself belongs to the fifth century, it is possible to suggest the following interpretation of what Antiphon is saying. Physically, and by nature, there is no difference between human beings – our needs and our physical equipment are the same in every case. But we are capable of developing in different ways as a result of subsequent influences – we can then be either Greeks or barbarians, either intelligent and civilised or pleasure-loving and stupid. By stupidly admiring the sons of noble fathers and ranking them above those from humble homes we behave in the manner of barbarians, as if we ourselves have become barbarians and lost the intelligence appropriate to us as Greeks. This solves the problem of the sequence of thought in the passage and has the advantage of enabling us to keep the more accurate translation of the sentence italicised. In the absence of the remainder of the passage in the papyrus, it can, of course, not be claimed to be certain.

In the story quoted earlier Socrates was presented as saying not merely that he was glad that he had not been born a barbarian, but as equally glad that he had not been born a woman. At Athens in the fifth century the political, economic and legal position of women was indeed extremely weak, all powers being substantially in the hands of men. Socially and in terms of personal influence no doubt the position was often very much better,[8] but that was all. So it is not surprising that the new thinking of the sophistic movement should lead to the posing of questions concerning the rights and position of women in Greek societies, though there is no evidence that this led to any actual movement for the improvement of their position.[9]

The starting point was no doubt the realisation that here as elsewhere actual social arrangements were not fixed inexorably but were merely relative. So in the *Dissoi Logoi* II.17 (DK 90) we read that the

---

[8] see the challenging article by A. W. Gomme on 'The position of women in Athens in the fifth and fourth centuries B.C.', *Classical Philology* 20 (1925) reprinted as Ch. 5 in his *Essays in Greek History & Literature*, Oxford 1937.

[9] Wilamowitz, 'Lesefrüchte', *Hermes* 35 (1900) 548 = *Kleine Schriften* IV.126 as against Ivo Bruns, *Frauenemanzipation in Athen*, Kiel 1900 = *Vorträge u. Aufsätze*, Munich 1905, 154.

Egyptians do not think the same things seemly as other people do, since in our country we regard it seemly that women should weave and work with wool but in theirs they think it proper for men to do this and for the women to do what the men do in ours. In Herodotus II.35 we are told the same thing as an example of how the Egyptians have different *nomoi* from the other people, and Oedipus in Sophocles' *Oedipus at Colonus* 337 refers to the same thing when he wishes to express his admiration and thanks to his daughters, who have taken on the burdens of their unhappy father in what would now be called a reversal of roles between male and female.

Pericles himself, we may take it, was not in sympathy, as Thucydides assigns to him in the Funeral Speech (Thuc. II.45.2) the statement that has become famous concerning the *aretē* of women, namely that they should not fall short of their natural character. Then great will be their reputation (*doxa*) and greatest of all will be hers who is least spoken of either for her excellence or in blame by masculine lips. This advice has, to be sure, often seemed gratuitous, and inappropriate to the occasion of the commemoration of Athenians who have died in battle. It is possible that it was inserted by way of reply to Gorgias (DK 82B22) who had said that it is not the beauty of a woman, but the opinion in which she is held (*doxa*) that ought to be known to many, which was perhaps to be associated with the importance that he attached to opinion (DK 82B26).

But all these are merely scattered references. What is of first importance is the evidence of Plato and its relation to that of Aristophanes. In the *Republic* Plato had argued that it is the duty of every person to devote his energies to fulfilling that function for which he is by nature best fitted (423d). When he comes to Book V however, he reveals his awareness that the question of the position of women involves a whole swarm of arguments (*logoi*) which have so far in the dialogue remained asleep (450b1). His own view is that the only difference between men and women is one of physical function in reproduction. Apart from that both men and women should follow the same range of occupations and perform the same functions in the community. For this they must receive the same education. But if men and women are to lead the same lives, the family will need to be abolished. Breeding will be arranged scientifically on a communal basis, the children will be cared for in state institutions, so that both women and children will be 'common', as belonging to the state rather than to individual husbands and parents.

After a thoroughgoing criticism of the Platonic scheme Aristotle states in his *Politics* II.7 that a number of other constitutional schemes have been proposed, by private individuals, by philosophers and by statesmen. But all are less radical than Plato's, and no one has introduced the revolutionary proposal of community of wives and children or common meals for women. On the basis of this statement it has sometimes been supposed that Plato thought out and invented the whole scheme for himself. At the very least, however, he had been anticipated in certain details. Herodotus (IV.104) had related that the Scythian Agathyrsians practised a kind of community of women in order that men might be brothers to each other, and, being all nearly related, might not feel envy or malice one against another. Euripides in his *Protesilaus* (fr. 653N) had referred to something similar, and Aristotle himself (*Politics* 1262a19) refers to a practice of the same kind in Upper Libya. This makes it clear that the idea was known, and had attracted interest well before Plato produced the *Republic*.

But this is only the beginning of the problem. The idea of a political revolution achievable by women (using the weapon of a sex-strike against males) was the theme of Aristophanes' *Lysistrata* produced in 411 B.C., and about 392 B.C. in the *Ecclesiazusae* a further revolution by women is described, where the programme of the women contains quite remarkable similarities to what we find in the *Republic*. An extreme hypothesis would have it that there must therefore have been an earlier version of the *Republic*, whether published or unpublished, available to Aristophanes by 392 B.C. since the version which we have is likely to have been completed not before about 375 B.C.[10] Perhaps it should not be a matter for too much surprise to find that almost exactly the reverse of this hypothesis has also been maintained. The chorus in the *Ecclesiazusae* (577–579) are made to declare that the city of Athens is in need of some clever invention, and they invite consideration of things that have neither been done nor spoken of before. Praxinoa then unfolds her programme in a passage of dialogue over a hundred lines in length (583–724). All property, all foodstuffs and all money are to belong to the community, with the result that poverty will be abolished. There will be complete sexual freedom and all women will be shared in common among the men. The resulting children will regard all men as their fathers. There will be no law-suits

[10] so e.g. Gilbert Murray, *Aristophanes, a study*, Oxford 1933, 188.

161

as there is no private property, and punishment when required will be by exclusion from the communal meals.

The detailed parallels with what Plato says in the *Republic* are indeed remarkable,[11] and it is not only possible but also quite likely that Plato knew the play at the time that he was writing the *Republic*. The only plausible alternative is a common written source for both treatments, but if such had existed it is strange that no one in antiquity seems to have mentioned it, apart from the general statement that Plato drew the contents of the *Republic* from the *Antilogika* of Protagoras. It is accordingly most likely that the *verbal* similarities are to be explained by Plato's use of Aristophanes' play. But it is *not* likely that the whole programme was something simply invented by Aristophanes. Because of the highly selective and accidental sieve through which the literature of the fifth century has had to pass before becoming accessible to us, there is a constant danger of underestimating the vigour and range of the written and unwritten discussions going on over matters of public interest. While we are unable to make particular attributions it can be taken as virtually certain that revolutionary theories about the rights and the position of women were in the air throughout Aristophanes' lifetime. Otherwise he would not have devoted at least three comedies to such issues, namely the *Lysistrata*, the *Thesmophoriazusae* and the *Ecclesiazusae*. Just what was in many people's minds can fairly be gathered from the elaborate account of the disadvantages afflicting women in Medea's first speech in Euripides' play (*Medea* 230–266) which begins with the declaration that having to buy a husband is bad enough: being his physical slave is even worse. Here, as has been said,[12] 'She contrasts the physical and social conditions of women's existence with the freedom enjoyed by men. A complement to this account of present conditions is furnished by the confident vision in the first strophe and antistrophe of the next chorus. A turn is coming, the future will be better' (410–430). All this has its place within the story of the play itself. But it would scarcely have been possible for an audience to have listened to what was being said without also being conscious of its wider implications.

---

[11] see the list drawn up by J. Adam in his commentary on Plato's *Republic*, Vol. I, Cambridge 1902, 350–1.

[12] F. Solmsen, *Intellectual Experiments of the Greek Enlightenment*, Princeton 1975, 73.

13

Religion and the gods

The sophistic movement as a whole has sometimes been regarded as characterised by a revolt against religion, a profound movement of the human spirit away from a belief in the divine towards a rationalist and humanist outlook on the world. This view has perhaps been to some extent influenced by the rather superficial analogy between the 'age of the Sophists' and the eighteenth century *Aufklärung* or Age of Enlightenment. But the truth is rather different. Greek religion had never been in any sense a unitary entity. At no period during the period of its independence was the Greek world organised as a single state and there was never anything remotely approaching what could be described as an organised church even in the separate city-states. There was never any authoritative writing like the Bible or the Koran, there was neither one Creed, nor a plurality of Creeds. Nor was there any uniformity in cult, ritual or mythology. All varied from age to age, from place to place, from class to class and even from family group to family group. Apart from the mystery religions it was predominantly a religion not of another world but of this world, tending always towards an anthropomorphic polytheism in which the gods were thought of as human in form and largely human in mind.

All this is elementary and well-known, but seems often to have been virtually forgotten in discussions of the sophistic movement. From Homer onwards there was a continuous process of intellectual discussion and reinterpretation of everything concerning the gods. The Presocratics repeatedly sought to equate the Divine with whatever any one of them identified as the ultimate source of power in the universe, and almost regularly speak of the Divine as all-encompassing, all-governing and so on. The implications of this way of looking at things were destructive of traditional anthropomorphism and Xenophanes did not hesitate to make these implications open and emphatic and in addition to attack the validity of divination. On the most probable view, Xenophanes had denied the possibility of any knowledge at

163

all about the gods, thus anticipating the famous statement of Protagoras discussed below. No man, he said (DK 21B34), has ever had, or ever will have sure knowledge about the gods and all the things that I say. For even if he should chance to give expression no matter how much to the complete truth, he himself does not know that he has done so, but only opinion is available to all of us. Heraclitus did not hesitate to attack ritual purifications and phallic worship, and both Pindar and Xenophanes anticipated Plato in rejecting myths in which the gods were depicted as thieves, cheats, adulterers, gluttons and seducers.

As has been said the achievement of this philosophy of the Presocratics may well strike us as 'the emergence of a radically destructive and fundamentally anti-religious force such as we often attribute to reason and to science. If one thinks of religion not as a form developing with a life of its own, but simply as a bare fact of history given once and for all, as is very plausible in the light of the Christian conception of a single and final revelation by God, this view is perhaps correct. But Greek religion is much richer and less restricted in its development. It does not consist in any revealed teachings reconcilable with rational thinking only to a limited degree; it springs rather from a lavish profusion of mythical views of the world, the characteristics of which are constantly changed and revised with each new shift of perspective.'[1] Small wonder then that no one took the slightest objection to what poets and philosophers had been saying over a considerable period of time. As we shall see, the sophists were doing no more than continuing the discussion along very much the same lines.

Yet later tradition was to identify a whole list of alleged atheists from the sophistic period, Diagoras, Protagoras, Prodicus, Critias, Euripides, to whom was also joined the names of Euhemerus and Theodorus from the end of the fourth century B.C. (see e.g. Cicero, *De Natura Deorum* I.117–119). This tradition was coupled with another according to which a whole series of prosecutions for impiety (*asebeia*) were brought against the exponents of such views – Protagoras, Socrates, Phidias, Anaxagoras, Euripides and Theodorus are all mentioned, and in a number of cases prosecution was said to have resulted in exile or even death. In the case of Protagoras tradition declared that the book in which he wrote concerning the gods was

[1] Werner Jaeger, *The Theology of the Early Greek Philosophers*, Oxford 1947, 173–4.

ordered to be burnt in public. It is probable that there is some exaggeration and even some degree of fiction in all this.[2] But the evidence can hardly be dismissed as a whole. As we have seen already in Chapter 3 there was considerable hostility to sophists in general and it was natural that what they said about the gods should be used as part of the general campaign to discredit all their activities. There may also have been an element of delayed reaction to the ever-widening sweep of rationalism, sharpened by fears in the war situation confronting Athens from 432 B.C. onwards. But above all the motivation was political opposition, first to Pericles and then to those who admired and would continue his policies after his death.

A very large part of the hostility to the sophistic approach to religion arose in relation to the famous statement of Protagoras (DK 80B4), which in its fullest form seems to have been as follows: 'Concerning the gods I am not in a position to know either that (or how) they are or that (or how) they are not, or what they are like in appearance; for there are many things that are preventing knowledge, the obscurity of the matter and the brevity of human life.' It was on the basis of this statement that Protagoras acquired the reputation of having been an atheist, and the Epicurean Diogenes of Oenoanda said outrageously that when Protagoras said he did not know whether gods exist, this is the same as saying that he knows that they do not exist. Of course all that the passage asserts is the need for Protagoras to suspend judgment on the matter. We are told that the statement came at the the beginning of one of his writings, but not whether or how he further substantiated it. In view of its importance however it is appropriate to discuss the possible ways in which Protagoras' mind may have been working, when he wrote the words that were so extensively quoted.

First, attempts have been made to interpret it in the light of the man–measure doctrine. It has been suggested that what Protagoras ought to have said, if he supposed that everyman's truth is the truth which appears to him, was: gods exist for those who believe in them; they do not exist for those who do not believe in them. To this it has been replied that according to the man–measure principle, gods exist for some and not for others, and consequently for Protagoras himself

---

[2] see on this the discussion by C.W. Müller in the second part of his article, 'Protagoras über die Götter', *Hermes* 95 (1967), reprinted in C. J. Classen, *Sophistik*, Darmstadt 1976, 323–40.

suspension of judgment was the only possible course.[3] But this is probably to misunderstand the position. There is nothing to suggest that Protagoras ever attempted to exempt himself from the operation of the man–measure principle. He is *not* saying here, however, that the truth is as it seems to himself, or for that matter as it seems to anyone else. What he is saying is that he cannot arrive at any (seeming) truth in this particular case. Gomperz is probably right in supposing that his reasoning is likely to have been: 'Hitherto no one has seen gods; but human life is too short, and the field of our observation too restricted, to affirm or deny with certainty the traces of their activity in the world of nature and man. Accordingly he withheld his verdict.' Thus Gomperz. Pericles also is credited with saying that we do not see the gods, but only make inferences about them (Stesimbrotus quoted by Plutarch, *Life of Pericles* 8, 9). Whether Protagoras would have gone quite so far as to say that no one had seen a god might be doubted – but he would probably have agreed with Xenophanes in supposing that no-one could know whether he had seen a god or not.

The charge that Protagoras had been an atheist clearly rested on the contention that in his famous statement it was the existence of the gods that he was at least doubting if not clearly denying. This is certainly the way in which his words were usually taken in antiquity as well as subsequently. This is sometimes regarded as supported by the antithesis between the first part 'that they are or that they are not' and the second phrase, sometimes omitted but likely to have been part of the original, 'or what they are like in appearance'. So the first part is taken as concerned with their existence, and the second with their qualities and characteristics. But the matter is perhaps just not entirely certain. Cicero in one place (*De N.D.* I.63) translates the first part as if he had supposed that the construction was that of an indirect question, so not 'that they are or that they are not', but 'as to how they are and how they are not', although elsewhere in the same book (I.2, 117) he took it as an indirect statement, and so as referring to the existence or non-existence of the gods.

In the man–measure sentence we have seen that the Greek conjunction introducing the subordinate clause, which is the same conjunction as that used in the sentence about the gods, is now usually taken to have referred to the manner in which things appeared to the man acting as measure, rather than to their existence. We have also seen

[3] W. K. C. Guthrie, *History of Greek Philosophy*, III, 234, referring to Jaeger, and to Theodor Gomperz, *Greek Thinkers*, Vol. I (Eng. trans.), London 1901, 457.

reasons to doubt whether the verb 'to be' when used absolutely had really developed any fully existential meaning before the fourth century B.C.

It may be noted that the question of the existence of the gods is not mentioned in the hostile parody by Timon of Phlius early in the third century B.C. (see DK 80A12). Such an interpretation of the sentence about the gods is not excluded by the addition of the second phrase 'or what they are like in appearance' since the whole could be understood as saying 'Concerning the gods I am not in a position to know either the manner in which they are or are not, or their visible form.' Certainly the second phrase, 'I am not in a position to know the visible form of the gods' suggests that they were there credited at least with existence. But the meaning may of course have been, 'or if they do exist, what they look like'. Whatever be the truth of this matter, what Protagoras said was almost immediately taken as in fact intended to refer to the question of the existence or non-existence of the gods, and it is noteworthy that Charles Kahn, in his major discussion of the uses of the verb 'to be' in Greek, accepts the sentence as involving perhaps the earliest surviving technical use of the verb as an existential predicate.[4] On this I remain unconvinced. All that can properly be inferred from Protagoras' surviving words is that he gave expression to the view that it was not possible to discover the nature of the gods, a kind of scepticism neither exceptional (see below, p. 170), nor offensive, at least to educated opinion, in the second half of the fifth century B.C. The true position is perhaps as has been well expressed by M.P. Nilsson, when he wrote with reference to this period 'Belief in the gods had faded, but was not extinguished. If the fun went too far, it could blaze up into religious hysteria, as at the departure of the hazardous expedition against Syracuse and the notorious prosecutions which followed in connexion with the mutilation of the Hermai in 415 B.C.' (*Greek Piety*, Oxford 1948, p. 78).

While the statement we have been discussing is by far the most famous expression of Protagoras' views on the gods, it is not the only piece of information that has survived. Among the list of Protagoras' writings is a work entitled *On Things in Hades*. In the myth put into the mouth of the sophist in Plato's *Protagoras* the gods existed before there were any mortal creatures, and it was the gods who, when the time came that was set by fate for their generation, moulded mortal

[4] *op. cit.* p. 302.

creatures inside the earth after they had made a mixture of earth, fire, and elements which blend with earth and fire. They were then assigned various powers useful for survival by Prometheus and Epimetheus. After some delay man acquired the gift of fire and so was brought up to the light of day. The story continues (322a3–5) with the words: 'Now when man had come to have a share in the divine Moira, in the first place, in virtue of his kinship with god, alone among living creatures he came to have respect for gods, and he set himself to construct altars and images of gods, and in the second place he quickly proceeded to an articulated distribution of voice and names.'

The orthodox interpretation of this passage verges on the perverse in that it has tended to argue either that the expression 'in virtue of his kinship with god' should be excluded from the text on the grounds that it is inconsistent with Protagoras' declared agnosticism, or that if it is retained it is evidence that the myth was the work of Plato rather than of Protagoras. But the myth as a whole is built about the activities of Zeus, Prometheus and Epimetheus, and the fact that it *is* a myth deprives it of any possible conflict with Protagoras' agnosticism. The divine distribution or Moira in which man has come to share is not so much the gift of fire, though this is included, as wisdom (*sophia*) which was always associated with the divine, and the kinship with the gods is probably something which *results* from man's participation in the divine wisdom. In fact the whole of the myth both here and elsewhere is presenting no more than a kind of projection or reflection at the divine level of forces identifiably at work amongst human beings in this world.[5] Exactly the same applies in the case of the bestowal of *aidōs* and *dikē* which forms the next stage in the myth – their gift represents the acquisition through learning of those qualities in human beings which are the condition of the maintenance of ordered human societies.[6] This means that his concern with religion was not primarily to conduct a polemic against traditional views of the gods, but rather to treat religion as a positive human phenomenon with a valuable function to perform in societies.

The sociological interpretation of religious beliefs was a feature also of the doctrines of Prodicus, though the scrappy, late and scat-

[5] so Part I of the article by C. W. Müller for which see above p. 165 n. 2. For this sense of Moira, see E. G. Berry, *The history and development of the concept of Theia Moira*, Chicago 1940, 49 ff.

[6] see my article 'Protagoras' doctrine of Justice and Virtue in the *Protagoras* of Plato,' *Journal of Hellenic Studies* 73 (1953) 42–5.

tered nature of the references make it difficult to go beyond mere description of what he had to say. Like Protagoras he was concerned with the origins of religion at early stages in the development of human societies. He said two separate things, of which the first was that the things that nourish and benefit human life were the first to be considered gods and to be honoured. The list of such things included the sun, moon, rivers, lakes, springs, the four elements, bread, wine, water, fire and so on with each of the things that are useful.[7] A number of these came to be identified with members of the Olympian pantheon, such as Demeter, Dionysus, Hephaestus and Poseidon. But some of these figure also in the second thing that he said, namely that the discoverers of new crops, foods and shelter and other practical arts were also enrolled in the ranks of recognised gods, and one mutilated source seems to suggest that Prodicus regarded this as a second stage. Certainly Prodicus stressed the importance of agricultural practices in the development of sacrifices, mysteries and initiatory rites and claimed that this was the source of the very concept of the gods for human beings.

Criticisms of the traditional doctrines about the gods found in the poets and attempts at radical reinterpretations were not confined to professional sophists. Herodotus (II.52 ff.) had speculated at some length about the origins of the gods, their names and their functions. According to one account Protagoras had read aloud the beginning of his book on the gods in the house of Euripides, and there was even a story preserved in the Life by Satyrus, that Euripides himself had been prosecuted for impiety. In quite a number of his plays there are criticisms of various kinds that are levelled against the gods. Sometimes these go no further than the conviction, expressed with varying degrees of passion by different characters, that the gods must be good, not evil. At other times profoundly unfavourable behaviour by a god or gods is made into the central theme of a particular drama, as is surely the case with Artemis in the *Hippolytus*, Zeus in the *Hercules Furens* and Apollo in the *Ion, Electra* and *Orestes*.

All this may however be regarded as in a way the natural stuff of Greek tragedy, the problems raised by the relationship of man to god, and god to man. Euripides was however associated with and influenced by the sophistic movement in deeper ways. It was in fact no accident that he came to be called in antiquity 'the theatrical philoso-

---

[7] DK 84B5 together with additional passages in Untersteiner, *Sofisti, Testimonianze e frammenti* fasc. ii, pp. 194–6.

pher or philosopher of the theatre' (Athenaeus, 158e, 561a), and that
Wilhelm Nestle could entitle his major study of him published at Stuttgart in 1901, *Euripides der Dichter der Aufklärung*, though he was
well aware that he is first and foremost a dramatist and is not to be
treated as simply a lecturer expounding sophistic ideas. This may be
illustrated by a further selection of some particular passages. Bellerophon, in his angry protests against the injustice of divine rule, is
made to say (*Bellerophon* fr. 286):

Does any man say then that there are gods in heaven? No, there are none. If
any man says so, let him not be fool enough to believe the old story. Let not my
words guide your judgment, look at matters for yourselves. I say that tyranny
kills thousands and strips them of their goods, and men who break their oaths
cause cities to be sacked. And in doing so they are happier than men who
remain pious day after day. I know of small cities that honour the gods, and
they are overwhelmed in battle by numbers and are the subjects of greater
cities that are more impious than they.

In another fragment (292.7) we are told 'if gods act basely, then they
are not gods'.

These lines are contrasted by Nestle with the position we more commonly find in Sophocles. 'It is assumed by both poets that God and sin
are mutually exclusive terms. But from this assumption they draw
opposite conclusions. Sophocles infers: "It follows that everything the
Gods do is good": and in order that there may be no remaining doubt,
he adds: "even when they bid us go beyond what is right." Euripides'
conclusion is different: "In that case the sinful gods of Greek mythology are non-existent."[8] But if then there are no gods, what are we to
suppose? One possible answer is given in terms that might have come
directly from an exponent of sophistic theories. In the *Hecuba* 798 ff.
we find Priam's widowed queen, Hecuba, appealing to Agamemnon
for mercy in a passage that has been much discussed: 'We are slaves
and, yes, it may be, weak. But the gods have power and so has *nomos*
which is the master of the gods. For it is by *nomos* that we believe in the
gods and recognise in our own lives a distinction between things that
are right and things that are wrong.' Some have supposed that Euripides is here referring to the divine law which stands above the gods.
But the statement 'it is by *nomos* that we believe in the gods' seems a
clear reference to the *nomos–physis* controversy, and this means that
Euripides is here prepared to explain the gods as owing their existence

[8] Nestle, *Euripides* 126.

to human belief. This need not mean however that their existence was merely subjective to individual human beings. In the *Frogs* (889–894) Aristophanes makes Euripides say he prays to gods that are different and that are special to himself and these are listed as 'Aether, my source of nourishment, Pivot of my tongue, Intelligence, Nostrils keen of scent.' Here it is likely that at least the reference to Aether has a serious point, and probably that to Intelligence also, in view of the invocation found in the *Troades* (884–887) in the mouth of Hecuba: 'Oh vehicle of the earth, oh thou who dost recline on the earth, whoever thou art, hard to know even by conjecture, Zeus, whether you be necessity of nature or the power of reason in mortal men, it is to you I pray.'

All this may serve by way of prelude and background to the remarkable dramatic speech (DK 88B25) put into the mouth of Sisyphus, the grandfather of Bellerophon. The passage has commonly been attributed by scholars to Critias, on the authority of Sextus Empiricus, supported in modern times by that of Wilamowitz. But, as has been stated earlier (Chapter 5, p. 53 above), the arguments for ascribing it to Euripides are rather stronger, not least because Euripides is known to have written a satyr-play entitled *Sisyphus* when he won second prize with a tetralogy, that included the *Troades*, in the spring of 415 B.C. (Aelian, *V.H.* II.8). The speech begins with the words that had clearly become standard, since they are found also at the commencement of the myth of Protagoras in Plato's dialogue of that name. Once there was a time when the pattern of human life was without order, animal-like, and enslaved to force. This was succeeded by a second stage when human beings established laws imposing punishments in order that justice might rule and hubris be held in check. Such laws were in fact successful in controlling acts done in public, but acts of violence continued in secret. So there followed a third stage – some man who was both clever and wise invented fear of the gods in order to frighten those who were secretly evil, whether in actions, words or thoughts. For the gods, who dwell in the heavens above, possess divine powers which enable them to inform themselves of misdeeds under each of the above three headings, even that of secret thoughts. The teaching of this wise man was not merely extremely useful – it is spoken of as concealing the truth with an account that was false. But the result was that lawlessness was extinguished by laws.

If we had only the above account it would be possible to suppose that the falsehood mentioned in it consisted merely in the attributing to the gods of such extreme powers of supervision over mankind. But Sextus quotes two further lines, which he says occurred a little later on: 'Thus first did some man, so I would suppose, persuade mortals to believe that a race of gods exists', and this would seem fully to justify the inclusion of the view thus expressed under the heading of atheism.

14

Conclusion

In a remarkable passage at the beginning of his *History* (I.10.2) Thucydides speculated that if the city of Sparta were to become deserted and only the temples and foundations of buildings were left, future generations would, as time passed, find it very difficult to believe that it had really been as powerful as its reputation suggested it had been. Not dissimilar is the case with the sophists. Neither they nor their writings survive and the few fragments that are quoted, like the traces of the foundations of buildings in an ancient city, are, on the surface and when looked at superficially, unimpressive in comparison with the mighty edifices of Plato and Aristotle which survive intact or virtually intact. When set alongside these, the original constructions of the sophists were surely vastly inferior. But when we investigate the surviving traditions about them more closely, and make use of the tools of study available to us, the result is surely not unimpressive. What is needed is a process of quasi-archaeological reconstruction on the basis of the traces that survive. Often such notional reconstructions will be uncertain and open to challenge. But the traces are there and it is wrong to try to pretend that the superstructures were either small or even not there at all.

In earlier chapters, on this present occasion, no attempt has been made to analyse, or even to survey, all of the material that has survived concerning individual sophists and the various doctrines with which they were credited. Even so the first impression must be of the very wide range that was covered by the sophistic movement. It has often been said that the main function of the sophists was to prepare the way for Plato, and this is regularly said in such a way as to suggest that they are therefore of only limited importance. But virtually every point in Plato's thought has its starting point in his reflection upon problems raised by the sophists, virtually every dialogue in one way or another has one or more sophists either visibly present at or covertly influencing its discussions. And this is true even if Socrates is wholly excluded from the company of his contemporaries for this purpose. Virtually all aspects of human activity, all the social sciences can be seen to have been the sustained subjects of sophistic debate, and in many cases for the first time in human history. This is something often better recognised by modern specialist writers in various branches of sociology than by those more directly concerned with classical antiquity. What we are studying are the fragmentary remains and traditions of a great movement in human thought.

If we ask what is the most marked single characteristic of the movement as a whole, the answer must be the sustained attempt to apply reason to achieve an understanding of both rational and irrational processes. But before reason can be applied directly to the solution of problems it is necessary first to establish a rational structure or framework within which the problem becomes capable of being approached by the investigator. It is easy to underestimate the really immense difficulties which this presents when previous attempts are all but non-existent. It means that largely unexplored questions of epistemology, logic and metaphysics seem to interpose themselves increasingly between the thinker and the immediate subject under discussion. It is not important that in a number of cases the responses on such matters by individual sophists seem naive or inadequate. What is important is that they did respond, when earlier Presocratics had come to grief because they had not even begun to see the nature and complexity of the problems confronting them, and had instead proceeded with a headlong rush towards the particular answers which most appealed to them on any given occasion.

It is probable that the historical and intellectual importance of the sophists is now generally recognised to a much greater degree than was once the case. It is hardly a matter of dispute that they taught and discussed grammar, linguistic theory, moral and political doctrines, doctrines about the gods and the nature and origin of man, literary analysis and criticism, mathematics, and at least in some cases the elements of physical theory about the universe. But were they philosophers? This is still not generally admitted. It depends partly on the definition of philosophy. Here the ghost of Platonism is still active. For Plato the sophists rejected what he regarded as the ultimate reality and were attempting to explain the universe in terms of its phenomenal aspects alone. For Plato the phenomenal world was a sham world, lacking in reality, and so lacking in the essential requirement for a genuine object of knowledge. But in the modern world where the majority of scholars are not Platonists, and in general do not even wish to look for reality in the direction where Plato believed it was to be found, it is something of a paradox that the Platonic condemnation still remains largely unquestioned. The time is surely long past when the rejection of any transcendent reality can be taken as evidence that the search for truth has been abandoned.

To this it may be replied, that is all very well. One can indeed search for truth without a commitment to transcendent reality. But what if the sophists were the equivalent of modern journalists or publicists at their worst – not interested in transcendent reality to be sure, but equally not interested in empirical truths either, but concerned simply with what can be given enough appearance of truth to persuade or deceive an audience? This would suffice to explain the wide range of matters discussed by the sophists, and it is indeed the traditional view of the nature of the sophistic movement.

Such a contention relates in part to the motives of individual sophists and this is difficult for us to determine. But to the extent that it involves a judgment about the actual writings of the sophists it admits in principle of a definite answer. If we had more of their writings we might expect that the answer would be clear and beyond dispute. As it is we must, as so often in the study of antiquity, proceed by inference from inadequate and incomplete evidence. This means that there is certainly scope for disagreement. What seems to me impressive however is the clear indications that survive of a range of technical doctrines under discussion in what we would now call the spheres of philosophy and sociology.

We live in an age which is sceptical and suspicious, and it sometimes seems that to express admiration for anything or anyone is to lay oneself open to charges of either naivety or dishonesty. Certainly expressions such as the glory of Greece or the greatness of the Periclean age at Athens are no longer exactly fashionable. The idea that Greece reached its highest point in culture and civilisation in the second half of the fifth century B.C. and that this was followed by a long decline resulting above all from the weakening of Athens that followed her defeat in the Peloponnesian war is also suspect. Despite this it is still legitimate to express cautious approval of Athenian achievements in art and architecture during this period. Likewise the literature of the age and above all the tragedies of Aeschylus, Sophocles and Euripides exercise a never-ending fascination. The stature of Thucydides as a historian is in no way diminished. What is needed is a recognition that in all probability the sophists were a no less distinguished and important part of the achievement of Periclean Athens – important in their own right and important also in the history of philosophy. In view of the nature of the evidence more study is required to substantiate this view in detail. But it is hoped that the present survey may have done something to suggest the correctness of this view, at least in its general outline.

Select Bibliography

I Texts and translations

Diels, H. and Kranz, W. *Die Fragmente der Vorsokratiker* Vol. II, 6th edn Berlin 1952 (and later reprints), Section C 'Aeltere Sophistik', cited with the abbreviation of the authors' names as DK.

Dumont, J.P. *Les sophistes, fragments et témoignages*, Paris 1969.

Sprague, R.K. *The Older Sophists, a complete translation*, Columbia S.C. 1972.

Untersteiner, M. *Sofisti, Testimonianze e frammenti*, fasc. I–IV, Florence 1949–62, fasc. I–III 2nd edn 1962–67.

II Treatments of the movement as a whole

Classen, C.J. ed. *Sophistik* (Wege der Forschung 187) Darmstadt 1976 (contains also an extended bibliography on the sophists, pp. 641–710).

Guthrie, W.K.C. *A History of Greek Philosophy* Vol. III, *The Fifth Century Enlightenment*, Cambridge 1969, of which the first part was also published separately under the title, *The Sophists*, Cambridge 1971.

Kerferd, G.B. ed. *The Sophists and their Legacy*, Proceedings of the Fourth International Colloquium on Ancient Greek Philosophy at Bad Homburg 1979, Wiesbaden 1981 (*Hermes*, Einzelschriften Heft 44).

Levi, A. *Storia della sofistica*, Naples 1966.

Nestle, W. *Vom Mythos zum Logos*, Stuttgart 1940, 2nd edn 1942, reprinted Aalen 1966, Chapters IX–XII.

Untersteiner, M. *I sofisti*, Turin 1949, 2nd edn Milan 1967 (in two vols.), English trans. of first edition, *The Sophists*, Oxford 1954.

III Name, concept and origins

Kerferd, G.B. 'The first Greek Sophists', *Class. Rev.* 64 (1950) 8–10.

Kerferd, G.B. 'The image of the Wise Man in Greece in the period before Plato', in *Images of Man in Ancient and Medieval Thought*, Studia Gerardo Verbeke dicata, Leuven 1976.

Vlastos, G. 'Plato's testimony concerning Zeno of Elea', *Journal of Hellenic Studies* 95 (1975), at 150–60.

IV Discussions of some individual sophists

ANTIPHON

Bignone, E. *Studi sul pensiero antico*, Naples 1938.
Kerferd, G.B. 'The moral and political doctrines of Antiphon the sophist, a reconsideration', *Proc. Cambridge Philol. Soc.* 184 (1956) 26–32.
Morrison, J.S. 'Antiphon', *Proc. Cambridge Philol. Soc.* 187 (1961) 49–58.

CRATYLUS

Anagnostopoulos, G. 'The significance of Plato's Cratylus', *Rev. of Metaphysics* 27 (1973/74) 318–45.
Derbolav, J. *Platons Sprachphilosophie im Kratylos*, Darmstadt 1972.
Goldschmidt, V. *Essai sur le Cratyle*, Paris 1940.

DISSOI LOGOI

Robinson, T.M. *Contrasting Arguments, an edition of the Dissoi Logoi*, New York 1979.

GORGIAS

Dodds, E.R. *Plato Gorgias*, Oxford 1959.
Irwin, T. *Plato Gorgias* translated with notes, Oxford 1979.
Kerferd, G.B. 'Gorgias on Nature or that which is not', *Phronesis* 1 (1955/56) 3–25.
Newiger, H.J. *Untersuchungen zu Gorgias' Schrift Über das Nichtseiende*, Berlin 1973.

HIPPIAS

Kerferd, G.B. 'Plato and Hippias', *Proc. Classical Assoc.* 60 (1963) 35–6.

PRODICUS

Binder, G. and Liesenborghs, L. 'Eine Zuweisung der Sentenz οὐκ ἔστιν ἀντιλέγειν an Prodikos von Keos', *Museum Helveticum* 23 (1966) 37–43, reprinted in Classen, C.J. *Sophistik*, 452–64.
Kerferd, G.B. 'The "Relativism" of Prodicus', *Bull. John Rylands Library* 37 (1954) 249–56.

PROTAGORAS

Capizzi, A. *Protagora, le testimonianze e frammenti*, Rome 1953, 2nd edn Florence 1955.
Kerferd, G.B. 'Plato's account of the relativism of Protagoras', *Durham University Journal* 42 (1949) 20–6.
Kerferd, G.B. 'Protagoras' doctrine of Justice and Virtue in the *Protagoras* of Plato', *Journ. Hellenic Studies* 73 (1953) 42–5.

McDowell, J. *Plato Theaetetus* translated with notes, Oxford 1973.
Mejer, J. 'The alleged new fragment of Protagoras', *Hermes* 100 (1972) 175–8, reprinted in Classen, C.J. *Sophistik* 306–11.
Müller, C.W. 'Protagoras über die Götter', *Hermes* 95 (1967) 140–59.
Taylor, C.C.W. *Plato Protagoras* translated with notes, Oxford 1976.

SOCRATES

Gulley, N. *The philosophy of Socrates*, London 1968.
Vlastos, G. *The philosophy of Socrates*, New York 1971.

THRASYMACHUS

Kerferd, G.B. 'The doctrine of Thrasymachus in Plato '*Republic*', *Durham University Journal* 40 (1947) 19–27, reprinted in Classen, C.J. *Sophistik* 545–63.
Maguire, J.P. 'Thrasymachus – or Plato?' *Phronesis* 16 (1971) 142–63, reprinted in Classen, C.J. *Sophistik* 564–88.

V *Some particular themes and doctrines*

Beck, F.A.G. *Greek education 450–350 B.C.*, London 1964.
Derenne, E. *Les procès d'impiété intentés aux philosophes au Vème et au IVème siècles*, Liège 1930, reprinted New York 1976.
Dodds, E.R. *The Greeks and the Irrational*, Berkeley 1951.
Evans, J.D.G. *Aristotle's Concept of Dialectic*, Cambridge 1977.
Gigante, M. *Nomos Basileus*, Naples 1956.
Graeser, A. 'On language, thought and reality in Ancient Greek Philosophy', *Dialectica* 31 (1977) 360–88.
Heinimann, F. *Nomos und Physis*, Basel 1945.
Kahn, C.H. *The Verb 'Be' in Ancient Greek*, Dordrecht 1973.
Robinson, R. *Plato's Earlier Dialectic*, Ithaca N.Y. 1941, 2nd edn Oxford 1953.

VI *Addenda*

Cassin, B. *Si Parménide, le traité anonyme De Melisso Xenophane Gorgia*, Lille 1980.

Index